MOIRA

MOIRA
A TRUE STORY

Dr. Martin Obler

NEW HORIZON PRESS
Far Hills, New Jersey

Copyright © 1993 by Dr. Martin Obler

All rights reserved. No part of this book may be reproduced or transmitted in any form whatsoever, including electronic, mechanical, or any information storage or retrieval system, except as may be expressly permitted by the 1976 Copyright Act or in writing from the publisher. Requests for permission should be addressed to New Horizon Press, P. O. Box 669, Far Hills, New Jersey 07931.

Library of Congress Catalog Card Number: 92-060567

Obler, Martin, Ph.D.
   Moira

ISBN: 0-88282-120-2
New Horizon Press

1996 1995 1994 1993 / 5 4 3 2 1
Manufactured in the U.S.A.

Of all the tyrannies on human kind,
The worst is that which persecutes the mind.

—John Dryden

CONTENTS

	Acknowledgments	ix
	Author's Note	xi
	Introduction	xiii
	Prologue: The Robbery	xv
1	The First Session	1
2	Meeting Mardoff	11
3	Other Demons	15
4	Family Ties	24
5	A Return to Moira's Past	41
6	A Clash of Wills	66
7	Echoes	77
8	Suspicions	82
9	Jarring Memories	93
10	Jarring Realities	101
11	Setting the Stage	113
12	The Hot Seat	122
13	Acting Out	137
14	Illusion or Love?	149
15	Confrontations	159
16	Theories and Reality	173
17	The Nature of an Illusion	187
18	Unsettling Confrontations	197

Contents

19	Transfer and Transference	208
20	Further Problems	220
21	Warning Signs	227
22	Seeming Answers	249
23	Ultimatums	263
24	Breaking Away	280
25	Final Partings	297
26	Reckonings	307
27	Resolution	314
	Afterword	318

ACKNOWLEDGMENTS

It took three years to research and write this book. I did not write it alone. Officially I am the sole author, but two persons collaborated with me—and contributed greatly to form and material. The first five chapters were written with the help of my daughter, Dita Obler, who helped shape the overall concept and direction of the work. A successful businesswoman trained in sociology, Dita is able to understand human beings on profound levels. The clarity of thinking she forced on me through her talented rewriting skills and deep-cutting insights was invaluable. They helped me present a more honest and serious account than I would have on my own. I am proud of her contribution both as a writer and gifted thinker. And for no extra charge, she will, by the time this book is published, have presented me with my first grandchild!

The second part of this book, chapters six through the end, was written by in collaboration with Peter English. I have known Peter for over twenty years and selected him because of his exceptional talents as a professional writer and profound awareness of psychology. His contribution to the book was enormous. Peter not only rewrote large sections to make it more readable but added his own insights to my concepts. He and I had originally collaborated on *Two-Way Mirror*, in which he contributed an essay on group therapy. At present we are discussing a new collaborative work on two perspectives of a psychoanalysis.

I respect Peter's sharp appetite for emotional truth, both of himself and of the world, and his capacities for significant connections to many kinds of people.

Many dear friends and colleagues gave generously of their time and effort to this manuscript. Their editorial and content suggestions were invaluable. They are too numerous to mention, but I am grateful for the extensive help they offered.

Finally, I am thankful beyond measure to my wife, Robyn, and four children, Dita, Gil, Alicia and Ricky, for their patience and loving support.

AUTHOR'S NOTE

This book was inspired by and is based on my real experiences. In order to protect others and myself, I have taken the liberty of changing some people's names and identifying characteristics, adding scenes or altering them when necessary. In some cases, the people in this book are composites and, in some instances, chronology has been altered.

Introduction

After all these years, I still hear the screams. Are they the screams of a life wasted? Of a lost woman's mind and spirit? Or are they screams echoing from my own childhood, where my mother and father struggled over power, sex, and domination when the real issue was poverty.

Do I hear Moira's screams and confuse them with my sister's? While aware that my sister was considered mentally ill, I never understood what was actually wrong with her. It is easy to forgive myself for that confusion. I was only four years old at the time of my sister's breakdown and six when I last saw her at the institution. But in Moira's case, my confusion and guilt remain with me to this day.

She was my first patient. As her therapist, my job was to determine the nature of her mental illness. Moira and I were to work as a team, unraveling and reconstructing her identity. I could not know it then, but the relationship was to be prolonged and intense.

PROLOGUE

The Robbery

As she entered the bank, Moira noticed the dark-haired, intense-faced young man looking about nervously. Almost instinctively, she fingered the glistening silver handle of her police revolver and felt a quiver of excitement as if something was about to happen.

While she was standing at the teller window, the alarm rang. The man, now clutching a brown bag and brandishing a gun, screeched orders as he rushed to the exit—a revolving door.

Within a matter of seconds, Moira pulled out her pistol and started in pursuit. She reached the revolving door just as the robber was about to emerge on the street. The door jammed, knocking the gun from his hand. He turned and their eyes locked.

The muscles in Moira's stomach and pelvis tightened. The door came free and the gun slid onto the sidewalk. The man began running down the street. Moira emerged from the door, raised her pistol, and took aim. Just as she was about to shoot, she felt her eyes drawn irresistibly to the man's gun lying at her feet on the pavement. She could not take her eyes away. Unable to stop her preoccupation with the gun, Moira knelt, as if hypnotized, to pick it up.

A burning sensation shot through her back. The intensity of it took her by surprise. She gasped. She had never experienced this feeling before. Dizzy, she swayed back and forth thinking she might faint. Suddenly, she snapped back into the situation at hand. She started to run after the robber but then stopped. It was futile to go on. It was too late. The man was gone.

Frozen, Moira stood on the sidewalk staring as the red flashing lights and screaming sirens of patrol cars arrived at the scene.

ONE

The First Session

The chill wind stung my face as I approached the Lewin Clinic's Flatbush address. I welcomed that bracing air with a sense of relief.

Growing up on the streets of Brownsville, I had learned that during the long, hot summers the air in Brooklyn acquired a uniquely heavy quality. As the citizens of Brooklyn slowed their pace down to a crawl, the air followed suit. It almost seemed to be holding its breath while a certain oppressive stench accumulated.

In this stale Brooklyn summer, the melting pot became a literal and tangible presence as a million immigrant families prepared their suppers. The odors poured into this syrupy atmosphere, where they were mixed and baked by the hot sun. The result is a sensation like no other.

The promised summer wind never seemed to arrive. It was the cooler autumn breezes sweeping down from Canada on days like today that finally brought relief.

I knew this neighborhood like no other. Here were the Italians, Irish, and Jews I grew up with, fought with, and made love to. In spite of having escaped into the more sophisticated world of academia and Manhattan, it was here I had an allegiance and emotional connection. So it was here

I had returned to build the foundation of my private psychotherapeutic practice.

The date was October 10, 1963, my first day as an interning psychologist. And despite my familiarity with the neighborhood and the people from whom I would draw my patients, I was nervous and apprehensive.

For though I was married and had begun raising a family of my own, as a third-year student in the clinical psychology program having just completed my comprehensive examinations and now beginning supervised psychotherapy with outpatients, I was struggling for financial and psychological survival.

Today my long years of preparation had reached a pinnacle. My work life would finally begin. My excitement was palpable. Myriad questions crowded together in my mind. Could I do it? Was I ready? Would I be successful? My stomach clenched and unclenched. First, a feeling of elation, then a feeling of nausea passed over me as the clinic entrance and my prospect for the future loomed only a few feet before me.

I walked the short distance. Now I had reached the front door. Pausing for a few moments to gather my courage, I took a deep breath. Then I pulled the door toward me and stepped inside.

Entering the shabby waiting room, I looked around. Immediately my attention was drawn to an attractive woman in a blue uniform sitting stiffly in the farthest corner of the room. She was in her late thirties or early forties with long wavy tawny-blond hair, which she kept attempting to push back under a navy blue cap. I wondered if this was my first patient. The woman appeared very tense and kept shifting in her chair as if she could not get comfortable.

Even from a distance she looked to be in great pain. Staring at her, I felt strange and self-conscious. Seeing me, her expression grew sad, and she leaned forward as if she were pleading for help. Petrified, I looked away. Looking down I saw my hands shaking. What if all people seeking help had this same stricken look? Panic rose in me again. I forced myself to take a deep breath. I repeated to myself almost ritualistically, *Cut it out, you're the therapist. Remember they need you. They need to feel they can depend on you.* This seemed to calm me. Slowly I walked toward the receptionist's desk.

"Gail, could I have my first patient's folder?"

Gail, a pleasantly plump, coffee-skinned woman who acted as a mother substitute for all the interns, smiled reassuringly.

"Of course, Dr. Obler. Your patient is already here," she nodded in the woman's direction.

"I'll be ready shortly," I said in a loud, unsteady voice.

Retreating to the cubbyhole that served as my office, I sat down and examined the case record that Gail had given me. The record had been prepared by my supervisor, the renowned Dr. S. Mardoff, whom I'd yet to meet. All the graduate students said he was rough to work under, but they also agreed his clinical reputation would open many previously closed doors for me. He had conducted all the initial psychiatric interviews personally and was responsible for the diagnosis of each patient.

My first assigned case was Moira McCarthy. Dr. Mardoff described her as "a hysterical personality with schizoid features, suffering from psychosomatic reactions in her lower back." His notes revealed that Moira lived in Bensonhurst, a middle-class neighborhood in Brooklyn. Most of Moira's extended family worked for the police department, and she had joined the force, an unusual place at that time for a woman from Moira's background, after two of her children were born. She had worked as a beat cop, a policewoman on foot patrol, for about three years before becoming injured, apparently as a result of an altercation with a criminal while on duty. After three months of extensive medical evaluation and personality testing, the department had insisted she come to the clinic for treatment.

Gail buzzed on the intercom. "Your patient is waiting, Dr. Obler," she said patiently.

I tried to get up but couldn't move. I seemed frozen in my armchair.

A short while later Gail buzzed again. This time more insistently. "Your patient is waiting, Dr. Obler," she repeated.

When still I did not respond Gail walked back to get me. "Ah," she said recognizing the look of fright on my face. "Let me assist you." Hooping her arm through mine, she propelled me out of the chair. Together we set out for the waiting room.

I tried to gather whatever composure I could as I approached Moira. She must have been wondering where I had been, for she looked at me strangely.

Awkwardly, I greeted her, "Hi, my name is Marty Obler. I'll be working with you as your therapist." My voice broke like an adolescent's on the last few words. Gail burst out laughing. Moira seemed speechless, but beads of sweat formed on her forehead.

Silently Moira and I walked down the corridor to the treatment room. Suddenly I noticed again how drab our surroundings were. The rooms and halls were small and bare, painted a now peeling institution yellow. There were neither windows nor pictures on the walls. I looked over at Moira to see if she had noticed the shabbiness, too. But she seemed completely absorbed by the task of making it down the hall. She walked hunched over, wobbling unsteadily. She reminded me of the old people in my neighborhood slowly creeping along the street.

Nothing in Moira's appearance suggested that she might be a policewoman. Her body language spoke of a shy and inhibited woman, a woman filled with fears, beaten down by life. A great many of the young women I grew up with in Brownsville had aged this way before their time. Powerless in most aspects of their lives, they seemed to absorb most of the blows life had dealt them, experiencing each blow as an almost physical sensation.

I was so tense by the time we reached the treatment room, with its loud wall clock, stark lighting, and worn cracking plastic chairs, that for the first time in a long while, I felt the need to touch something to stop my trembling. I thought I had learned to control this compulsive behavior from my childhood. Obviously, I had not. I had the first glimmer of recognition that there is little real difference between therapist and patient. The difference lies simply in the tools we each have available to us. My training was indeed such a tool. I only needed to be one step ahead of them in learning how to live successfully.

When I looked over at Moira I saw that she too was shaking. I wanted to embrace her. I felt a new compassion for her based on my identification with her. In that moment, I knew that our friendship had begun.

Moira chose a chair in the opposite corner of the room from the scarred desk and chair obviously meant for me. She was attempting to put as much distance between us as possible. I considered turning around the client chair facing the desk, thereby sitting closer to her. But I wasn't sure that was an acceptable option. Wasn't the doctor supposed to sit behind the desk? I ended up behind the desk not because I respected her choice to protect herself with the distance, but in reality to hide behind convention and protect myself.

Moira, whose back was obviously paining her now, had trouble sitting comfortably in the hard plastic chair. She tried to draw little attention to herself but could not keep still. She fidgeted constantly and played with her hair, which kept falling over her startling green eyes. Each time it fell she pushed it back with reddened, work-worn hands. In contrast, her skin was pale and parchment fine. Her lanky body, long neck, and delicate eyes and mouth were dominated by an aquiline nose. The clinical report indicated that she was forty-two years old.

I looked at her face carefully as we exchanged small talk. Had life been kinder to her, she could have been a beautiful woman. The tension and pain reflected in her strained expression and twisted body showed that life had not. Still, though faint lines of age had begun to etch themselves around her eyes, she had remained remarkably handsome.

After a while we sat in silence. I looked at her, wondering what to talk about next. She stared off into space.

I tried to read meaning into her silence but couldn't tolerate the tension between us. Out of desperation, I broke the silence and repeated inanely, "I'm Martin Obler and I've been assigned to your case. I'll be your psychotherapist. How can I help you?" I smiled nervously, got up, walked over to her, and again awkwardly offered my hand to shake.

Moira forced a smile and clasped it.

"What's happening to me?" she asked still holding onto my hand. "I don't belong in a loony bin like this. I'm a cop. Do you know what being here could do to a cop?"

I felt uncomfortable and drew my hand back. How was I supposed to help her? I was supposed to be the one in control, the one to offer comfort. I repressed the impulse to jump in and try to rescue her. I let her proceed instead.

"I'm a good person," she said.

"Psychological problems have nothing to do with morality," I interjected. "Good or bad are issues for the Church, not for psychotherapy."

Moira seemed stunned when I mentioned the Church. She continued, "The police department is my entire life. And now, they force me to come here. Where I come from, people think this is the same as being put away."

I nodded sympathetically. "That's just old-fashioned prejudice."

"That's fine for you to say, but what have I done to deserve this? I am honest and I don't ever cheat or lie. I am terribly afraid of losing my job. They don't trust me anymore. It's not that I was malingering—I have real pain. There was an accident and my back got hurt. But I don't want to talk to you about that."

* * *

Once again we sat in silence. The tension between us had shifted. While Moira's stress had grown, I had slowly begun to relax. Having a psychotherapeutic dialogue was familiar territory for me. I had experienced these kind of exchanges in my own personal therapy. As long as the focus was on her, I could feel comfortable. I just had to switch roles and play it the way my therapist did.

Another long pause ensued. Then an unusual thing happened. This time when Moira shifted in her seat, her body seemed to take a new stance. The contorting back pain appeared to relinquish its control. Deftly, she opened the top few buttons of her blouse and pushed her skirt up ever so slightly. Then she languidly sat back, crossing her legs. The shift was very subtle. At first I did not consciously notice it. Preoccupied with my own thoughts, I was startled when she suddenly spoke in a low, husky voice very different from her earlier one. There were intonations of a strange new accent, perhaps European or British.

"You look like a kid, Doc," she said, her emerald eyes locking with mine. "But I know we'll get along. Just let me handle this." She continued, assuming a power and force that had been absent in her before. "The second I saw you out there in the waiting room I could tell how scared you were. I could see the fear in your eyes. You know, back where I come from, we have the strength to face almost anything. Just sit back, my doctor friend, and I'll take care of everything."

I was suddenly petrified. Control of the situation had again shifted abruptly. I no longer felt empowered by her earlier vulnerability. I had no experience with this kind of change. Was she just trying to manipulate me? How was I supposed to respond? Should I acknowledge the difference? Should I ask prodding questions? I didn't know.

Was this the same passive, almost pathetic woman I had walked with from the waiting room? Her new manner was dominant, aggressive; I felt flustered. Matters were getting out of hand here. I tried to reestablish my position as an authority figure by directing the conversation onto another topic.

"Moira," I said trying to make my voice as forceful as I could, "tell me about your back pain. When did it begin? What happened?"

Her face reddened. She waved my remarks away with a sweep of her hand. But she neither reacted fearfully nor retreated back into her original timid character. Instead, she erupted. "Read the record, Yoyo! Don't give me any bullshit! You know about my back pains, why they forced me to come here—my supervisors and all those test results. It becomes very tedious doing everything for you. If I knew why I suffered these back pains, I wouldn't have to come to you for help. I would go back to Chester and get away from those awful pricks I live with. Don't get the mistaken impression that this police job is any great shakes. Shall we continue?"

I gasped, stunned by her outburst. This definitely was not the woman I had met just a short while ago. Although I was confused by the seemingly unconnected flow of her statements, I tried to follow her lead.

"By all means, return to Chester," I hastily interjected. "I'm sorry about those stupid questions. I'm kind of new at this, but I thought that it might help in getting to know you. By the way, who is Chester?"

Completely ignoring my question, Moira responded aggressively, "All you have to do is ask, if you want to get to know me. Now let's try and fit the pieces together if we can."

"Sure, let's do that," I mumbled weakly.

As soon as I said that, her face changed quickly again. The red flush that had come over it when she was angry was gone. In its place was the pale, agonized face of the timid woman I had met in the waiting room. Her body stiffened again. She looked pained and uncomfortable as she moved to the edge of the plastic chair. She didn't respond to my words.

I didn't know what to do next. So I just sat there. Finally, I glanced over at the ticking clock on the wall and noticed gratefully that the time for our session was coming to an end.

"I didn't realize that the time flew by so quickly," I said anxiously, fumbling with my words. "We didn't really have a chance to talk about it, but I assume you know that our sessions are scheduled for forty-five minutes. I have another patient waiting. Maybe we can set up a contract to work with each other at the next session. Then we can start fitting the pieces of your life together." I smiled weakly as these pretentious words slid out of my mouth.

Wearily she nodded, "It's okay, Dr. Obler. I appreciate your help, but I know that I'm just wasting your time listening to my trivial problems." Her voice was now weak, hesitant. That strange, affected accent was gone as well.

We shook hands and I walked her out to the waiting room. I felt like a failure as a therapist. I wondered if Moira would ever return. I was greatly relieved when Gail introduced me to my next patient. For the rest of the day I didn't make the same mistake. I took refuge in that classic analytic pose—silence.

At 6:30, when my last session was over, I walked wearily out to the waiting room and leaned over the reception desk.

"How was it?" Gail asked gently.

"Terrible," I said dejectedly. "I'm ill-equipped to be a therapist. In fact, I'm in worse shape than the patients I'm supposed to be helping."

Gail looked at me sympathetically. "It couldn't have been that bad."

I shook my head. "Worse. My first patient threw me for a loop."

"Moira?" Gail asked.

I stroked my forehead thoughtfully. "I don't know if she was putting me on, playing with me, or what. I thought I understood mental illness, but I couldn't read her at all." I sighed heavily, "I botched it so badly she may never come back."

"You're pretty distraught, Martin," Gail said, watching me. "Maybe you should schedule an appointment with Dr. Mardoff."

I nodded gratefully. "The sooner the better."

"How's first thing tomorrow morning?" she asked, scanning her appointment book.

"Good. Thanks a lot, Gail." I patted her shoulder.

She smiled. "Now get some sleep. The first day's over."

"Thank God," I said, walking quickly toward the same door I'd entered with such high hopes that morning.

TWO

Meeting Mardoff

He strode into the room, a silver-haired, ruddy, and militarily-erect man in his early fifties. He was perfectly cast for his supervisory role: meticulously dressed in a double-breasted gray flannel suit and a navy blue regimental tie adorned by a Phi Beta Kappa key.

"What is it, Obler?" he asked with a trace of annoyance he made no effort to hide.

"I'm sorry to bother you, sir," I said hesitantly, trying to gather my thoughts together so they sounded intelligible.

He looked straight into my eyes. "Never hesitate to bother me. I am your supervisor." He drew the word out so long I flinched. "I am here to answer your questions."

"Thank you, sir," I said gratefully.

"Well," he said crisply, "let's hear it!"

I cleared my throat. "I'm having difficulty with one particular patient," I finally began. "The other patients seem fairly straightforward, but she's very different. I do not understand how to approach her."

"We call them *clients* these days," Mardoff corrected sharply. "I assume that you are talking about Moira. Don't be fooled by initial appearances. What kind of difficulty are you having?"

"She seemed to take on a new personality midstream,"

I explained earnestly. "One moment she appeared passive and vulnerable and the next she was forceful and inaccessible. We've spoken in class about a new diagnosis—alternating or multiple personalities. I've been wondering if that could apply here. It was just so strange."

Mardoff frowned. "Don't let her play games with you. It's an old trick—many women play it this way to catch you off guard," he instructed. "If you get hooked, you'll never establish a positive working relationship. She will never build trust in you if you don't establish who is in control quickly. I believe my report clearly outlined the diagnosis of hysteria. As a new trainee, she probably hoped to snag your interest by putting on a good show. That way you won't be able to observe the boredom and isolation she feels as an aging woman. Hysterical women often use such attention-getting devices. Be careful, seduction is their major weapon."

I swallowed hard. "The idea of Moira manipulating me had crossed my mind," I said slowly, "but I had discarded it." My first image of a helpless and distressed Moira rose in front of me. In the next moment it was supplanted by a second image—the one of the dominant and aggressive Moira I had glimpsed later in the session. I grimaced. I prided myself on not letting people play me for a fool. Had she? I studied Mardoff. He certainly knew what buttons to push.

"How do you suggest I proceed with her?" I asked. I felt foolish having been so gullible. While I still had a few doubts about his interpretation, I was awed by the confidence he displayed. His argument was certainly classic.

He fingered the Phi Beta Kappa key. "Just sit back. Respond neutrally," he instructed. "Don't react to her play-acting and games. It is imperative that you encourage a healthy behavior on her part. It is the only way the transference can unfold properly. Hysterics would like nothing better than a little acting out with their therapists."

I nodded obediently. I was overwhelmed by Mardoff's competency and professional astuteness. He was the epitome of psychiatric stature in both appearance and command of technique. He was the image of the perfect practitioner. I had no doubts that I wanted to be like him.

I thought I detected a note of hostility in his initial evaluation of Moira, but if so, it was well disguised. Anyway I couldn't be sure, even if it had been there, on what it was based. Perhaps he had negative feelings toward schizoid women or some broader category. I wondered if Mardoff was ever accused of being a misogynist, as Freud had been.

I watched him. He had begun speaking again, quietly but intensely, his strong eyes riveting me.

"Repressed females like Moira redirect their anger at men through their sexuality. If the seduction approach is not successful, hypochondriacal or bodily complaints usually follow," he continued. He was of course referring to the symptoms of pain in her back. "She must be experiencing difficulties in her married life. I would guess that sex with her policeman husband is problematic. Do not misinterpret there; that isn't to suggest that she ever actually enjoys intercourse. In general, hysterical females do not. They just use sex as a means to hold onto their men. Most often, they will turn to aggression when their sexual overtures are not successful. This aggression serves to mask their fragility." He added rather meanly, "She certainly succeeded in doing that in your first session."

I recoiled. Obviously he was experiencing a sense of anger at having to consider the trivia I brought up when bigger and more vital issues demanded his time.

"I know I'm just wasting your time listening to my trivial problems," I flushed. The words had fallen out of my mouth before I had time to consider their meaning. I suddenly remembered these were the exact words Moira had spoken to me at the end of our session. I wondered why they had come to mind.

"Please go on." Mardoff was the epitome of graciousness now. "I am very interested in your making a good beginning here."

I relaxed a bit. I was lucky to have such a distinguished

man as a supervisor. I really wanted to know more about his thinking on hysteria. "Is that why she played out that aggressive role after appearing so weak walking into therapy?" I questioned. I also wanted to impress him with how much theory I had accumulated in graduate school and so continued without waiting for his reply, "Yes, of course, I see your point. You've identified her symptoms as fitting the classical Freudian description of psychosomatic rechanneling," I continued. "In your intake report you mentioned that you felt she might be malingering in order to get out of her job. Are her back pains developing from sexual repression, or is she pretending to have pain to avoid working?"

Without missing a beat, he confidently responded, "The answer to your first question is, yes. As for the second, yes to the first part and yes and no to the second. It is commonly understood that rage and anger develop when individuals are forced into obligatory sexual relations with their partners. Having no easily accessible avenue to adequately express these feelings, they often develop bodily ailments. This is a direct result of blocking these feelings. I believe that she was predisposed to this type of situation and then started using these symptoms as a secondary gain value."

His articulation of the professional jargon was superb. I was clearly no match for this man. Still, I felt even more driven to prove myself to him. I wanted to show him that I was an exceptional clinical student. I started to speak, but Mardoff glanced at his watch and cut me off authoritatively.

"I'm afraid I really must go. At your next session with Moira I strongly suggest you explore the origin of her back pain."

He started to walk away. At the door he paused, "And, Obler," his intense eyes were back on me, "I strongly recommend you avoid any appearance of warmth or support." Without changing his expression, he lowered his voice which still carried across the room. "Warmth could be misinterpreted by her as interest in her seductive behavior."

I felt my face redden. Before I could reply he had waved with a flourish and was gone.

Three

Other Demons

In the interim between meeting with Mardoff and my next session with her, I thought obsessively about Moira. While much of what Mardoff said made sense on a theoretical level, it did not match my perception or intuitive sense about her. I felt that though the power had shifted several times during our first session, neither Moira nor I were really in control.

Despite what Mardoff had said, Moira did not seem to be faking the second character that had emerged during my initial meeting with her, and even if she was, I couldn't see Mardoff's point regarding her manipulation of me. She had not acted seductively during our interaction. The switch in her personality was between an aggressive self and a weak and passive self. In neither case did I pick up sexual signals. The strong feelings she evoked in me were compassion, fear, and anger. I didn't understand why Mardoff was so certain that seduction was the means she would use to empower herself. I needed to explore this much further with Mardoff and determine what was going on.

"What about the rapid and intense shift in her behavior?" I asked at the start of my next session with him. I was hoping that this time Mardoff would see my point. "Such changes must signify something more important than hysteria or manipulation," I continued. "You pointed out that hysteria is brought on by repression, but the second character Moira played was not at all repressed but actually quite powerful and assertive. The question I kept asking myself was, Can she assume different states of consciousness at will or is it without her awareness?" I took a deep breath and gathered up my nerve. "I recognize that I'm new at this, but my gut feeling after rethinking that initial session is that we might have a dual or multiple personality on our hands." I leaned forward expectantly.

"Your imagination and need for excitement is getting the better of you, Mister Obler." Mardoff smiled condescendingly, but his tone indicated impatience, almost annoyance. "Though you may not share my confidence, you may rest assured that my judgement skills are based on many years of experience. I am quite certain that I would have picked up something so irregular in my initial interview with her. Are you completely lacking confidence in my judgement?" He paused and gave me an icy glare. I shivered involuntarily as he continued, "Furthermore, you must be aware that there are very few documented cases of multiple personalities that have withstood scientific verification. Most often, as with Moira, they are shown to be nothing more than malingerers, or, in some cases, they turn out to be chronic criminals feebly attempting to avoid responsibility for their action."

"Dr. Mardoff," I felt myself flushing. Aware that I was on rugged ground, I chose my next words with care. "I am aware that only 263 cases of the disorder have been properly documented," trying to show him that I had done my homework since the last meeting. "Still, doesn't the possibility exist here? In any case, this patient is clearly in deep trouble. She seems driven to reveal a side of herself that may have been disguised for years. I don't think she is aware of the changes in her self-presentation. Of course, this is just my feeling. The hidden part of her was just begging for support. I am convinced that Moira needs warmth to soothe those very deep scars. I wonder if she suffered sexual abuse as a child. I feel certain that her behavior is not contrived. In your opinion, couldn't this serve as an alternative theory—a kind of antithesis?"

"I see that you are eager to fall for the female seduction bit," he interjected irritably, dismissing my hypothesis with a wave of his hand. "Neurotic women use whatever weapons they can unearth to perpetuate their neuroses. An example from the natural world might illustrate my point more effectively: Consider the case of the black widow spider. At first encounter, the female spider presents a powerless facade to the male spider. Trapping the male in her web, however, she then proceeds to destroy and devour him. He hasn't been watching carefully enough, has he? He's been caught off guard." Mardoff smiled disagreeably.

After waiting a minute for the analogy to sink in, he continued. "Moira is well aware of power dynamics and how to play them. With most of her family in the police force, this is probably her way of competing for power with her supervisors or husband. Most certainly, she has developed the back symptoms as a means to manipulate them, to force them to take care of her."

Mardoff said sourly, "That's how these women operate, since they don't have the arsenal to deal effectively with men in a more direct way." His lips tightened. "You need to read Freud more diligently. This type of behavior is practically set in stone. It has been this way for ten thousand years. I strongly suggest that you avoid this supportive nonsense. Your job is to patiently wait for her to open up. It will all be there waiting for you, the whole mapping of her defensive structure."

I sighed, listening to him hammer home his points again and again. I had to admit that he was very persuasive. He spoke with an undeniable authority. There was just a hint of an implied threat, a sarcasm, carefully disguised with humor, probably meant to scare off the less experienced. However, I remained unconvinced. My experience with Moira during that first session was simply too powerful. The memory of our exchange felt completely different from what he was describing.

Despite my convictions, I knew that it wasn't in my best interest as a clinical student to struggle with Mardoff. Still, I suspected that on some level this conflict was fated to emerge.

There was something about Moira that was so vulnerable, so unforgettable. While I knew that she reminded me of someone, I wasn't able to pinpoint who. Mentally, I went through the roster of possibilities. Could it be my schizophrenic sister Shirley or maybe it was the second of my three sisters, Libby, or my frightened mother. I looked through Mardoff, who was still talking. My mind spun backwards.

My parents were immigrants. Having few or no family contacts, both my parents were quite alone in the world. Each was getting on in age and neither had found a suitable partner. My father needed a woman to cook and clean for him. My mother was poor and uneducated. Her world view began and ended at the edge of the tiny Polish farming village where she was born. Nothing in her upbringing could adequately prepare her for her ultimate arrival in the great and bustling metropolis called New York.

Sent by her family, she arrived with thousands of other travelers at Ellis Island. It was the early part of the Twentieth Century. The expectations had changed dramatically. In Poland, surrounded by an extended family, she had been given neither choices nor responsibility. She had simply done what she was told. Illiterate, unskilled, alone, she spent her life attempting to cope with her new reality.

As a small child my mother spoon-fed me haunting stories of her arrival in the great and terrifying black hole known as the New World. These tales left me with permanent reminders of the precariousness of life and confirmed how frighteningly alone we all are.

My mother's natural passivity was reinforced by the many ordeals she survived during those early years.

The marriage broker arranged everything—the introduction, the meetings, the marriage itself. This was a common practice within the Jewish community at that time. It was one of the many customs that had trailed the immigrants in their move to the new world.

From the very beginning, my father and mother's match was a poor one. They had little in common. After a time my father secured employment as a steam fitter at the Brooklyn Navy Yard. He was let go when he contacted smoke poisoning on the job. Thereafter he was only able to work as a pushcart peddler selling thrown-away potato sacks. Most of the family income and resources came from welfare supplements and food supplies given to us as handouts.

My mother's fear and loneliness were exasperated when, with the responsibility of four children to feed and clothe, she still faced the same poverty she had known all her life. Her dreams of a better life with a man to take care of her quickly crumbled. In her frustration and fear, she made crystal clear her belief that a man's only real value to his family was as the bread winner. Since my father was unable to support us, she emphasized, he disqualified himself as a man.

My father began to drink. He became physically and sexually abusive to my mother. His outrage at her was expressed through beatings and sexual encounters bordering on rape. They grew to hate each other.

They never realized that each despised and resented the other for things beyond their control: loneliness, isolation, poverty.

My sister Shirley was the product of their first year of cohabitation. As the first born, Shirley received the brunt of their mutual anger. Temperament and genetic predisposition may also have contributed to make Shirley more vulnerable than the three children to follow. Libby was their second child, born a year and a half after Shirley. Then, three and a half years later, my sister Selma was born. I followed approximately five years later.

I say approximately because everything concerning facts, dates, or time sequence was not easy to determine in my family.

Unable to read or understand the official documents given to her, my mother was incapable of keeping any valid records of important events in her children's lives. Even the record of my birth remains somewhat of a mystery. I was born on the last day of December. Since my birthday fell on the last day of the year, I was always curious as to the time of my birth.

My birth certificate just recorded the date. My mother could only remember that I was born in Brooklyn Jewish Hospital. I questioned her continuously throughout my childhood. After many years of prodding, the only other information my mother came up with was that right after I was delivered, there were loud noises outside and people yelling. I decided that I must have been born just before the start of the New Year.

I had the same problem obtaining accurate information concerning events surrounding my siblings. My oldest sister, Shirley, embarked on a path of emotional self-destruction before I was born. The only information my parents could supply was that sometime before my fourth birthday she was removed from the house. She was shipped off to a state institution on Long Island.

After she was sent away to the hospital, my parents denied her very existence. They pretended it was some other family that had a crazy daughter. At times, they actually claimed that they had three children instead of four.

My only memory of Shirley dates from a trip I took with my father to visit her. I was six at the time. At the asylum they brought out my sister in a drab white hospital gown. She had wild, long brown hair flowing about her shoulders. Her eyes were piercing, and she looked like the crazy women I'd seen in my neighborhood.

I had always been frightened of them. These were the women who could be seen roaming the street, screaming incomprehensible accusations and muttering things to themselves. When my father introduced my sister Selma and me to Shirley, she ran toward me and clawed at my eyes. Only my father's timely intervention saved me.

Later, from the pieces of the puzzle I managed to put together, I realized that Shirley must have been psychologically and emotionally brutalized by my parents. She became the target of their hatred for each other. In those days, poor people shipped their disabled children to the state mental institutions. During the height of the Great Depression, resources were so scarce that it came down to a basic question of family survival. One had to cut one's losses. Poor families could not realistically carry the additional burden of psychotic youngsters.

During the time that Shirley remained in the family, her presence acted as a kind of shield for Libby and Selma, my other two sisters. My parents had assigned Shirley the role of pawn in their war against each other. In contrast, Libby and Selma simply suffered physical and emotional neglect. Yet, given the alternative that Shirley faced, they fared comparatively well during that critical time in their development. Their psychological problems surfaced later.

In adolescence, my second sister, Libby, would often display sudden and vicious anger. This was primarily directed at my father. Sometimes, her anger could be understood as an expression of rage over not getting her own way. At times, however, the anger was sudden, unpremeditated, and filled with fury.

Out on the street all day selling his potato sacks, he would return home cold and worn out. Frequently, after finishing a long day of work, my father would rest quietly on the living room radiator.

Most often, Libby would simply regard him with hostility and disdain. Occasionally, she would burst into a sudden fit of rage. She was not psychotic at the time. Still, even as a child, I realized that her anger seemed to have no connection to what was happening between them. It appeared to be coming from some internal place in Libby as foreign to my father as to me. I could only imagine that she hated my father because she sensed his underlying rejection of her.

I was the fourth and last child in my family, and as the sole male child in a Jewish family with origins in Eastern Europe, I received the only love that any family member ever got. In addition to the strength secured through that love, I was also the strongest of my siblings by temperament. By age eight or nine, I had already developed the skills to effectively intercede in fights between my parents. I could also mediate conflicts between my siblings and parents.

Of course, my being a male and having better coping skills did not entirely protect me. As all the vulnerable children in our household, I too suffered painful emotional scars living in that disturbed environment.

Now sitting in Mardoff's office and only half-listening to him, I felt the past and present mingle in my mind. I wondered if it was Shirley that Moira reminded me of, rather than Libby, or could it be some combination of both of them? Moira's extreme vulnerability reminded me most of Shirley, the weakest link in my family chain. Still, the interesting thing about Moira was her strange combination of mood swings and seeming shifts in personality. She seemed at one moment so vulnerable and sensitive and then at the next moment to show an assertive confidence and control.

Years of fearful fantasies about my sister's experiences in the mental hospital drove me now. *At all costs*, I thought watching Mardoff intently, *I must shield Moira from a fate similar to Shirley's.*

I returned to the present. Mardoff was shaking his finger at me. Involuntarily I drew back from my formidable mentor and at the same time tried to focus on what he was saying so vehemently.

I felt overwhelmed. How could I engage Mardoff in battle? I was an inexperienced student; he a consummate powerful professional. Yet I could not seem to give in to his powerful but, in my opinion, mistaken theories. A new strategy was necessary—one that could successfully reconcile the opposing desires within me. I needed to keep Mardoff on my side, yet do the kind of therapy I believed was in Moira's best interest.

I played for time. "In your opinion, what is the best approach to use if she continues the play-acting manipulation again at the next session?" I asked Mardoff hesitantly, trying to figure out which step to take next. "Should I let things flow and not intervene, or do I point out to her that I'm onto her game?"

"As long as your responses are neutral and do not interfere with the process, it doesn't matter," Mardoff testily replied. "In other words, if you decide to take an active role, remember not to interpret, just question. Do not, under any circumstances, show any warmth or support to this histrionic woman."

Why does he keep calling her a histrionic woman, I wondered? This really puzzled me. It was clearly too early to draw a conclusion of this kind. I reminded myself not to question his judgement or threaten him. At all cost, I must avoid direct conflict or confrontation. Patronizing him seemed to be the best tactic.

"I feel much more comfortable now. Thank you for the advice," I responded, using my best grateful student tone and getting up to leave. "I've taken too much of your valuable time already," I said humbly.

"Quite alright, Obler. Just put into practice what I've suggested," he paused a moment and fingered his Phi Beta Kappa key again, then went on, "and you will find that both your patient and you," he fixed his ice blue eyes on me, "benefit."

FOUR

Family Ties

Moira arrived exactly on time for our next session. The form-fitting heather grey suit that she was wearing enhanced her attractive figure. Her back pain was not evident, and she looked almost cheerful. "I've felt so much better all week," she said, "I'm eager to begin." She was very animated and excited. She described the many changes she experienced in handling things. "Even my back doesn't hurt so much," she said in a breathy, throaty voice.

"But it still hurts," I said.

"Yes it does, but you've helped me so much already. You can't imagine how awful it was before."

As we sat facing each other, what she was unable to articulate in words, she expressed through her body. As she struggled for the words to describe the changes in her, her body spoke clearly of her pain.

Somehow, I got a sense that the pain was long standing. It was not just a manifestation of the power struggles she was having in the police department. Perhaps Mardoff was right that her back pain was just a symptom of hysteria. However, I suspected that the source of the hysteria lay elsewhere.

Watching her I thought about Mardoff's speculation. I felt more than ever that they were projections of his own personal underlying struggles, just as mine were. I would have to isolate Moira's real issues from mine and his in order to help her. If only I could find out more about the true origins of her back pain. I had the feeling I would be able to make a good beginning.

While the robbery incident had undeniably triggered a serious psychosomatic outbreak, I felt certain that her problem did not begin there. I wondered if the incident was symbolic for Moira in some way, or was the pressure of her unexamined anxiety simply too much for her, like a time bomb, which erupted within her that fateful day?

As she continued to talk about the healthy feelings that had arisen within her during the prior week, I wondered if the powerful and aggressive personality I had glimpsed in our first session would re-emerge during this one. I secretly yearned for that other personality to appear, so that I could discover whether my suspicions that she had multiple personalities was true.

However, Mardoff had cautioned me not to interfere with the unfolding process. I made the practical decision to follow his advice. Moira spent the remainder of the hour rattling on about how well she felt. Apparently one meeting with me had worked miracles, curing all her ailments. We ended the meeting on a positive note, "I look forward to our next session," she said smiling. Her clear green eyes met mine directly. When she reached out for my hand I felt the electricity, and startled, I realized what a sensual woman she was.

The next few sessions with Moira were uneventful. She did not want to explore either the robbery incident that had set off her back pain or any emotional conflicts she had in the past or present with her family. The only significant thing she told me was that she had very little memory of the robbery that triggered her psychosomatic injury.

"My home life, marriage, and mothering are very satisfying," she insisted. "Work is going well and I can't see any reason for being in therapy." She seemed to have forgotten what happened between us during the first meeting. Our contacts were superficial and lacked intimacy.

I was impatient with Mardoff's advice to sit and listen. I felt trivial and inconsequential. I wondered what the purpose of therapy was. My classes at the university were far more interesting than the work I was doing with Moira or any of my other assigned patients.

Although all the other graduate students in my classes kept making grand declarations in public about how fascinating their cases were, comparing notes with my close colleagues in private, I found that most felt inwardly disappointed. Therapy wasn't living up to our expectations. We weren't doing the kind of work we'd imagined. The romantic images we saw portrayed in Hollywood movies about therapy and therapists did not match our reality.

One afternoon, I, along with many of the students, decided to cut classes and go as a group to a movie at a museum. It was the classic film *Snake Pit* with Olivia DeHavilland. When I saw the saddened faces of the lonely mental patients dancing together on the dining room floor of the hospital, I cried uncontrollably. I fantasized that one day I would be the great therapist who could rescue them.

I could not seem to stop crying. Later that afternoon when I saw my analyst, Jill Holiday, I complained, "I've never felt more emotionally frail than I did watching the movie. The warmth, sensitivity and strength of the hospital staff overwhelmed me.

"The professors in the clinical program insist on the importance of maintaining strict neutrality in the therapeutic process. They emphasize the need to concentrate on the transference and countertransference issues that would surface with our patients. They tell us we must avoid emotional identification with them, we must remain objective. But I'm not sure it works," I said.

Jill, a tall, auburn-haired, thirtyish woman, looked at me sympathetically. "Have you thought out the possibility of a connection to your sister Shirley?" she asked. "Was she so alone?"

I was unable to trust myself to answer, and so I cut the meeting short.

At a rap session the next day with my fellow students, I brought up my own discontent with how I was performing. It became clear that many of the others also felt uncomfortable with the theoretical prescriptions they were being taught. "I feel lost," Hal, a sandy-haired guy, said. "I'm uneasy with the cold, indifferent posture being recommended by our mentors."

"I feel confused and ineffectual," Maria, a Spanish girl with large ebony eyes, contributed.

My fellow students reported that a large number of their patients had dropped out after only a few weeks of therapy. "How are we to help people if we scare them away from therapy?" asked Brian, a gray-haired older intern. "Wouldn't significant patient attrition reflect badly on us?"

These opinions fed my natural inclination to encourage warm supportive relationships with my patients. I recognized that this approach would not be successful with everyone, but I felt particularly strongly about implementing such a plan with Moira. I hoped that by building trust based on caring, she would feel more comfortable with me and start to open up.

I felt concerned about the conflict between the standard theories and practices professed by my teachers and my own instincts. While I understood that a patient's trust was built through a belief that the therapist refrained from passing judgments, was indifference the only means to communicate objectivity? How was I to handle the scorn of the authorities when I exhibited signs of warmth toward patients? Like a stubborn puppy, I decided to address these concerns once again with Mardoff.

We met on that Wednesday morning before the clinic opened. "Dr. Mardoff, I don't feel anything important is happening in therapy with Moira. She just goes on and on about the enormous progress she is making and how well she feels in general. Then she says that she doesn't need therapy and isn't sure why she has to keep coming. I just sit there acting neutral as you suggested, but the meaningless chatter continues. Moreover, she never mentions a thing about her strange behavior during our first meeting."

I paused, took a deep breath, and then continued, "Some of the other interns are feeling the same way. Most of our patients are not sophisticated and have very little idea about the therapeutic process. I was wondering if you thought we should reconsider our strategy? My thought was that by showing support, we might encourage a greater degree of trust, opening up real feelings during therapy. Perhaps a little warmth, to help them feel it's a friendly atmosphere?"

Mardoff's face turned white with sudden rage. "While you are correct that many students feel the way you do," he responded arrogantly, "it stems from their own unresolved needs. An accepting and warm environment, when confronting tension, may make the therapist more comfortable. However, it is counterproductive for the patient. We are doing therapy for the patients, are we not?"

Mardoff seemed to be getting more and more heated. He went on, "You must recognize that it discourages a true transference process from occurring. The patient's repressed experiences cannot emerge. I will not continuously repeat myself, Mr. Obler. You must avoid imposing this unnecessary interference. You must remain objective and uninvolved emotionally during the course of treatment."

I felt troubled. "But isn't each patient to be regarded as an individual whose needs and experiences vary from other patients? Isn't it possible that some patients require warmth to build trust? Without that trust, couldn't the patient's resistance actually obstruct the emergence of the transference? If it helps Moira trust me, makes her feel more comfortable, and solicits more meaningful material for treatment," I pleaded, "wouldn't that encourage her to work more effectively?"

Mardoff tipped his chair back. "Perhaps, Mr. Obler,

you should examine your real motives in the situation." In a flash of anger, I suddenly realized that, strange as it seemed, I was relating to Mardoff in the same way Moira related to me. Mardoff assumed a position of power. He was the authority. He alone knew what was going on. There were no questions of perception or judgement, but only of fact.

In my churning thoughts were frustration, confusion, and anger. In my exchange with Moira, the same dynamic was evident. I held all the answers. Moira must please me or I'd ruin her chances at work. My unresponsive, analytical pose must keep her guessing—which answer does he want, which answer will win me my freedom? For expediency's sake, both Moira and I recognized that we had to try to get along with our authority figure. We each had good reason for the fear and anxiety we felt.

Mardoff's lips had tightened. "She's trying to manipulate you. She wants to seduce you into becoming her friend. But this, in fact, defeats the purpose of the therapy," Mardoff suggested cleverly.

He added, his eyes fixed intently on me, "By becoming the good parent, and not the parent she experienced as a child, you delay the transference process. You hinder the emergence of the most important early deprivations with her parents. By remaining neutral, neither offering nor denying her support or warmth, you reproduce the conditions that set off the nucleus of her pathology. Eliciting these conditions and helping her gain insight about her role in this dynamic, you can assist her in rechanneling the neuroses into healthier sublimations."

Mardoff continued, his words snapped out like a command, "Do not fall so easily into the traps of the inexperienced therapist. Do not permit yourself to be seduced by the recent, and may I add, marginal literature. Psychoanalysis has a historical perspective, years of solid research, conclusions based on well thought-out and tested theories."

He concluded with a flourish, "Providing affection and warmth to female patients only feeds their neuroses. It's just like in a marriage. By nature, women need men—their fathers, brothers, husbands—to set limits for them. Women can't recognize boundaries; they demand attention ceaselessly until the man establishes the line. That's ultimately what most want and need."

I nodded. I was impressed by how well he applied psychoanalytic theory to support his own conclusions. Still, underneath it all, I felt I detected an undercurrent of hostility toward women. Was this hostility inherent in psychoanalysis itself, or was it attributable only to Mardoff's own perspective? I didn't know.

While I questioned his opinion, my own insecurities did not permit me to openly challenge him. Maybe I was just missing some essential information, or maybe my stubbornness was getting in the way. Was I misunderstanding his point on purpose? I knew that I would have to back down, at least for now.

"Dr. Mardoff, I must thank you again for your patience. It's not easy for a new student to know how to correctly handle these difficult cases. Of course, I will follow your advice and remain neutral with my patients. Thanks for putting me back on the right track," I indulged him. "Do you think I should mention what happened in our first meeting to Moira? She hasn't shown that other assertive personality since then."

He tapped his fingers drill-like on the desk, "Mr. Obler, you don't seem to be grasping the concept. Strict noninterference is your best strategy. I strongly recommend not mentioning it until she brings it up." We ended the supervisory session abruptly.

At my next session with Moira, I followed Mardoff's advice and said nothing. To my surprise, Moira began to describe the events surrounding the emergence of her back pain. My self-confidence was shaken. Maybe Mardoff was right after all. I listened carefully and without interruption to her story of the robbery.

"What happened after you felt the back pain?" I finally asked.

"Nothing. I just remained frozen there on the sidewalk. I stared at the flashing red lights of the patrol cars arriving on the scene. Then I saw my husband's face. . . . Would you believe that his patrol car was called to the scene?"

Her face contorted as she recalled her colleagues arriving. It became obvious that her memories made her intensely uncomfortable. She began to shake and tightly clutched the arms of the chair. Saliva formed on the edges of her mouth. At first, I thought she might be experiencing some kind of seizure, but she continued talking.

"Now that is what I call fate, my dear," she said. Her voice was very strange. I sat upright, my eyes widening as she continued. "Can you imagine those pricks arriving with my idiotic husband. As if it was not enough to be humiliated by that fuckin' thief escaping! Now I had to face my husband's ridicule as well. You should have seen the looks on their faces."

As she spoke, Moira's accent changed. The normal Brooklyn-Irish inflection in her voice was gone. In its place was an affected British diction that clashed with the vulgar language. It was the same voice that had emerged in our first meeting.

I took a deep breath, wondering what I should do next. Mardoff had cautioned me not to interfere. He said to permit her the room to acknowledge these changes herself. I looked at her despairingly, because she did not seem conscious of the changes in her voice or demeanor.

"Why did you feel humiliated when your colleagues and husband arrived?" I stiffly asked. "I would think that you would welcome their support—particularly in a dangerous situation like that."

"You don't know my husband and his friends at the precinct," she answered, leaning toward me plaintively.

However, she had returned to her normal voice. "Those cops don't support any of the women on the force."

I tried to contain my surprise. Was she aware of what she had said or not? Could she be conscious of her personality change as well? I had no tangible evidence either way, but somehow, despite the contradictions, I felt that she was oblivious of any such change. I decided to try a gentle prod.

"You sounded very angry at them before. You even called them pricks and idiots. Could you tell me why?" I asked softly.

"Pricks and idiots?" she asked, her face and neck flushing in obvious embarrassment. "What are you talking about?"

Was she putting me on? Minutes before, she had acknowledged her previous statement. Yet now, she was acting as though it had never happened. I studied her intently. She seemed completely sincere.

Totally flustered, I once again contemplated my next move. My confidence shaken, I had to rethink my whole strategy. Should I follow Mardoff's instructions or my own intuition? I remembered a classmate's advice to avoid direct confrontation. Bypassing the whole subject seemed the safest course of action.

"You mentioned first noticing the back pain when you were chasing the robbery suspect," I responded, ignoring her question. "I was wondering if any other symptoms of physical distress come to mind, I mean prior to the incident?"

Moira gave a wan smile. "Not that I remember, but what does it matter anyway? I'm a loser any way you look at it. Nothing I do ever works out," she said dejectedly.

"According to my mother and sister, I botch up anything I touch. Look how I handled my gun while chasing the thief during the robbery. That was really competent behavior, wasn't it? My husband and those other officers tried to console me as best they could. I just bring it all on myself. I know that their scorn was my fault. My feeling humiliated is my problem, not theirs. After all, if I can't do the job right, I don't deserve to be an officer."

"Moira," I said and looked off into the distance, "perhaps," I stopped short. Though I was trying to hide my feelings and appear neutral, I knew that my body language communicated the disapproval I felt of her self-denigration. I didn't want to censure her but could not seem to help myself. I went on, "It sounds like you're trying to cover up something. Could it be anger toward your husband for not supporting your behavior during the bank incident? Do the attitudes of your male colleagues toward women officers bother you?"

Moria's whole body started trembling. The motion was similar to the spasmatic body movements she had exhibited during our first session. As I watched her I realized that I had made a mistake confronting her. She was clearly too fragile. Now the damage was done.

Moria's face turned ghost white. Her trembling stopped—her body became rigid. The only movement I could detect was the gritting of her teeth.

Suddenly she screamed out, *"That fucking pig!* When we got home, he really gave it to me. He told me what a fool I was—have always been. Then, he beat me till there were welts all over my body." Moria's voice was shrill and out of control. "Clever man, he made sure to hit me where nobody would notice the swelling." She paused and the rage seemed to abate as she continued, "But he does it all the time and I guess I deserve it." Again she paused and then sighed, "He's my darling."

At first, I felt by successfully summoning Moira's suppressed personality, the one that I had witnessed during our first meeting, I now had the means to vindicate myself with Mardoff. Here was the angry, aggressive woman who had been completely absent from our sessions since that first time. I wished that Mardoff were here to observe this new personality. I wondered to what degree she controlled her behavior? "He's my darling," she repeated in a despairing whisper.

I sat there silently, waiting for her next move. I knew that eventually I would have to respond to her. Thoughts whirled about within me. I could casually mention some element of her aggressive outburst again or return to her back pain as I had done before, or I could feign disinterest and move on to something completely different—that might throw her off guard.

I felt driven to determine whether or not this was all a game for her as Mardoff had implied. One alternative would be to reject the neutral approach and play back with her. I might reflect back to her some of her own uneven behavior or I might even try a direct confrontation. I could feign anger at her denial or I could try to corner her into admitting that she has been pretending all the time.

All of those things were possible, but I didn't feel competent enough watching her to try any of them. I returned to the relative safe ground of her back pain. In response, she laughed. Then, with a frozen smile on her face, she stated calmly but in that strange affected voice, "The fucking thing never stops killing me. Killing me . . . like the rest of them."

I gasped. Now what was I going to do?

The mere possibility that Moira might be totally unaware of these shifts in her personality was incredibly seductive. Still, the fact that Moira was conscious of at least some of the content of her statement indicated that she could be acting deceptively. Did I want her to be unaware of herself for my own needs?

It was all so confusing! I couldn't make up my mind: Was she acting deceptively or was she unaware that she was sweet and passive one moment and belligerent and assertive at another? I felt pressured by the fact that the session was drawing to an end. I needed some kind of closure, and I suspected that Moira felt the need as well.

"Have you consulted a physical therapist about your back pain?" I asked her. She shrugged noncommittally. Then trying to be off-handed, I added, "By the way, why do you refer to your back pain as 'the fucking thing'?" Moira looked at me for a long moment, then she stood up and without saying another word strolled out of the office.

I sat there transfixed until Gail announced my next patient.

The day before our next session, I had two dreams. All my other dreams in the year previous to these concerned my own activities. This time they concerned Moira. I even considered sharing them with her, despite the therapeutic inappropriateness of doing so. When I met again with Jill, my analyst, I told her about them, but I didn't mention them to Mardoff.

"In dream one," I said softly, "two women were running toward me. Their arms were stretched before them and they were moving through heavy fog. One of the women was smiling radiantly. She handed me a black handgun. The second woman seemed distressed because though her arms were stretched towards me, her hands were empty. For some reason, I had to choose between these women. I knew to Freudians my choice represented a powerful unresolved oedipal yearning.

"Even though we had not talked extensively about her parents during the sessions, I felt that the two characters represented Moira's mother and father. In the dream as in reality she was trapped between their opposing emotional demands. The mother demanded complete obedience and left little room for Moira to enjoy the pleasure of childhood. So, for reasons yet to be determined, Moira displaced her pleasure needs as a child onto fantasies of sexual contact with her father.

"I believe Moira's father's police gun is symbolic of her unconscious sexual desires. Thus, she asks her mother to let her play in the dream and when her mother refuses, Moira turns to her father. When her father rejects her need to be involved with him, she turns to me, hoping I can resolve the conflict." Jill was silent, but I continued.

"At first, Moira is the woman handing me the gun. When she discovers her father isn't there for her, she becomes the distressed woman. She suppresses her sexuality. During our sessions, I must have picked up these powerful oedipal strivings and conflicts in Moira and incorporated them into my dream about her.

"Perhaps," I said rubbing my chin thoughtfully, "the two women in the dream also represented her elder sister and mother. Her mother was portrayed as domineering and controlling—destroying her during her teenage and adult years. I interpreted Moira's crying at the end of the dream as her helplessness to do anything about the domination and rejection she felt."

I continued to speculate wildly. "Perhaps the gun that she saw lying on the bank floor precipitated her back problems. Maybe it was connected to these oedipal repressions, especially the statement in the dream 'The fucking thing is killing me.' Thus, 'fucking thing' represented both sexual cravings and the back injury."

I looked searchingly at Jill. "I recognize that these heavily biased Freudian interpretations are just conjecture. Nevertheless, I feel that in reality, they could be reflections of Moira's conflicts that I had gleaned from her during therapy." Jill nodded but said nothing. I went on.

"In my second dream, I entered a darkened church, a Madonna appeared at the door. It was Moira—pale and hollow-eyed. She beckoned me to the altar. I was unable to move. My feet seemed weighted. 'But I am Jewish,' I said. 'It's alright,' she replied, 'We must all suffer our sins as children of the Lord.' On the altar was the gun from the other dream. It appeared as a sacred object next to a portrait of Jesus on the cross. In the dream, I could see the gun, but it remained hidden from Moira's view. She searched about for something and saw the gun. Kneeling down, she kissed it and then offered it to me. I refused her gift, feeling it was sexual. As a professional, I knew that I wasn't supposed to get involved with her. She became angry and shouted, 'You fuckin' pig! You're all alike . . . you men.' Then she shrieked and pulled at her hair.

"I interpreted the second dream as consistent with the first. The only addition was the sexual tension between Moira and me. I felt that subconsciously either she was attracted to me, or I to her, or both. Since she also had spoken a little about her Catholicism, I felt there was a connection between her symptoms and religious guilt.

"I knew that I should talk with Mardoff about my dreams, but I hesitated. How would I feel if he slashed my analysis to shreds? What if my interpretations had no theoretical significance or validity? I felt that I could not risk making a fool of myself in front of him.

"I've been thinking about the shift in Moira's character in my second dream," I said to Jill. "Obviously, they represent the two personalities she revealed during our sessions. I am fascinated by the contrast between them."

Jill finally decided to intervene. "Why do you think that your last three sessions have been completely devoted to this one patient? We've discussed your perceptions and reactions, gone over in detail your dream interpretations. What we seem to have accomplished is avoidance of your personal life. I wonder if you have any thoughts about this?" she said pointedly.

Jill made a single comment about the dream. "Martin do you think that the dream might be the expression of your desire to assist Moira? Could it be an indirect means to compensate your sister Shirley for your inability to help her when you were a child? Did your fear of Shirley evoke also feelings of guilt and inadequacy?"

"I thought that I was supposed to discuss any significant thoughts or feeling," I said defensively. "While I may have been obsessing about this patient, I have been thinking about her constantly. I feel that Moira represents some conflict in my own life. Your observation that I have drawn an association between Moira and my institutionalized sister seems right on target.

"It's all I've been thinking about for the past week and

a half since I had the dreams. I'm confused as to how to resolve it. I know I ought to tell Mardoff, but I'm scared. I'm not sure how he will react to my interpretations. What will he think, knowing that I have been dreaming about a patient—one that I believe he is hostile toward?"

Jill looked at me intently. I rushed on as if in a soliloquy. "You think I'm being narcissistic, don't you? I know that a preoccupation with one patient can be interpreted as the therapist's need to play the savior/rescuer role. You think that I am getting off on my own need to feel brilliant and show off." I paused, and took a deep breath, then let it out. "Maybe you're right. But I don't think about anything else. All my other patients bore me. I've been neglecting my wife, ignoring my kids. Still, I can't get my mind off it. I am electrified by the possibility that I'm working with a multiple personality."

Jill's eyebrows went up. "Why don't you continue telling me what you speculated about in your second dream," she softly asked. Apparently, she had changed her mind concerning the importance of what I was saying.

I nodded. "I wondered if Moira's repressed sexuality was symbolically represented by the handgun in the dream." I keep thinking that the gun in the bank is in some way connected to her husband or her father. They are both policemen. Might the sight of the handgun on the sidewalk have aroused explosive sexual feelings—feelings that have been repressed because of her fear of them?" Jill was silent. She rubbed her chin thoughtfully.

I continued, "The gun near the crucifix might be guilt about these feelings. In the dream, she identified with the martyrdom of Jesus. That's the martyred person I see most of the time in therapy. Moira seems uptight and sexually suppressed until the other self emerges. Then she begins to express her anger and sexuality. The two seem inextricably tied in Moira."

"An interesting speculative analysis," Jill replied leaning her lean sinewy body toward me. A smile played across her face. She added gently, "Don't you think it may be a little early to express such strong and definite ideas regarding her diagnosis and treatment?"

My own voice rose heatedly. "Are you suggesting that I should focus more on my own needs in the situation? Figure out what is driving me with Moira, find out where it comes from in me?"

"Perhaps that would be more useful to you. Probably more accurate as well," she responded tautly.

"Isn't it the case that many of your patients express their confused and ambivalent feelings toward their parents through symbolic acts of self-destruction? Maybe the source of Moira's back pains are the conflicts she was having with her parents as a child."

My breathing grew heavy. "Could my neurosis of needing to touch people or things to reduce my anxieties come from similar unresolved conflicts? Perhaps it's in the nature of being human that you choose to hurt yourself symbolically when you can't hurt your parents for hurting you."

I continued pontificating, "I recognize that these interpretations sound pat and based on simplistic Freudian theories. I know that I have little evidence from the content of my sessions with Moira to believe they're true. Yet, I truly feel they are."

"Martin," Jill said quietly, "this session is almost over. I recommend strongly that you do not explore your dreams with Moira without discussing them first in supervision."

"I understand," I said noncommitally.

However, I had already made my decision: I would never share these feelings with Mardoff. I knew that Mardoff would disapprove and maintain that Moira had been successful in manipulating me. I also knew that I would discuss the dreams with Moira despite Jill's counseling.

I was not sure whether those decisions were foolish. Interpreting one's own dreams to a patient is a highly unorthodox behavior in most psychotherapeutic practices. Was I justified in taking this approach with Moira? I wasn't sure. I just knew I needed a working alliance with her, and I felt that this was the way to achieve it.

Even though I was going to share my dreams about Moira with her so she would trust me, I still did not completely trust her. I questioned whether she was putting on a powerful performance—playing games with me—but I knew the only way to establish a connection between us was to put myself on the line first.

When Moira arrived for our next session, she behaved as though nothing unusual had happened at our previous meeting. She seemed surprised when I told her I had dreamt about her. "Please tell me what you think they mean," she said.

I carefully selected only those portions of the dreams and interpretations that I felt would be useful for her to know. I chose them not to threaten her, but to hopefully lead to an examination of her own past. Moira seemed to understand. "I am glad you are so honest with me." A soft smile played around her mouth. "I can see you've been thinking about me and care about my pain. That means a lot," she said, reaching out for my hand as we faced each other at the door. During our next few meetings, she began to freely explore her family history with me for the first time.

FIVE

A Return to Moira's Past

"My parents," Moira said softly, "immigrated to the United States from a poverty-stricken Ireland. They were to have six children in as many years. I was the second born and also the second daughter; three brothers and a sister were to follow."

"How did they get along money-wise?" I asked.

"They were more financially stable than most of our immigrant neighbors. As a New York City policeman, my father brought home a moderate income and had relative job security. Although six children must certainly have placed a large burden on them, they were able to adequately feed and clothe all of us, which is more than a lot of people living around us could do—what with the country in a recession and all." Her gaze swept the room and then focused intently on me. I fidgeted in my chair.

"Following my father's example, all three of my brothers joined the New York City Police Department at the first opportunity. Of the three girls, I alone chose to pursue a career outside the family. My sisters became housewives like my mother before them."

"Was becoming a police officer a difficult decision?" She nodded.

"A really tough one for me. At first my family opposed

it, and I almost gave in to them; but I told myself I had to be brave. Somehow I was. Even though, as you can imagine, not many woman were employed by the NYPD at that time."

"Did you have any encouragement?"

"The only people who really believed in me were my mother's parents, who had arrived in this country a few months after mine did. They were quite religious in the traditional sense, but they also believed in self-reliance. I guess it was their values, which made a real impression, that led me to believe I could do it."

I leaned toward her. "Wasn't your mother religious?"

"My mother never really seemed to believe in the Church unless she needed to hold it up to us as either a punishment or a reward."

"And your father?"

She smiled, "My father hated all religious institutions. My mother always said he didn't care about anything but his drinking buddies on the police force.

"Anyway, my grandparents fought with my mother all the time about the way she was raising us—twisting the Church's teaching to suit herself in front of Moira and her sisters and brothers. They accused my mother of exposing us to evil.

"On the surface my mother seemed to ignore what my grandparents said, often making fun of their naive, Old World approach. Still, she must have suffered terribly," Moira said, twisting the Kleenex she held and shredding it piece by piece.

"Maybe that was why she made my older sister, Janice, the family enforcer, and ignored the rest of us."

"That must have hurt you a lot," I said, empathizing with her.

Tears sprang to her eyes, but she continued. "We children were sent to my grandmother's house to be taken care of. It was my grandmother who washed and fed us. It was my grandmother who taught us how to take our first steps, speak our first words. At the end of each day we returned home in the late afternoon. Janice played the go-between, delivering directives or criticisms for mother."

"That must have been hard on you," I said.

"It got worse. While I was still in grammar school, my grandmother died. I had loved her dearly and suffered terribly at the loss. I guess as many children do, I felt responsible for her death. I kept thinking if I had only been a better and more loving person, perhaps my grandmother would not have died. My bad feelings were made worse by my mother, who kept saying she hated having us children back at home.

"As the eldest of the children who had been sent to our grandparents for daily care, I took the brunt of her dissatisfaction, most of the criticism. When we had to stay home I tried to understand and justify my mother and Janice's treatment."

There were tears in Moira's eyes, but she blinked them back. "My grandmother wasn't there for me anymore. The only thing I could fall back on was the teachings of the Church that she had tried to instill in me. I had heard many stories about the various martyrs and saints who followed in Jesus's footsteps, and I tried to be more like them."

She looked off into space. "They had all suffered without deserving, and I tried to accept the cruel way Janice and my mother treated me as helping me become more like the saints. I prayed to my grandmother to help me. I tried to be more like her."

"You must have missed her a great deal," I said.

She nodded but her voice hardened. "Each morning I got the younger children up and dressed. I prepared and served the family breakfast. When they were old enough, I took my brothers and sisters to school. Often I arrived late to my own classroom, only to be scolded harshly by my teacher. In the afternoon, I straightened up the house. Then I prepared an early dinner for my father, keeping him company while he ate."

As she talked of her father, Moira's face became mask-like. I leaned toward her, not wanting to miss anything that might be a clue to her inner turmoil. "Tell me about him."

"He was always speaking of how he deeply missed his beloved Ireland."

"In what way, do you think?" I asked.

"In Ireland, the rules had been so much clearer. As a young man, my father had lived in a small, close-knit community. He had grown up knowing everyone in town and had maintained almost all his childhood friendships. Working for minimal wages doing manual labor, he made enough to contribute to his parents household for his upkeep. Whatever was left, he could freely spend at the local pub with his buddies. Until he married, he was neither expected nor permitted to interact with girls."

"And then what happened?"

She grimaced, "Everything changed after he married. He was expected to spend more time at home and less with his drinking buddies. His wages were no longer enough to support his new family. Neither he nor my mother knew about or had any access to birth control. My mother soon became pregnant. My father quickly realized that he had to do something to make more money." She left the sentence hanging for a moment then began again. "In a sudden move, they left for the United States."

"That must have been difficult," I murmured.

She nodded. "When my father arrived in this country, he tried to find friends like those he had left behind to drink with and talk to. The only ones he had were his colleagues at the police department. This was a time when Irish immigrants dominated the New York force.

"While he had not known these new friends from childhood, after a few drinks it didn't seem to matter that much. They were the only people he could seem to feel connected to. He would spend long boring afternoons at home waiting to meet his friends at a local pub before work. When evening arrived, he would leave while my mother complained vehemently.

"I think he ran from her as much as from the boredom.

My parents had been manipulated into marriage by small-town rumors that they might be involved sexually. Both sets of parents pushed them to get married to avoid scandal.

"Now, after many years of marriage, all they both seemed to feel was anger and resentment. They remained together because they were Catholic, but they spent most of their time trying to avoid each other. My mother told me they only had sex to have children and after the birth of their sixth child, they didn't want any more. I think my father felt a lot of guilt about hating my mother."

"Why do you say that?" I asked.

"Well, he withdrew from all of us. The only person he ever talked to was me, when I prepared dinner. I would listen to him talk about his experiences on the police force. He loved to tell me about the criminals he arrested." Moira's face was animated now. "To me it was fascinating."

As I listened to Moira recreating her father's stories, I was reminded of the days I had spent with my own father when he recounted exciting stories from his past. I thought once again of the similarities in Moira's and my lives. Both our families were filled with turmoil, Moira's even more than mine. In a way we both provided outlets for our parents' frustration. Yet watching her now I could not help but think that Moira's role was much more painful than mine. Though my family was troubled my father had loved me unconditionally. Suddenly my mind came back to the present.

"Even though when we were alone my father spoke to me of his own adventures, he had already enlisted in the unspoken family pact in which I was chosen as the primary target," Moira said. "And although he didn't criticize me as Janice and mother did, he never stood up for me either. I guess he couldn't, or they would have been on his back, too."

"Still, it must have hurt you," I said.

"I guess," she shrugged, "but what was the use?"

"In the late afternoons, after my father left for the local pub, I continued with the family chores. Sometimes when my mother and Janice were out of the house, some of the younger children would offer their help. However, at other times they would avoid me. I guess they were fearful of mother's anger. She had a raging temper. It wasn't their fault," Moira said looking at me for confirmation. "They were so young."

"You were, too," I said quietly.

"But it was my responsibility to look after them so they wouldn't get in trouble, and I didn't always do that."

"You were a child, too," I said once again.

"But it was my fault," she insisted.

I said nothing.

"As time passed, my father drank more and more heavily. Sometimes he hit us." I winced but Moira didn't notice. "Never mother, or the rest of the family, colleagues, or even adult strangers, just us kids."

"Most batterers," I said quietly, "always manage to stay enough in control of themselves to select 'safe' targets."

As if she had not heard, she went on. "More often than not, he hit me."

My thoughts churned. This may have been because, like my sister Shirley, she was the weakest link in the family chain, or perhaps Moira's father resented his dependence on her—resented that it was Moira and not his wife who fulfilled his emotional needs.

"Didn't anyone notice?" I asked.

Moira shook her head. Her voice breaking, she said, "Neither my teachers at school nor any of my family ever questioned me about my frequent bruises. No one ever offered to help or comfort me."

"Did you ever tell anyone?" I asked.

Moira seemed unable to go on. "No, I never talked about it till now," she finally said.

* * *

At my next meeting with Mardoff I tried to talk about Moira's abusive childhood. Mardoff laughed at my compassion for her. He scoffed at my suggestion that the outrageousness of her behavior during stress might be an indicator that Moira had been sexually abused as well. But to me, the often sexual nature of her outbursts while in her alternate personality, seemed a clear sign that somehow sex was a key concern.

"You may recall, Mr. Obler, that Freud rejected the seduction model in his psychoanalytic theory before the turn of the century," Mardoff sneered. "He realized, even if you don't, that fantasized sexuality, not actual seduction, was central to the core of the neurosis." Mardoff had a way of discounting any theory I proposed to explain Moira's multiple personalities.

Once again, I accepted Mardoff's recommendations and avoided directly addressing what I believed were the key issues. Although I began to develop more confidence in my abilities through my continued contact with Moira and other patients, I was still willing to bow to Mardoff's expertise. With Mardoff's approval, I decided on another approach to Moira—the Church.

We both felt the Catholic Church had played a pivotal role in Moira's life. At our next session I asked her about it.

"As a teenager, I would often go to my room early," Moira said. "There, I would climb out the window to escape to the peace and solitude of the local church."

'A good Catholic is born to suffer,' a priest pointed out to me one day as he illuminated the purpose of martyrdom during confession. He said, 'You should be grateful for any circumstances that, though perhaps seemingly difficult to live though, provide you with the avenue to a state of grace.'

"I tried to do just that. I never talked about what was happening in my family except during confession. But since I was primarily responsible for the beating I received, it was my duty to report them there. Although the priest and nuns were therefore aware of the beatings, they never intervened, reported it to the authorities, or made any attempt to stop the abuse. I felt they agreed with me."

I tried to challenge the logic of her rationalization. "Why," I probed, "did Janice and the other children escape this treatment if indeed it was essential for all your ethical and religious development?" Moira could not see the paradox. "As I see it, either they had been neglectful in their duty to provide proper ethical teaching to your siblings or they had been wrong not to offer you protection from abuse."

"What are you saying?" Moira's voice rose heatedly. She responded as if I were trying to rob her of a valuable gift, one she had worked hard to acquire. "I loved it at school, the nuns reinforced and rewarded me for doing such a good job at home. They always said that I would earn God's approval through accepting burden and self-sacrifice. I must not think indulgently of myself, but of the family good."

Moira told me that corporal punishment was not uncommon at the parochial school she attended. Moira somehow managed to stimulate the nuns' ire more frequently than the other children did. Unlike the other children who received beatings for misbehavior, Moira received the beatings because she was "proud." This pride manifested itself as obedience in its most literal form and a complete embracing of a martyr role.

As Moira patiently explained the twisted logic to me, I felt as if I would explode. "No, no, no!" I screamed at her. "Look at the contradictions. You were being given top honors as a student, yet somehow your teachers regularly found fault with you. Can't you see that they were simply taking out their frustrations on you? Isn't martyrdom supposed to be achieved when evil seems to triumph but the victim remains true to God? How could your teachers justify their treatment with promises of Heaven? When will you let your anger emerge?"

I knew that my outburst was inappropriate and that I would only succeed in alienating Moira. However, I was simply unable to control my own feelings of outrage. Once again, I found myself over-identifying with her. Again, I was acting out what I imagined were her feelings of oppression.

Looking inward for the source of my rage, I remembered an incident from my childhood. One Saturday, after morning prayer at the local synagogue, the Rabbi asked me to help out. He offered me the honor of putting away the Torah, adding that I should turn off the lights and lock the door afterward.

Even as a child, I knew that turning a light switch or locking a door were forbidden by religious law on the Sabbath—the day of rest. The Rabbi had tried to exploit what he thought was my childish ignorance. He was willing to exchange my place in heaven for his own convenience. He would not incur the wrath of God for his offense—I would.

After that, I refused to return to that synagogue. My parents had to find another one for my Bar Mitzvah. I came to hate all forms of religious hypocrisy. Thinking of it I was once again struck by how much my own experiences affected what I viewed as important in Moira's experience. On a deeper level, I began to question whether it is possible for therapists to suppress their own issues and or values.

Like any scientist, mustn't we examine and acknowledge our biases? Wasn't it more realistic to expect therapists to confront their issues directly and utilize the power of the examination to help a patient? Certainly that approach would be more fruitful than expending the energy denying their importance?

Wasn't power and control the primary issue in therapy? I felt intuitively that the distance Mardoff suggested that a therapist must always maintain was really an underhanded bid for power. It was all part of the doctor mythology—as if we were above it all, exempt of feelings and needs.

* * *

A week or so later, Moira began to speak of her one and only childhood friend, Marcia. "As often occurs, opposites attract. Marcia was everything I was not—confident, outgoing, and outspoken. She always thought she deserved the best of everything," Moira smiled. "Marcia scolded me for putting up with the treatment I received both at school and at home."

When I heard Moira describe Marcia, I was overjoyed. This could be my avenue to Moira. Thinking back to my own childhood, I recalled that I too had had such a friend. In my case, however, the friend had been imaginary.

Until I was around seven years old, my sister Selma was a surrogate mother to me. Suddenly, and for no reason I could fathom, Selma began to act as if she hated me. To compensate for this devastating rejection, I began to pretend that I had a new playmate.

Like Marcia, my friend was aggressive, able to conquer the world, able to deal with the pressures and stresses of daily life. My friend offered me an escape from the aching loneliness of my parents' neglect, as well as a place to direct all my overlooked tender and loving feelings. Eventually I became stronger. I didn't need my friend to soothe away my fears anymore. I wondered if Marcia served the same purpose for Moira.

Remembering my friend, I listened more intently to Moira now. "In order to spend time with Marcia, I willingly risked my mother's anger. I used to imply that I had to stay after school to help the nuns; in truth, I would escape with my fantasy friend and explore the neighborhood. Roaming the streets with Marcia, I felt daring. Never in my life had I felt this way, before or since."

I nodded, "Yes, I know how you felt."

"Unfortunately Janice and my mother quickly noted the change in me." Moira grimaced. "They discovered that Marcia was behind the change in me and immediately forbid me to see her. Of course, I complied."

"That must have been very difficult," I said.

Tears came to Moira eyes. "I never recovered from the

loss of my friend. The only way I could stand it was, every time I saw Marcia at school I pretended she was transparent."

Shocked, I sat upright. "What did you do then?"

"I turned to God," she said quietly. "By the time I entered high school, I talked all the time about Catholic virtue and my schoolmates took off as soon as they saw me," she laughed.

"You have a lovely laugh," I said, "I wish you'd use it more often."

Moira sighed, "Anyway I desperately desired another confidant. I would walk through the schoolyard each afternoon fantasizing that one of my classmates would approach me with an offer of friendship. No one did. I only had God."

She twirled a bit of her lustrous blond hair and looked off into space. "Anyway, my newly found vocation, serving the Church, left me little time to relax after completing my Church duties and household chores. As I went about my household tasks I would repeat my prayers over and over. It was a kind of mantra. At least I didn't feel as alone all the time, but I still had no one. Even though I filled up the spaces, my loneliness was there, behind all the busy work waiting for me. It was that way for several years.

"Then one day at home, I watched a television program from England. Something about the program reminded me of a film I had seen with Marcia many years earlier. Like Marcia, the central character of the film was a bossy schoolgirl. I had almost forgotten my friend. At least I thought I had." Moira flushed and stammered. "I, uh," she lowered her lashes, "I began to fantasize about Marcia and this bossy British character. Secretly, I would pretend that we were all friends. After awhile the girl and Marcia seemed like one person. Can you understand that?"

"Of course," I murmured, "go on."

"Well, after that, if things seemed too awful to bear, I turned to my new fantasy friends. I could call upon these newfound 'friends' whenever I needed help—" she paused and took a deep breath, her green eyes seeking mine as if for sympathy or at least for confirmation that I didn't condemn her. "When Marcia or the British girl appeared, the world was at my command. I felt powerful and happy."

"Moira, I think this is a good place to stop for today," I said. "I'm afraid your time is up."

As Moira rose to leave, she paused for a moment looking at me. "You know, I didn't want to come here," she said quietly, "but I'm glad I did, and I'm more than glad it was you they picked to see me. You're very special, you know."

I felt my face flushing. "Moira, you're very special, too."

"I wish," she half-whispered quickly going out the door.

As the weeks went on Moira seemed to confide in me more and more.

She related two discrete incidents from her adolescence that seemed of particular significance because of the feelings of intimacy and connection to another person that Moira expressed when relating them to me. They involved interactions with her father.

"One day," she said quietly, "my father invited me into his study. Normally, his study was off-limits to our family. Even my mother did not enter this room. It was his private sanctuary. Often, he slept there in order not to disturb mother when he came in late from his night shift.

"Well, to my surprise, on this occasion my father showed me citations for bravery that he had been awarded by the police force. Also, he showed me his handgun collection. 'Look at these,' he proudly exhibited the weapons. 'Aren't they beautiful,' he said lovingly, 'so strong and powerful.'

Moira paused and her eyes met mine. Talking about this incident seemed difficult for her, so I said, "Please go on, don't be afraid."

"Well, as I listened to my father, a wave of anticipation

and excitement ran through my body. I felt exhilarated. As I looked at my father's face, I saw for the first time a kind of pride and power. Then," she paused again, and I leaned forward, sympathetically, "he gently reached out and touched my face. Without knowing why, I began to cry. No one had ever touched me that way before. I felt a special bond between us. Still, I didn't understand why he hid this bond and let mother and Janice hurt me." She winced and rushed out as if not wanting to linger.

When next we met, Moira wore a soft yellow dress and her cheeks were flushed. She seemed anxious to begin, her words rushing out as she told me about another incident. "On this day, my father told me about his childhood in Ireland for the first time. He spoke of his own father, a farmer and a gentle man. He described his father as a giant of a man, a man who worked the family farm alone and was able to support his immediate and extended family by his efforts.

"In the early 1900s, Ireland faced economic depression. His father was forced to auction off the farm. He became a tenant farmer. With his family facing impoverishment, his esteem as the family provider suffered. He was a sensitive man and he withdrew emotionally and distanced himself from everyone he knew.

"When my father was ten years old, his father died. He had never been close to his mother, who now became head of the family. She was a harsh, cold disciplinarian." Moira shivered as if recalling the torments in her own life. "My father retreated further inward as his father had done before him. He distanced himself from his family. By the time he reached adolescence, he had begun drinking."

"I see," I said rubbing my chin thoughtfully.

"My paternal and maternal grandparents had been neighbors in Ireland. While growing up, my father had always been told by his mother that he was to stay away from the neighbors. They were not to be trusted. However, when it became convenient, his mother pushed him into marriage with their neighbor's daughter." She stared off into space and was silent.

"Moira," I prodded her, "Tell me more."

She nodded. "My father did not want to marry his prospective wife but felt he had no choice. He despised himself for his inability to stand up to his mother." I stared at Moira, reflecting on her words and her life. "Following in his father's footsteps, when he experienced himself as a failure, he withdrew from his natural instincts of warmth and affection. By the time he escaped his mother's iron hand, it was already too late. The pattern had been set. When he immigrated to this country, he simply isolated himself further, establishing no connection to his wife or children. He managed to almost exactly duplicate his father's life."

Moira's eyes sought mine. Touched by these memories of intimate moments shared with her father, Moira had one of her most penetrating insights: "Do you know," she asked slowly, "his relationship with his mother was almost the same as mine is. We both let ourselves be tyrannized. Even those special moments I shared with my father were doomed from the start. Neither of my parents can tolerate that kind of closeness."

"Go on" I said gently.

"When I completed high school, I submitted to my mother's demand that I obtain immediate employment. I looked for a job to help support the family." She grimaced. "Going to college and meeting people was never discussed as a viable option. My mother would never allow such indulgence. Only Janice was permitted the privilege of having personal desires or goals."

Moira's beautiful green eyes narrowed. "A bitter dispute broke out between my parents over the selection of work for me. Taking a rare stand, my father stated that he wanted all the children to join the police force. My mother was furious. The hours on the police force would limit my availability for household chores.

"Finally, my parents struck a compromise; I was compelled to accept. I would be permitted to become a policewoman but would also continue all of my usual chores. The chores would not be delegated to the other children as my father had first suggested." She let out a heavy sigh. "There was no escape for me. No one seemed to question whether it was fair or right."

"Weren't you angry?" I asked, watching her face darken.

She nodded. "Sure, but I didn't fight it. I figured that anything that even momentarily allowed me to get away from my mother's abuse was worth it."

We stopped there. The session was over.

The next time we met I immediately brought up her job. "That must have been a big day for you," I said.

She nodded. "My first day on the force, I met the man I would eventually marry. A fellow officer. In those days, he was known as a skirtchaser," she bit her lip, "but at least he seemed to be interested in me."

"You're a lovely woman. Why wouldn't he be?" I asked.

She blushed. "He was after me all the time and," she paused, "no one else was. Later I found out he was dropping misleading hints about me to our co-workers; he gave the other officers the impression that we were already involved. At first I was oblivious to this. I did not understand why the other officers stayed at arm's length. By the time I learned about it, it was too late."

"You were very young," I said.

She shook her head. "I had no desire to marry at that point. I knew that I had a lot to learn about the world and was terribly excited to finally have achieved adult status, but he," she paused, "my husband-to-be convinced me that my only escape from my mother's clutches was through him. In addition, my mother seemed to like him. I was afraid that if I turned him down, my mother would punish me by making me leave the force.

"A few weeks before my engagement was to be announced, I began to have grave misgivings about my future husband. I realized that I was trading one problem for another. I broke off the relationship." She stopped.

"Then what happened?" I asked.

"Well, early one morning, my ex-fiancé followed me home after we had both worked a night shift." She stopped again, her face pale; she began to shake.

"Are you alright?" I asked, leaning forward. "Do you want a drink of water?" She didn't answer.

"Moira," I said, "aren't you feeling well? Can I do something, get you something?"

"No, I'm okay." She continued, her voice almost a whisper, "With nobody in sight, he approached me. In front of my parent's house, he attacked. . . ." She stumbled over the words, "He clutched at me and forced me to submit to him."

"He raped you there," I said, horrified.

Mutely, she nodded. I poured a glass of water from the pitcher on the desk and handed it to her. Gulping down a little, she continued. "A neighbor awoke because of the commotion. She told my parents. They insisted on our marriage. My mother said I would be undesirable to other men. She beat me and then I gave in.

"From my mother's perspective John was a perfect future son-in-law. He was strong and forceful, yet willing to listen to her. They understood each other perfectly. Actually they were a lot alike," Moira said defeatedly.

"She let him marry me, but she stayed the boss. She set the rules. She decided I would continue to do the chores in her household. After completing these, I was to take on new responsibilities as a wife, and soon after, a mother.

"As soon as the wedding was over, my mother and husband insisted that I take a leave of absence from the police force. I was expected to have children immediately. I became pregnant. I had three children at one year intervals."

"That must have been difficult," I said.

She sighed, "Inside I resented the demands that my children imposed on me. I longed to return to my job. After the birth of each child I became very depressed, and it was during these periods that people began to comment on the strange accent I used when very agitated."

"I see" I said.

"I was confused by their observations. I explained that it was a sign of my depression. I tried to convince my husband that I was not mocking him or his acquaintances but was simply unaware of the accent. He did not accept my explanation and beat me instead. Of course, these were not the first beatings I had gotten from him."

She hung her head. "I felt like a complete failure by then. Ever since I got my period, I have never felt sexual desire. The only sexy feelings I remember happened one afternoon spent long before in childhood with my friend Marcia."

"Moira," I stood up, "we'll talk about that next time." I hated to stop there. It seemed so difficult for Moira to recall feelings of desire, and it took several meetings before I could get her to address the subject again. Finally she did.

"Marcia and I were going through some dress-up clothing when we came across Moira's father's police revolver. Marcia referred to it as a black "dick"—like in Dick Tracy. She said that you fight criminals with it.

"We began to play a game where I was a policeman and Marcia, a fugitive. We pretended to shoot at each other. After a while, Marcia started getting silly and pointing at the gun giggling, 'It's like the boy's thing that hangs between their legs. The thing they squirt with.'

" 'What thing?' I asked, not making the connection between the word *dick* and Marcia's reference. Although I had younger brothers and I had seen them naked, no one had ever referred directly to a penis before.

"They want to put it in here," Marcia said to me, as she

pulled down her panties and exposed her genitals. A flush of excitement came over me. Feeling confused and overwhelmed, I quickly repressed the sexual sensations. Still, I never forgot how I felt in that moment. It was the only passion I have ever felt."

The warnings by the nuns and priests at school and her mother about touching—oneself or others—had left a deep impression on Moira. When her husband felt her sexual withholding, he became enraged. Passivity was one thing—he enjoyed feeling that he was in control—but he felt that Moira was rejecting his advances and his masculinity became threatened. His frequent sexual attacks bordered on rape.

Over time, Moira's husband learned to gain immense pleasure from the pain she experienced during intercourse. "Every time I cried out in pain, he'd get more excited. He kept saying I welcomed this punishment, maybe even enjoyed it.

"Eventually, every time we had sex he tried to hurt me physically." Moira went on to tell me that to protect herself from this horror, she often dissociated during sex. "I thought of the wonderful afternoons with my friend Marcia strolling through my neighborhood."

When listening to Moira describe her sexual interactions with her husband, I felt ambivalent. Even though her husband's behavior was unacceptable, I felt angry with her —not him.

I wondered if my feeling was connected to my mother's attitudes toward sex. Throughout my childhood, my mother repeatedly told me that men were dogs. They only wanted to steal their pleasure from women. Submitting to them sexually was abhorrent to her.

As with my mother, I wondered why Moira stayed in an intolerable marriage. Moira's sexual passivity disturbed me as well. Why had she put these limits on her own enjoyment? I tried without success to separate my feelings of anger toward my own mother and my feelings toward Moira. I felt that I might be projecting my own issues onto

Moira, and I knew I had to separate my problems from hers if I was to really help her.

At our next encounter, I tried harder to do this. Moira sat slumped in the seat across from me. She continued speaking about her marriage.

"After four years on leave, I told my husband that I wanted to return to work. I felt by then that I had failed as a mother. My mother and Janice criticized me on that score constantly. In addition, I felt that my mother was steadily taking control of my children. They seemed to have little devotion and loyalty toward me anymore. They only listened to my sister and mother."

The children's fear of their father alienated them even more from their mother. They sensed her weakness and inability to offer them protection from his storming behavior. Instead, they turned to their grandmother for protection. Following her lead, they ridiculed Moira in front of their father sensing that in this way they might gain his approval.

"My mother loved the children's rejection of me," Moira said bitterly, "and their connection to her. She felt it was justice done."

"In what way?" I asked, confused.

"Well, she always felt her mother had stolen my affection from her so many years ago. And that I, being no good, had turned her other children against her as well." Moira turned to me. "What's wrong with me?"

I sat silently. I was frightened by her helpless feelings —her acceptance of this nonrelationship with her children. Later that week in analysis, Jill pointed out the source of my anxiety. "As a child," she said, "one of your deepest fears was a fear of your own mother's abandonment. Unlike Moira you overcompensated for these fears by denying your underlying helplessness."

It was then that I recognized my internal contradictions. While I compassionately accepted Moira's limitations to fight her mother and husband, I could neither accept nor understand her withdrawal from her children.

"So," I said slowly, "if I empathize with Moira, I might

have to acknowledge my mother's incapacity and, in turn, empathize with her. What next?" I asked angrily. "Am I expected to forgive her? That's too much for me. I'm not ready to forgive my mother," I said, stalking out.

I didn't have to confront my own demons, at least not then, because at our next session Moira explored another subject: her police work.

"After my third child my husband reluctantly agreed that I could return to the police force. The other officers were nice enough, and simple daily adult contact eased some of my loneliness. My husband was on his best behavior in front of our colleagues.

"However, it wasn't long before the strain of combining high-stress police work and the exhausting responsibility for two households' worth of chores began to show. I was getting close to a nervous breakdown. My partner began to notice my bizarre behavior. Often I would mutter to myself. Once they overheard me carrying on a two-way conversation in the ladies room when no one else was there. My partner spoke to the day sergeant about it, and the day sergeant proposed I take a long vacation. I refused, but things deteriorated.

"As tension mounted at work and at home I began to suspect that the department would soon take action. I feared that I would be transferred to another precinct, or worse—placed at a desk job. Then the bank robbery incident occurred. Three weeks after that, the precinct captain demanded that I enter therapy immediately. That's how I got here."

Exploring her past resulted in immediate psychological and physical benefits. As Moira began to move around free of back pain, the shame she had experienced because of her handicap disappeared. The anxiety of being labelled "disabled" diminished. Her overall demeanor was calmer. Moreover, the changes in her personality revealed during our earlier sessions were not evident any more.

Although finding out about the past was an integral element of the recovery process, I was aware that the changes Moira exhibited were essentially superficial. I knew that we had only touched the surface of her problems. Outwardly, she was willing to explore her past. She had even begun to recognize and articulate feelings of anger. Still, she did not truly integrate the meaning of the extreme abuse she'd experienced. She resisted any attempts to understand the abuse on a more profound level—to see her family as abusive. The origins of her psychological problems were still unexamined. I decided to confront the issue.

At our session that Tuesday, I asked, "Don't you think your mother behaved cruelly or even sadistically toward you?"

Moira jumped up, her face livid. "To manipulate me," she spat out. "Even you're trying. All this supportive behavior. It's just a tool used by therapists to encourage patients to find fault with their parents."

I sat there letting her vent her feelings. Perhaps Mardoff had been correct. Would a neutral pose as a therapist have tapped more directly into the repressed rage? My rationale had been based on the premise that until Moira received the warmth and nurturing withheld from her during her childhood, she would be unwilling to explore any repressed conflicts with her family. I had reasoned that if I openly shared my own painful childhood experience, I could develop a trust based on common experience. Then, she might be willing to expose her feelings. My plan had not met with success. Moira had only acquired minimal insight into her real problems. I decided to opt for a more classical approach the next time we met.

At the next session, Moira wore a dark blue suit, which set off her blond hair. She started the session by firmly stating, "It's quite a relief to be free of the back pain. I am really enjoying my job and my family."

I decided not to respond to her remark. She interpreted my disapproval correctly from my body language. We were both aware that her back was better and did not have to rehash the obvious, as we had done so long ago in our first sessions. We now found ourselves staring speechless at each other, silently waiting for something to happen.

After fifteen minutes, the pressure of the silence became too much for Moira. Her mouth and jaw began to contort, with the lower and upper parts of her mouth moving in different directions. Her eyes began to open and close continuously. It looked almost cartoonish. Instead of slouching in her usual position in the chair, she sat upright and started to rub her hands against her hips. I was shocked when she spit on the floor.

"You bloody fucking bastard," she screamed, followed by a string of vulgar and suggestive street expressions.

"What are you trying to say?" I asked after a few moments of trying to regain my composure. While the expletives she used were fairly clear in meaning, the vulgarity seemed odd coming from her.

We sat silently and inspected each other. Suddenly she glanced around the room as though familiarizing herself with the surroundings for the first time.

"God forgive me . . . God forgive . . . ," she said, as though pleading with me to forgive her.

"Forgive you for what?" I asked. "For having sexual feelings?"

Her body jerked violently in response. "Would you like a child?" she shouted in a very clear British accent. Suddenly, she lifted her skirt and exposed black exotic, fancy undergarments. "It's yours for the asking," she jeered.

Bewildered and shaken, all I could think of was, What is this repressed woman doing wearing black undergarments? I wondered if they represented some strong sexual passion that I had been unaware of all along.

"So you are interested in sex," I said, attempting to act

as though I were unmoved by her explosive comments. She frowned at me disgustedly. Slowly, her persona began to change again. She still seemed angry but without the contorted facial expressions. The old Moira was back.

She smoothed her skirt down tucking it in so it covered her knees. "I was sent to you to get rid of my back pain. I'm not here to give you a cheap thrill."

"I notice that your British accent has suddenly disappeared," I replied, trying to focus attention on her use of accents.

"British? What British accent? What are you talking about?" she agitatedly asked.

I leaned forward and said in a firm voice, "Don't you notice that you speak sometimes with an American accent and at other times with a British accent? Even your face changes expression. You appear more in command when using the British accent."

"I do?" She shook her head. "People always make jokes—teasing me about mimicking or something—but I never really get the jokes. I don't understand what they are driving at. I thought that maybe it was some reference to a movie or television show that I haven't seen. Do I really do that?" She looked genuinely scared now. "Am I nuts? Don't crazy people behave this way?"

I pressed on. "It seems to come out at times when you are tense," I observed. "What's even more interesting is that your British character seems much more self-confident. Typically you come across . . . unassertive, unassuming, passive. When this other personality emerges, you seem very assertive, even aggressive. You were using your British accent when you lifted your skirt before."

"I lifted my skirt?" she gasped, looking at me incredulously. Her face was flushed. Obviously, she was having trouble believing me.

"You're kidding, right?" she half whispered. She hung her head, as if ashamed. "I wouldn't ever do something like that. I pride myself on always staying in control."

"It's interesting that you feel that holding back your sexual feelings is being in control," I pointed out.

"I don't believe that that is what I said. Wasn't it you, doctor?" she replied challengingly in a very heavy British accent.

"There it goes again—the British accent," I quickly interjected. I was hoping she would see that she was using it. "You're sure that you are not aware of speaking with an accent?"

She was becoming agitated, perhaps envisioning a further probing of her personality changes. I felt unnerved as well.

Not knowing where to start or what to focus on, I jumped around illogically. "Look, do you accept that your accent keeps changing? Don't you think that exposing your underwear is acting out your sexuality? Anyway, after all, you must have chosen those seductive panties before coming here this morning. Or, do you always wear that kind of underwear? Are you in an altered state?"

"I don't know, I don't know. I have these memory lapses. Sometimes when I wake up, I find my hand rubbing down there," she paused, "Do you know where?" She averted her eyes from my stare.

"Can you tell me more about these lapses?" I asked hesitatingly. She didn't answer. Her reference to masturbation had obviously embarrassed her.

I took a deep breath. I needed time to digest what had taken place. So much had emerged during the session that I felt mentally fatigued. Still, I knew instinctually that we had made a breakthrough. Looking at my watch I noticed that the hour was almost up. Afraid that any mention of masturbation would ignite feelings we wouldn't have time to sufficiently address, I gently placed my hand on hers to indicate that the session was coming to a close. "We'll continue next week," I said softly.

The next few months of therapy continued to be productive. It became clear to me that the roots of Moira's problem resided in her family's failure to provide a caring, nurturing and safe environment. As her story unfolded, evidence accumulated that she had been physically, emotionally, and perhaps sexually abused.

SIX

A Clash of Wills

In session, the stage was set for therapist and client to continue a meeting of minds. In supervision, the stage was set for doctor and student to continue a battle of will.

At our meeting that Tuesday, Mardoff impatiently admonished me for pushing too quickly in exploring Moira's past. He vehemently protested, "Clearly, she was not ready for it." As we spoke I bucked his authority at every opportunity, challenging him even when I knew that I was lacking information or simply outright erroneous in my assessment.

Now, it is not unusual for supervisors and supervisees to participate in subtle power struggles. Perhaps the obvious gap in knowledge and experience between mentor and student inflames in the student the need to test the boundaries of the mentor's knowledge. As for the mentors, their investment lies in justifying a career-long commitment to a particular therapeutic model. They have a legacy to leave behind. What better way to ensure the success of that legacy than through the continued application of their ideas by their student disciples.

However, at this meeting, the degree and intensity of the conflict between Mardoff and me was unique.

"Can you not see," he said, his voice rising to a credendo punctuating his word, "what harm you are doing her by confronting her rather than letting her find out herself? Plus," he said, "you are too rash—or worse." Mardoff defended his personal beliefs about therapeutic technique with a ferocity unprecedented in our relationship thus far. For my part, I too refused to yield any ground.

"A therapist must be emotionally involved with a patient in order to enhance the interaction."

"Nonsense, have you learned nothing?" He slammed the table with his clenched fist. "What about the problems of countertransference?" We argued on and on.

"I warned you about these manipulative women," Mardoff reprimanded me. "This is a straightforward case of resistance. While her sexual provocations are offensive, her strategy is quite apparent. She's pathetically trying to seduce you as a means of avoiding facing herself."

His face was white with rage. "Your schizoid hypothesis is way off base. Initially, she makes feeble attempts to change her routine. When this fails, she utilizes this obvious parody of a multiple personality transformation to confuse you.

"While you are apparently an easy fish to hook, it's still the old seduction game. Stop this foolish overidentification. Keep exploring her symptoms. Avoid this female trap, Mr. Obler. Remember, her strongest desire is to be taken care of without having any demands placed on her."

I broke in. "How can we have any hope of eliminating her syndrome if we simply focus on her symptoms without dealing with the origins of her repression or the etiology of her sexual disturbances? Perhaps I haven't described our interactions clearly, since you seem to have some misconceptions. She's not trying to manipulate me through sexual seduction. She seems genuinely unaware of her strange behavior."

"Pursue the latest research on hysterics, Mr. Obler. You will find that the indications are clear. Examining the past with hysterics is basically a waste of time. They are incompetent when dealing with the analysis of dynamics. By concentrating on her back pain and its psychic functions," he continued, "you will discover the root of her hysteria. Eventually, not needing this function, she will most likely sublimate to a less debilitating symptom. Do your job, show no warmth or support. Help her see her pathetic behavior as the manipulation it is."

I cringed. "Manipulation? I think she is suffering terribly. While I agree that the conversion disorder is central to her pathology, there is a lot more going on here. The back pain is just the tip of the iceberg. She is frightened of everyone, even her family. While her husband physically brutalizes her on a regular basis, the rest of her family either ignores these violations or blames her for them.

"My support will provide her with a foundation from which to examine the origins of her illness and her reliance on abusive interpersonal relationships. With a little warmth and affection, I can really see her blossoming."

My voice rose emotionally, "I understand the theoretical validity of focusing on the selected dysfunctional organ and it's symbolism in conversion disorders. But, as Fenichel points out, in some cases of hysteria, you first have to build a working relationship in order to understand the central features of the neurosis. That's all I'm trying to do. I remain convinced that if I play an active supporting role, I will be the only person in her life who cares."

The room rang with Mardoff's bitter laughter. " 'Person in her life,' Mr. Obler? You are not—I repeat, not—a part of her life. Are you forgetting that you are supposed to be her doctor? Really, while there is no question that past explorations are significant, it's essential not to confound transferential components. Let's keep your pathetic support and warmth out of this."

Mardoff was clearly furious with me. "I warned you about her seductiveness. She's got you precisely where she wants. Warmth and support . . . the same old trick." He strode out of the room.

In contrast to Mardoff's combativeness, Moira seemed cheerfully at ease at our next session. Considering the way in which our last meeting had ended, I felt surprised. Her allusion at the last session to masturbation did not seem initially to bother her. She even brought the subject up herself. "Have you told Mardoff about my public display?" she asked. I tried to remain composed.

"A good deal of what is talked about in therapy is later reviewed during supervision," I replied noncommittally.

"How have things been since I saw you last?" I questioned her, wanting to change the subject. Even though she had raised the topic, she now seemed genuinely relieved to drop it.

She leaned forward, her face animated, her green eyes sparkling. "I have discovered new feelings—sexual ones. I wonder if it is because . . . of what we talked about during our last meeting. Childhood dreams and fantasies have resurfaced. . . . I remembered wishing my father would touch my body. I felt embarrassed about it. . . . Also, I was never aware before that I block my sexual impulses. When I get . . . excited, you know, in *that* area, I don't feel sick any more. I always used to feel bad." Moira dropped her voice in a conspiratorial whisper. "This week, I touched myself and I didn't even feel guilty. And it lasted a lot longer than with my husband," she added giggling. "Usually with my husband, it takes about thirty seconds. He gets on me, puts himself inside and then its over." She paused and looked at me conspiratorially. "Do you think I should have an affair?"

I was astonished by her growth in self-awareness, but she seemed to be covering a lot of ground quickly, maybe too quickly. I also recognized the courage it took for her to discuss these issues no less contemplate a relationship outside of marriage. I felt conflicted. What was my role? Should I encourage her to act out her fantasies? Or, should I simply recommend limiting them to analysis in therapy? If anyone in her family ever found out, she could crumble.

"Who would you have an affair with?" I inquired. "How would you go about it? I don't think it would be easy to deal with your family if they ever discovered you were having an extramarital affair."

Her green eyes narrowed. "Well, I haven't really thought about it carefully, but *you* might be right. You'd be someone I would consider," she answered very casually. Squirming in my seat, I was unable to hide my discomfort. She was clearly delighted with her power to effect my emotional response. "Don't get nervous," she laughed. "I know that it's against the rules. But, Mardoff isn't working directly with me. He's a rather good-looking man, don't you think? And I know he's interested in me," she continued.

"Mardoff? You can't be serious," I blurted out uncontrollably. Suddenly, I felt shaky. She was successful in her attempt to rattle me. My outburst was clearly inappropriate. I contemplated my next move. I knew that she was getting to me by playing me off against Mardoff. As a therapist, I was rendering myself ineffective by letting my own issues enter into the dynamic.

"Tell me more about your attraction to Mardoff?" I queried her forcefully.

"I'd rather not talk about that right now," she snapped. "There are more important things to talk about. I've made some important decisions. Ones that I know will change my life. . . ."

She went gallivanting off in another direction completely. "From now on, when my husband tries to censure me, I'm going to fight for my rights. I have tapped into a power within myself that I had never imagined existed."

She rushed on excitedly. "At work, I will stop punishing myself every time a superior criticizes me. I am going to demand to be returned to active patrol duty. I loath the desk job that I've been given because of the disability. Until then, I'm going to take walks during my break times. From now on I'll enjoy the 'sights and sounds' of the city."

She still didn't allow herself to pause or take a breath. "Even my children will realize the change taking place in me. They're going to start respecting me again. Instead of avoiding me. They will begin wanting to spend time with me. And they will no longer defy me."

I stared at her, but she would not meet my glance. "I'll

stop my unreasonable work schedule and renounce my mother's control over me. Life could become pleasurable for the first time." She smiled, her eyes feverish now. "I have had the power to fight the back pain that had disabled me. The family system set up by my mother and Janice will be defied." On and on she raced.

"Sounds really good," I said trying to keep the skepticism out of my voice. Although I was thrilled by her newfound assertiveness and impressed by the conviction of her resolutions, I felt that she might have difficulty implementing her plans. "But you still didn't answer my question about having sex with Mardoff, or me for that matter."

Moira shook her head vehemently. "Why are you insisting on pushing that point? I was just kidding, pulling your leg and fooling around. It's been my understanding that one of the goals of treatment is to achieve sexual freedom. I feel less inhibited and am very grateful to you. You have helped me feel more liberated. If I offended you in any way, I apologize. Believe me, that wasn't my aim!"

I took a deep breath. "I don't feel offended. Exploring your feelings and thoughts surrounding your therapist is an important and normal part of the therapeutic process. Any sexual fantasies you may have about my supervisor or me are useful to analyze."

She seemed upset and confused by my continuing to push the issue. "I want to tell you about an experience I had this week," she said suddenly. She ignored my attempt to direct our inquiry.

"What experience?" I couldn't help my curiosity.

"I'm not sure it really happened." She passed a hand across her forehead. "It was so weird. It could have been a dream, or maybe one of those states I find myself in that we've talked about. Though I don't think it was. I'm not really sure. Well, anyway, I went to my younger brother Bill's apartment. He had abandoned the apartment about two years ago. It was right around the same time he disappeared from the force. None of us have seen too much of him—except sometimes, I run into him in the oddest places.

"Once, when I was coming home from work, I ran into him outside the supermarket with a bunch of empty bags in his hands. He looked like a vagabond. We carried on a typical family conversation, you know, reviewing how everyone was doing. Neither of us acknowledged how uncomfortable we felt, not having kept up with each other and all.

"Another time, I thought that I saw him peering from behind a storefront entrance outside my mother's house. It all seemed so strange, his leaving the force, disappearing from sight and popping up periodically. He always seemed different, even as a kid . . . and everyone else thought so as well. He never seemed the creative type—a pretty uninspired fellow. I never wanted to know any of them—my siblings, that is. But with Bill in particular, well, he was always such a loner, following the others but never really participating in anything.

"Anyway, in his apartment, I began to rummage through his things. I came across a diary he kept. It was strange because he wasn't the kind of person who would write in a diary. I read part of the diary and even brought a piece of it that I ripped out—so it must be real, right? I didn't want you to think that I was making it up or was crazy."

Shyly she handed me a few crumpled pages. The writing was barely legible. Huge in some places, minuscule in others. I attempted to decipher the first few words. It looked like the writing of a schizophrenic—made up of incoherent sentence fragments, diagrams, and stick figures. The ideas were difficult to follow. I studied the pages carefully. Slowly, I started to piece together an intriguing message from the fragments.

I read the words out loud. " 'She loved. Wanted me to make love to her and relied on me to stroke her body. When she cleaned me and washed my body, I knew . . . and she knew that we wanted each other. I loved her more than my mother . . . Junuses . . . or the others. She let me put my fingers into her and it was good. My big stiff thing . . .'

"These pages are fascinating. Do they mean anything

to you?" I asked her, handing back the sheets of paper. It struck me that while the words had a straightforward sexual content, they evoked an almost religious undercurrent.

Moira ran her hand back and forth across her forehead. "The word *Junuses*. That was the way Bill referred to my sister Janice when he was just starting to talk," she said, adding with a puzzled expression. "I'm not sure why, but I think he was talking about me when he referred to the girl who wanted him."

"What was in the rest of his diary?" I asked. I was eager to know what else she had seen.

Moira tapped her long ivory fingers on the desk. "He referred to lies we all had lived with, but never specified what these were. He wrote over and over how much he hated mother, even called her 'The Tyrant.' He claimed that she terrorized the whole family." She paused and looked off into space as if she was seeing another time, another place. "There was a hand-drawn picture of all us kids stabbing mother with Janice looking on in horror. There was also something about plotting his 'sister's' death.

"He seemed to feel that our parents took out all their personal problems on us because they hated their own lives. He said that he was certain that our parents despised each other. Once he saw them having sex while mother repeatedly screamed, 'I hate you,' to father."

She sighed heavily. "He claimed that his sister and mother would rub against him and make funny sighing noises. Also that father had a big member and would put it into his little daughter Moira. Moira would imagine being with Bill."

I felt completely overwhelmed. While during most of the reporting she had seemed herself, suddenly she had referred to herself in the third person. What did this all mean? I didn't even know where to begin.

Today, we read and hear almost daily about the epidemic levels of child abuse. However, then the sexual abuse of children was a barely recognized phenomenon. While

Moira's cognition and ideations were fragmented, they all seemed to lead to the same conclusion—physical abuse.

I knew that if I consulted with Mardoff, he would pull out Freud's writing on unresolved oedipal issues. Essentially, Freud believed that an adult woman's unconscious fantasies of sexual relations with her father result in one of several hysterical responses. Still, in Moira's case, I felt an undercurrent of reality. Her memories sounded like someone's actual experience of abuse. The question remained, however: Was this Moira's experience or Bill's? So much of the puzzle was still missing.

"Do you remember anything else? Something that might help you decide if it was a dream or a real experience?" I asked.

"No, nothing else really. It's just that after I left his apartment, I kept thinking about this memory. It kept popping into my head; I wasn't really focusing on it."

"Tell me about it," I said.

She nodded. "I was in nursery school or kindergarten. The chairs were easy to climb and I could reach the table. It must have been snack time because I remember having something good in my mouth. The teacher put out the lights and said we were going to see a movie.

"I don't remember much, but I know that there was a girl just about my age. She spoke funny and later said that she came from a faraway place. I thought she had a wonderful way of talking. I loved her.

"I went home and remember telling my younger brother Bill about the movie. He kept asking more and more questions. I think that it was the same movie I told you about before. The one that I saw in fourth grade . . . about England . . . before meeting Marcia."

The connection between the frail, sulky Moira and this domineering British girl as a protection of her wish fulfillment seemed clearer to me now. I posed a question. "Could it be that your other personality, the one who speaks with a British accent, was inspired by the character from the film?" Quickly she looked away. I tried to get her attention back.

"Moira," I said watching her, "I also wondered whether your friendship with Marcia had offered you a similar means to self-expression. Since your family network was so oppressive, maybe you have merged the two characters and then adopted this new personality as your own when you needed to express a more forceful part of yourself."

Now I was racing ahead, consumed with my own insights. "Could this experience have occurred, but at an earlier part of your life? Are you blending past and present events, fact and fancy? At least some of your description seemed based on what were perhaps repressed sexual feelings harbored toward your younger brother. Could you have gone looking for your brother, worried about where he was and what had happened to him, and then subsequently imagined the rest?"

Instantaneously, her demeanor and voice changed. "They want my cunt. All of them," she sneered as saliva formed on the corners of her mouth. Then, she raised her skirt. She had nothing on underneath. Starting to masturbate, she shouted at me, "Mardoff wants it and so do you. Daddy is nothing. He lets that fucking Janice push him around. He isn't getting any of my cunt . . . I love it, I love it . . . put that big boy right here in me." She began to pant vigorously. She turned away, facing the opposite wall. She laughed hysterically.

I tried to think of something open-minded to say. I wanted to give her the impression that I was accepting of her actions. Not coming up with anything, I just sat quietly, silence descending on the room. After she climaxed, she lowered her skirt.

After a few minutes of silence, I volunteered, "It is normal to masturbate." I quickly added, "I hope you do not feel embarrassed about it." While it was a foolish thing to say in this clearly inappropriate situation, I was disconcerted and didn't know what else to do.

Moira acted as though she had peripheral knowledge of her behavior, but she seemed surprised to find her shirt pulled out of her skirt and self-consciously tucked it back in. She tried to flatten out her wrinkled skirt and flinched when her hand touched a wet spot. Red blotches appeared all over her skin. She seemed humiliated and lowered her head.

"It's okay," I responded ineffectually. I stupidly added, "People often become sexually stimulated and masturbate unknowingly. I'm glad you shared the experience with me." I knew that I had to say something. If I didn't help her feel more comfortable before the session ended, she would be in deep trouble after her departure.

I fumbled with my words. "Do you think that there may be a connection between the surfacing of memories having to do with repressed childhood sexual experiences and your need to masturbate here?"

"What are you talking about?" she shot back angrily. "All that gobbledgook you shrinks spout. Get me the fuck out of here."

Moira sprung out of her chair and marched out of the office. I felt a strong impulse to run after her but discovered that I was completely immobilized.

SEVEN

Echoes

When clinic hours were over, I tiredly made my way back to the cramped two-bedroom apartment in Harlem in which I lived. Although I was only twenty-five, I already had the responsibility of supporting a wife and two young children. In addition to my internship at the clinic, I held a full-time job as a social worker. With the help of school grants, we were able to get by, but a twenty-one-hour work day left little time or energy for my family.

My wife and I had met five years earlier in Tel Aviv. A mutual friend introduced us and we quickly became involved. Four years older than I, she was more mature and sophisticated.

I had found myself in Israel through the sponsorship of a leftist Zionist organization that I had joined. As a young adolescent, the organization offered me a coherent explanation for the poverty and injustice that surrounded me. I was presented with a whole new and unfamiliar universe of ideas—ideas that offered hope and possibility. A ninth-grade drop-out, I was introduced to a set of economic and political ideas that applied beyond the microcosm of Brownsville. These ideas worked on a world scale.

When I turned nineteen, the organization decided to send some of its members to Israel to learn firsthand the wonders of communal endeavor. We were to live and work as ordinary members of a kibbutz. Before leaving for Israel, we moved into the organization's central office, which was located in another part of Brooklyn.

Leaving home was a completely liberating experience for me. For the first time, I had contact with people from different social-economic classes. I met and learned to feel comfortable with people who were wealthier, formally educated, worldly—people more complicated and contemplative than my immigrant neighbors.

I hung out in Greenwich Village with a group of intellectuals. Never before had I met people committed to the exchange of ideas. We would spend days and nights in endless debate at the local coffee shops on MacDougal Street. On weekends, we would play basketball on Houston Street and roam the streets of the city arguing about politics and sexual freedom.

My real heroes of that time were not the intellectuals I met who offered me political ideas but the many women who offered me love. They initiated me to a radical new view of human relationships. Throughout my childhood, strangers had been viewed with suspicion and mistrust. Little or no emphasis was placed on communication and intimacy.

I made my first adult friends within the context of the loosely connected group I had joined. We were drawn together by our common need to compensate for emotionally impoverished childhoods. We sought in each other the nourishment and intimacy we had missed within our family network.

Many of us were later to pursue careers in the social service professions. To this day, virtually all my close friendships are with people who have made a life commitment to communication. Among my friends, I count mental health professionals, social workers, teachers, writers, and psychologists. We each in our own way search for a means to avoid the loneliness and pain that are an inescapable part of the human condition.

It seems that I can't remember a time when I wasn't consumed by fears of loneliness and alienation.

Before I left Brownsville for Israel, my preoccupation with finding someone to love left me flipping from relationship to relationship. I had sex with many young women and deluded myself that I had a boundless capacity to love. In my heart, I knew that a significant part of me still felt crippled. During most of time spent with my adolescent lovers, I fantasized about the woman I would marry. I became convinced that the eventual creation of a family of my own would make me feel secure.

By the time I got to Israel I badly needed a companion to assuage my loneliness in such a strange and foreign land. An unplanned pregnancy demanded that I assume the responsibilities of marriage and fatherhood by the time I turned twenty-one.

Thus, although I was to feel coerced into marriage because of my wife's pregnancy, I had finally secured the family stability for which I had hungered throughout my life. I had children of my own—children whom I could love and be loved by unconditionally. I felt this loving family could replace the hatreds I experienced in my original family and the brutality of poverty.

Although it was a struggle supporting a family of four while pursuing a clinical education, I told myself that the warm, supportive atmosphere of a healthy family gave me the foundation I needed to succeed. Divided between competing needs, I vacillated, constantly rearranging my priorities. While I thrived under my wife's support and guidance, I also felt tremendous resentment toward her for our mutual dependence and blamed her for the weight of my responsibilities. I circumvented dealing with the ambivalence I felt toward her by entering love affairs with other women.

The affairs I had at that time were not limited to sexual interactions. Driven by my need to feel nurtured, I became deeply involved with each woman. With each, I hoped to feel some magical relief from my anxieties and neuroses. I did not recognize my compulsive need to pathologically attach to women who reminded me of my mother. The fears of my childhood had been rechannelled from ritualistic behaviors to finding love objects.

At this time, I began to encourage weaker people to develop dependencies on me. The more dependent others were on me, the more protected I felt from my abandonment fears. My collection of dependencies included a wife, two children, lovers, friends, and even patients.

The power and domination I gained in these relationships disguised the helplessness and vulnerability I felt underneath. While I was convinced that most of my colleagues suffered from the same syndrome, they seemed more successful at hiding it from consciousness. Perhaps I was projecting my issues onto them.

In any case, we all took advantage of the protective shield offered by a professional identity. The undeniable ego gratification of being important to other people helped mask our fears of having limited skills as new and inexperienced psychotherapists. The illusions that our personal lives were under control and that we were indispensable to our patients combined to provide us with improved self-esteem and a sense that we were effective in our work.

In reality, at our best, we therapists can be only one step ahead of our patients. At times, we might think that we seem healthier because, after all, haven't we learned to hide our neuroses from public sight? Work in personal psychoanalysis helps to reinforce our misconception that we are better adjusted. As therapists, we alone have the awareness, courage, and education to confront our personal pathologies. We feel certain that we have cornered the market on personal growth and mental health. That is pure crap.

Each day, my life as an intern felt like a juggling act. I was torn between lovers and wife, employment and school, Mardoff and Moira. While I had great faith in my practical ability to negotiate these relationships, the larger conflict between security and freedom was harder to handle.

Being with my children was the only thing that seemed to offer me a respite from my all-consuming anxieties—

some semblance of peace. I kept reminding myself, "At least I have a family now. At last, I have a family of whom I am an integral member." However, as my work with Moira went on, I slowly recognized that not only Moira but I too was spinning out of control.

EIGHT

Suspicions

At our next meeting I attempted to help Moira see her British personality as the representation of a suppressed aggressive side of herself. I took Moira through the sequential phases of her relationship with this personality. First, the British girl was a storybook character whom Moira could admire and identify with. Then, she became Moira's fantasy friend—a source of comfort in an intolerable situation. Over time, Moira learned to incorporate the memory of the girl's aggression into her own psyche. This manifestation served to protect her inner world from dangerous outside forces threatening to annihilate her. The British girl became her hidden assertive identity.

I tried to show Moira that under normal circumstances she was able to contain this fragmented self. However, during times of great stress, her personal resources were strained beyond their limits. She could no longer stop this more powerful part of herself from emerging. It was in the midst of that meeting that I spontaneously decided to introduce Moira to her long lost friend. I rationalized that if she could integrate this stronger but suppressed part of herself, she would no longer feel so helpless.

As I sat there in that meeting, I remembered that in

some of Moira's dreams the British girl appeared as an aggressively sexual character. I asked Moira about it.

She erupted. "Stay out of my fuckin' dreams or I'll have to shove it to you," she screamed at me, using her British accent. "You want to fuck me little boy? I'm curious . . . tell me, just how big is your dickie? . . . I'm so hot for you . . . the way Mardoff is after me."

Why this allusion to Mardoff then? She had brought him up when the sexually aggressive side of her came out. Was there something going on that I didn't know about? Supervisory interactions were rarely discussed with patients. As far as I knew, she had no contact with him. When I asked Moira to clarify what she was trying to say, she refused to respond. "Oh doc . . . You fucking asshole, you prick! Your body is on fire. Your cock is loaded and ready to blow."

It was at that point that suddenly she shot backwards in her chair. It was as if the power of her words had somehow momentarily bridged the gap between these two sides of herself. I felt that perhaps she had briefly experienced the discordant merging of these two selves.

Suddenly the sound of the buzzer broke in. Gail was ringing to remind me that my next patient was waiting for his session. Although I went through the motions during the following session, I only devoted a small segment of my attention to it. I kept drifting obsessively back to the session with Moira and the memories of the prior session.

What was going on with Mardoff? I was convinced that there was some clue there. Moira's reference to Mardoff and sex resounded in my mind. It was pretty strange indeed. She said that she wanted both Mardoff and me shortly after she started masturbating. Was there a connection? How did all this fit together? What did it all mean? I couldn't wait to see Moira, or Mardoff for that matter, to try to assuage my suspicions.

In the intervening time, I checked the clinic records, searching through the list of phone calls. Had Moira tried to reach Mardoff? I couldn't find any evidence of it if she had.

I questioned Gail. She could not be sure but thought that she remembered someone who sounded like Moira asking for Mardoff.

I began to suspect that Moira and Mardoff were having an affair. Moira's references and intimation of having contact with him constantly occupied my thoughts.

My suspicions found a focus in Mardoff's constant criticisms of Moira during supervision and his insistence that she was a seductive hysterical personality. Why would he so rigidly ignore the overwhelming evidence I had presented? Hadn't I proved over and over again that she was a multiple or dual personality?

He must have a hidden agenda. Why would he do this . . . unless he needed her to be seductive? Mardoff must be invested in defining her as a neurotic. If she was erotically obsessed, couldn't he use that as the means for justifying their interactions and ensuring his own self-interest?

My mind went back and forth. First I told myself that I was becoming paranoid. Then I told myself my paranoia was justified. After all, I reasoned, Mardoff had rigidly adhered to the seductive hysterical diagnosis before one could logically conclude anything about a new patient. Could their clandestine meetings be occurring all this time behind my back?

The ongoing rumors and gossip at the clinic—clinical interns and clerical workers were constantly making suggestive references, implying all kinds of irregular activities—fueled my suspicions. Before this, I dismissed the rumors as bravado and boredom, but now I began to believe there was truth in them.

I tried reaching Moira by telephone when she did not show up for her next regularly scheduled appointment. At her home, a young-sounding male voice answered the call. In a disjointed conversation, he told me that he had neither seen nor heard from her. After contacting her precinct, I was informed that she had taken an unscheduled two-week vacation.

A supervisory session with Mardoff was scheduled for

the following afternoon. It was our last meeting prior to summer break. When I entered the clinic the next morning, I saw Gail sitting in her usual place.

"Marty," she said matter of factly, "I have two messages for you. Dr. Mardoff has pulled in your scheduled supervisory session two hours. He wanted me to let you know that he needed to meet earlier so that he could catch a plane to St. Vincent. Also, your patient Moira called, she said that she would not be coming to therapy for two weeks."

"Do you know approximately when she called?" I anxiously inquired. "And from where?"

"Around two hours ago," Gail responded. "I think that it was an international call—there was an operator on the line."

"Can we trace the call?" I asked heatedly.

Gail looked at me surprised. "What for? This is not a detective agency! I've got plenty of work to do without wasting time on stuff like that," she reacted angrily.

My imagination went wild. I began to fantasize about Mardoff making love to Moira in St. Vincent. Pictures crowded my head. I was seething with rage at the thought of Mardoff taking advantage of Moira's vulnerability. I rushed to his office and walked in without knocking.

"I think that I ought to let you know: Moira won't be coming to therapy for a few weeks." I nervously began the supervisory session with Mardoff. "By the way, I heard that you are off on vacation, too. Where are you planning to go?" I initiated the inquisition.

"To St. Vincent for two weeks," he replied coolly. I sensed that he was annoyed at my broaching such a personal subject.

"With your family?" I persisted.

"No, alone," Mardoff irritatingly responded. "My wife is a pediatrician. She is on call this week and next, and my kids are in summer camp."

I couldn't help myself. I plunged in. "Interesting . . .

isn't it a strange coincidence that Moira—and you—are taking vacations at the same time?" I asked sarcastically.

"What are you implying?" Mardoff shot back, his face turned crimson, his anger becoming more evident by the moment.

Suddenly, I panicked. In my mind I rapidly reviewed the information I had picked up around the clinic about Mardoff's marriage. Nothing. I had also heard that Mardoff was considered quite a catch by the female therapists and clerical staff. Rumors of his sexual involvement with pretty graduate students circulated regularly.

Until now, I hadn't paid much attention to these rumors. I had thought that the overabundance of rumors at the clinic was a normal response to a highly charged environment. I also knew that it was an unreasonable leap to assume that, since Mardoff was willing to have affairs with female therapists, he would also be willing to jeopardize his professional standing by initiating relationships with patients.

However, I was obsessed with my suspicions. I recalled a conversation with Jill, my analyst, the previous day. She had suggested that I was transferring to Mardoff a love-hate ambivalence that had its roots in my relationship with my father. On an unconscious level, I had always wanted my father to fight back against my mother's wrath. I loved my father. He was my only ally in a female-dominated, male-hating household.

My therapist suggested that while unconsciously I wanted my father to punish my mother by having affairs, I also feared his being involved with other women. What if he found a more satisfying relationship, someone who loved him better than I did? Would he take me with him or leave me in my crazy home? Again my fears of abandonment drove my inner struggle. The desire that my father escape the rejection of his marriage conflicted directly with my all consuming fear of being left behind. According to my analyst, I was reenacting this dynamic in my relationship with Mardoff.

Her interpretation, though logical, did not convince me. I felt strongly that the affair between Mardoff and Moira was real. Now, however, I realized I had gone too far. I had no proof, and if I accused Mardoff I might jeopardize my whole future. I pulled back. "Oh, I was just kidding —pulling your leg," I finally answered Mardoff. Suddenly I recognized in my response Moira's words to me during our last session, and this added to my embarrassment.

"You seem very agitated," Mardoff commented cautiously. "Is there anything bothering you?"

"I guess that I am just worried, since Moira disappeared after a very strange therapy session. I checked with her family and they didn't seem to know where she was. Then, I called her at work and they said that she had taken an unscheduled vacation. When Gail said that Moira had called from overseas and that you would be going abroad as well, I hastily jumped to a ridiculous conclusion.

"I guess I'm just feeling anxious that my favorite supervisor and patient both select to take holidays at the same time. I feel abandoned."

"Your attempts at humor are a bit off today, also," Mardoff remarked. "Can we get on with the so-called incident pending Moira's unexpected disappearance?" I quickly ran through my session notes with Mardoff. His reply was curt and to the point.

"You have consistently reported a high level of inappropriate seductive behavior on Moira's part. Why do you characterize these particular incidents as strange in comparison to her usual behavior?"

"Well, she started masturbating during the session . . . albeit without awareness on her part," I half-truthfully informed him. "She also told me that she wanted to have an affair with either you or me. I attempted to get her to explore her transferential feelings toward us but she refused, claiming she didn't really know you and it was out of the question with me."

"That's probably why she's been in touch with me," he

responded casually, but I noticed his jaw tightening and a nervous tick appearing. I bit my lip.

"What? Why the hell didn't you tell me? Did you ever hear of professional courtesy? You have no right to have kept me uninformed. She's my patient, not yours."

"I did not tell you because I didn't want to hurt your seemingly fragile feelings." He tapped his fingers drum-like on his desk. "She claimed that you've helped her a great deal, but at this stage of her therapy she needs someone more experienced than you. What do you think about her request?"

"Spare me your concern with my fragile ego. I'm more interested in finding out about her contact with you. When did she first contact you?" I replied accusatorially. "Was it recently or does it go back for quite some time?"

"Are you questioning my professional ethics?" he retorted angrily; his voice had a steel edge. "If it had not been recently, I would have informed you earlier. I had decided to wait until I returned from vacation so that we could strategically work together.

"But I must remind you, Mr. Obler, that you are playing a risky game if you start questioning the appropriateness of your supervisor overseeing your work with clients. You are just an intern." He said the last word so disparagingly I flinched. "You have not yet earned your stripes, so to speak. I advise you to deal with this as a personal problem and handle it in your individual analysis."

His play for power was both manipulative and obvious. My reaction was to fight fire with fire. "Life is very precarious, and I am prepared to take risks. I will protect any position that I believe to be morally correct. I will not compromise my relationship to a patient."

His face was white with rage. Recognizing that such a defensive response only highlighted my vulnerability, I abruptly shifted gears. "I'm not making any accusations, I am just letting you know that my client has been making all kinds of indirect references to having had contact with you. It's my obligation and responsibility to protect my patient. I am checking out her intimations with you. How would you recommend I deal with it?"

Mardoff pounded the desk with his fist. "I warned you from the beginning that you were dealing with a hysterical woman," he responded. "Are you purposely trying to destroy your own career? Certainly you are well aware that it is mandatory to report in supervision what happens in session. Until you graduate from this program, your patients are still my responsibility. You've impeded not only her therapeutic progress but the success of your supervisory training.

"These types of women thrive on attention. Their forte is in engineering competition between males. In this case, the competition was a bit lopsided—a knowledgeable and powerful supervisor versus a blathering idiot of an intern."

In that moment, I knew that he had me. It was stupid to challenge his authority. I didn't have a shred of evidence to back up my claims. My career was over if I couldn't fancy-dance my way out of this mess.

Retreating to childhood lessons, I examined my options. How could I rush into a fight I couldn't win? There was no question that this was a losing battle. I had to reestablish our roles as exemplary student and kind, understanding mentor.

I retreated. "Look, Dr. Mardoff, I want to apologize for my absurd accusations and outlandish behavior," I said meekly. "I've been under a lot of stress working with this patient. As you say, I've most certainly foolishly permitted her to manipulate and seduce me.

"Separation, anxiety, and fears of working without your supervision over the summer are creating an intense panic given my relative inexperience. I've discussed it in my personal analysis. My therapist feels that I am experiencing the transference process with you. This could explain my ambivalent feelings toward you and my eagerness to enter into this oedipal configuration. I beg you to forgive me. Please, help me out of this confusion."

"Why don't we wait until I get back from vacation before unravelling this quandary," he answered coolly. "In the interim, perhaps you can regain the detachment you need to proceed."

Two weeks later, Moira came back to therapy. I had not heard from her or her family during this time. My investigative attempts proved fruitless.

When Moira entered the room, her tension and agitation were apparent. There was a desperation and pain in her eyes that had not been there before. I have never forgotten that look or the words that followed. We sat in silence, and tears streamed down her face.

"Help me," she eventually pleaded. "Tell me what's happening to me. I'm missing so many days. When was I here last? I feel so frightened. I don't know what's going on. I know that you are talking about me when you speak of that aggressive British girl. I just have no memory whatsoever of being her. I want so much to be well."

"Where have you been since your last session?" I asked.

"I don't know. I only have flashes, bits and pieces. Everything else is a blank." Her panic was palpable.

"When did you call and leave the message about your vacation?" I asked, hoping to jar a memory.

"Called and left a message?" She said puzzled. "I don't remember doing that. I did have a dream about a wonderful vacation. I was on an island. I was with an older, sophisticated man. He was taking care of me, and I think we were sleeping together."

"Can you recall where you were when you had the dream?" I inquired. "Or, how about where you were before you came to session today? Do you remember that?"

"No, I only know this morning, I woke up in a hotel. I don't know how I got there. When I tried to pay downstairs, they said that it was already taken care of. I felt afraid because I didn't remember paying. There was dried semen on my clothes and my leg. I don't remember being with anyone. I went to my mother's house to wash and change. Then, I came directly here."

Moira jumped direction suddenly. "I really like the lady receptionist here. She's so nice. She was in my dream. I feel close to her. I think that we could be friends."

"Why did you go to your mother's house, and not your own, before you came to session?" I broke in. I wanted to know if there was any rationale underlying her decision.

"I was embarrassed and fearful of running into my husband. Can you imagine what it would have been like to run into him or my children?"

"What if you met your mother or Janice instead," I suggested. "Wouldn't that have been as bad or worse?"

"They don't scare me any more. I'm a lot more frightened by my memory lapses," she declared. "I don't know why, but I think that the hotel in my dream was in a foreign place. It is hazy and all I remember are shadows of things. I think the man had silver hair."

I flinched. "Was it the same hotel as the one before you came to session?" I said, wanting to probe further.

"No, that was much later," she said as the expression on her face changed dramatically. "Sometimes I wish that I was a man. Men can do almost anything. Maybe I am imagining the whole thing. The dream seems somewhere far away and different. The man was an older man. My father could shoot well, really well," she suddenly interrupted her own train of thought.

"Are you aware that you are having trouble sticking to one subject?" I asked, trying to speak calmly.

Moira responded strangely. She began singing and moving her body, rocking back and forth rhythmically to her own music. I listened to her words and realized that they were a raunchy caricature of a religious song.

The voice was not Moira's, but it sounded familiar. It sounded sophisticated and male. Was the voice Mardoff's, I kept asking myself? I sensed that Moira had entered a new space and was calling on a different personality.

"My father was the only one who was ever kind to me." Moira appeared to be phasing back to the personality who began the session. "The best times I can remember were with him. I would sit next to my father and watch him clean his gun. He would polish it until it shone like moonlight."

I decided to try and pull her back to the previous personality. "What happens to you when you sing in that voice?"

"What are you talking about?" She looked at me strangely. "I don't recall singing."

I stood up, watching her intently. "Our time is up now, but I'm concerned that you'll have another episode and will miss therapy once again. Maybe we could work out a way for you to contact me if you feel the start of a split in your personality. You could call me in that moment and I could bring you back in touch with reality. That way we could avoid any loss of memory. What do you think about that?"

"God damn it," she screamed. "Why couldn't my father help me? Why wouldn't he help me? Why did he let them . . . those bastards . . . do this to me? I was so weak and vulnerable." Then she got up and stalked out of the room.

Shaken, I barely got through the rest of the day. That night, I went to my lover after therapy. I told her about what had happened with Moira. As I talked about the man's voice that came out during the session, I remembered an event from childhood. I described the memory to my lover in great detail. I had not thought about it for over twenty-two years.

NINE

Jarring Memories

When summer evenings shifted from sweltering to unbearable, it became almost impossible to sleep. At those times, my parents permitted my older sisters to stay up late into the night. Their domain was extended to include the entrance steps of our tenement building. My sisters and their friends would sit out there for hours gossiping and giggling. My parents had to concede that only there were they likely to catch any stray breezes.

As the youngest, the best I managed to negotiate with my parents was the fire escape landing outside my mother's bedroom window. I convinced my mother that she could keep an eye on me better there than in the living room where I normally slept. Unlike today, it was still a reasonably safe place to sleep on hot summer nights twenty-two years ago in New York.

My memories of those nights sleeping on the fire escape are filled with a child's mixture of both excitement and horror. While I lay quietly, pretending to be asleep, my fire escape nights included hours of adventurous spying on my sisters and their friends and citings of pretty young women undressing at the open windows in the buildings opposite ours. They also included frightening displays of violence and anger among our neighbors fighting in the adjacent apartments, and the unseen but heard big-city night sounds of lonely people crying out.

On one particular night, an event occurred that would shape the rest of my life. For twenty-two years afterwards, I managed to keep this memory from my consciousness. I retained, however, an unnamed residual fear and anxiety, which I was able for the first time that evening to trace back to what had happened so long before.

I remembered overhearing some neighbors yelling about the "Shvartzers." Since my own parents used a mixture of Yiddish and English in our home, I knew that the Yiddish word *Shvartz* meant black. Our neighbors were talking about the southern blacks who had recently migrated north to the big cities. Several families had moved onto an adjacent street.

On the whole, the neighborhood seemed in agreement that these newcomers were a definite threat. Of northern and eastern European stock, our exposure to non-white, non-Western people was extremely limited. As with all unknowns, irrational fear spread quickly.

We said that they would "ruin our neighborhood," an expression we learned when it was first applied to us moving into a neighborhood. We wanted them to "go back where they came from"—also learned from accusatory jeers of those who had arrived before us. My childhood was spent quietly listening to the rantings of hatred among ethnic and racial groups fighting for the few crumbs available to the poor and helpless.

While half-asleep, I listened to the familiar exegesis on our newest neighborhood problem. Once fully awake, I realized that I was thirsty. I crept past my sleeping mother on my way to the kitchen to get myself a drink of water.

As I reached in the darkness for the light switch, I heard a noise. Even as a young child, my mother's paranoid fears of the world had infiltrated my psyche. I shook with fear expecting criminals or robbers or child snatchers. The tales of the terrifying pogroms and murderous cossacks rarely left my young mind.

I screamed for my parents, but nobody answered. I became panic-stricken. I realize now that my scream must have been a silent one. Suddenly, I heard something unexpected. It was the sound of soft crying.

I decided that I must be dreaming. Often, I awoke frightened in the middle of the night. It was always my father who comforted me, explaining that it must have been a bad dream, a nightmare. I gathered courage and switched on the light.

To my amazement, there was a little black boy standing by the window. He was standing in a corner, hugging the leg of a kitchen chair. He alternated between whimpering softly and sucking on his thumb, all the while big tears streaming down his face. We stared at each other incredulously.

He was much smaller than I. Although I was the youngest in my family and so did not have experience with younger children, he couldn't have been more than three or four years old—after all, I was almost five and he was smaller than me. I remember thinking that he must have lost his mommy and daddy.

My father came rushing into the room. He was probably awakened by the light. Seeing the strange boy, he grabbed him roughly. He hit the crying child hard in the face. I began to weep uncontrollably.

I watched my father and the boy through my tears. As I stared at them, my father half-carried, half-dragged the child toward the open window. The crazy anger in my father's face terrified me. I screamed. For some reason I was certain that my father was going to throw the boy off the fire escape.

My parents had warned me many times to be careful on the fire escape. They reminded me that it was a dangerous place to play if you didn't pay attention. It was easy to fall and get hurt. I gasped in horror as my father yelled curses at the child. I begged him to stop.

My father placed the boy on the landing of the fire escape. The boy just stared in terror at my father. My father screamed at him to climb down the ladder to the street below. This must have been the way he got into our apartment. Someone had lowered the ladder to street level. The crying child nimbly scampered down the ladder.

My father turned to me, yelling, "You must be careful of those people. They're dangerous animals. You should have nothing to do with them." I felt confused. Did my father think that I had brought the child into our house?

I started to shake violently. My father picked me up, hugging me closely to him as he plunked down on a chair. His heart was pounding against his chest. I can now recognize that his reaction was, at least in part, one of protectiveness toward me. But at that moment in the kitchen, I felt only rage and a sense of shame as I looked into my father's face.

Why did my father want to hurt that little boy? Wasn't he a little boy just like me? Would my father hurt me that way? Could I no longer trust him? Could I expect other people's fathers to hurt me?

I didn't really understand the connection between the boy in our kitchen and the talk about the "Shvartzers." Weren't they talking about grown-up black people, black men who were criminals, carried knives, drank cheap alcohol, gambled in the streets, and stole the few low-paying jobs around? We were just kids, this boy and me.

Later, through my involvement with civil rights and my own children, I came to understand the connection better—and also my early confusion. I realized that a child's view of prejudice and social injustice is probably the most objective and optimistic available.

My mother ran into the room, hysterical. She was joined by my two older sisters, who had heard the commotion from the street below. We all looked down to the foot of the fire escape. The little boy stood motionless, staring up at us and continuing to suck his thumb.

I cried out to him. "Run so they cannot hurt you. Run quick." I turned to my family. Through my anger, fear, and mistrust of my parents, I took my first, however hesitant, step toward adulthood. Without thinking of the possible repercussions, I pleaded with my parents, begging them not to hurt him.

I was shocked when my father responded by climbing down the ladder to the street. He carried the child back up to our apartment. He sat the boy down on a chair by the table. My mother brought food to the table and placed it before the child. We watched as he hungrily fed himself. In that moment, I loved my parents more than I ever have since.

The boy stayed with us overnight. In the morning, we went out into the neighborhood searching for where he lived. We stopped people in the street, inquiring, hoping to find someone who knew the boy. No one seemed to.

Eventually, the boy led us to the basement of an abandoned building. He lived there. There were two teenage boys sleeping on the floor whom we assumed to be his brothers. They stared at my family in sleepy disbelief, saying nothing. They did not seem to have noticed that the boy had been gone. We left the little boy there with them. Somehow I knew that I would never see him again.

About a month later, we heard that the boy had been found murdered. His body had been mutilated and he had been sexually molested. Rumors spread over the next few months that the rapist-murderer had severed his thumb from his hand. For many years afterwards I dreamed of a hand with no thumb. In my dream, as I looked closer, I suddenly realized it was my hand.

The repressed memory of that childhood incident haunted me after my last meeting with Moira. The connection between my feelings for that little boy and Moira did not escape me.

As the weeks passed, I felt my own need to help her intensify. I thought of Moira constantly and could not concentrate on other patients. I knew I was in danger of losing all sense of proportion. I did not exhibit the required and appropriate professional restraint. Still the fact of how unjustly she was being treated haunted me. I vowed to faithfully defend all fragile and helpless victims. I would end the brutality wrought on those too weak to defend themselves. Only then would I feel safe myself.

My obsessive preoccupation with Moira was interrupted surprisingly enough by Mardoff. I received a message from him a week before his return to the office. He requested that we reschedule our planned meeting for an earlier date.

We met at an early Monday morning breakfast session. For once, although he was suntanned and impeccably suited, Mardoff looked nervous and harried rather than debonair and composed. He wasted no time on amenities. "I have," he said forcefully, "spent a good deal of my vacation thinking about your training. I was very concerned because I feel that you have become too involved in the therapy with Moira."

Thoughtfully Mardoff stroked his chin with thumb and forefinger. "It is a complicated case, although I want to reiterate that hysteria is the root problem. I admit that perhaps it was a mistake to assign a borderline patient to a new intern. I apologize, accepting culpability in the situation." Of course, in this way, he was also able to once again challenge my competence and increase my sense of insecurity. I did not take issue with his interpretations.

I did not mention either Moira's search for her brother or the diary notes that she had brought in. I kept my sexual abuse theory to myself. I only hinted obliquely that something may have gone on with one of her brothers when she was a child.

I masked this mention of sexual contact within the family in terms of Mardoff's oedipal theory. According to Freudian theory, brothers and sisters often express sexual interest in each other at the end of the oedipal period. This is one mechanism useful in helping to resolve the intense emotions produced during this psychosexual state. Mardoff seemed to accept and appreciate my more moderate stance.

After a while when I felt Mardoff was no longer on guard and wary, I brought up the balance of Moira's partially remembered dream. Watching him closely, I told Mardoff of her reported fantasy of sexual contact with an older man on a foreign vacation. His face was impassive, his voice cool. "It is clearly a thinly disguised subconscious erotic transference to her father. In particular, it reflects her strong wish to be orgasmic." Mardoff leaned back in his chair. "I would also suggest that missing sessions is often a sign of unconscious resistance. In this case, the resistance probably developed from a fear that her erotic wishes could become reality during therapy."

Mardoff shook his head affirmatively as if agreeing with his own assessment. I said nothing. "In fact," Mardoff went on smoothly, "perhaps I made a mistake even accepting her call. I recognize that it may have further complicated the web of transferential sexual components." I was amazed by Mardoff's relative lack of defensiveness and impressed by the accuracy of his insights. Again I asked myself, had I been wrong in my suspicions about Moira and him? Mardoff was on the offensive again. "You need, Mr. Obler, to carefully examine once again," he drew out the last word, "countertransference feelings in your own analysis."

"I think," he slyly added, "you must learn to draw a distinction between the work you are to do with your therapist and the work you and I are to do in supervision."

I flushed. I felt my own anger rising. I sat up straight. I had no intention of being intimidated. If he wanted a showdown here and now, I was willing to accommodate him. "My interest in Moira is purely professional. It is yours I question," I said meeting his eyes.

Mardoff was on his feet, his chair flung back, his face flaming red, "Have you gone mad, Obler?"

"I don't think so," I said stammering. "I wonder if you are seeing Moira clandestinely."

"What did you say?" Mardoff strode over to me, his fists clenched, but I refused to be stopped.

I stood up and faced him, "Are the two of you lovers?"

Angrily Mardoff cut me off. "Really, you little ingrate, I will not permit this," he spat out. "You'd better get this straight. Stay out of my life, and if you ever," there was venom in his voice, "if you *ever*," he repeated, "so much as insinuate your suspicions to anyone, the only career you'll ever have is sweeping floors—if that.

"Now," he said ominously, "get out of my way. I'm going to give myself a week to decide what to do with you, and during that week, Obler, I strongly suggest you think seriously of the options open to me." He paused, "In fact, since you seem so obsessive, think of nothing else. . . ." His steel-edged voice cut through me. Without another word he was gone.

Mesmerized, I stood there trembling, considering what his next move would be.

TEN

Jarring Realities

During the next few days, Mardoff's parting words reverberated in my mind. Just as he had instructed, I thought of little else. Why had I confronted him? Had I expected him to confess? How stupid could I be? Mardoff was brilliant and powerful. I was dumb and naive. He headed the clinic, I was a lowly intern. One thing was blatantly clear to me: to achieve nothing I had stupidly jeopardized my future and Moira's. How could I hope to help her if I was taken off her case, or worse—thrown out of the clinic? Mardoff could easily crush us both without anyone being the wiser. Watching, waiting, I inched through my office hours. There was no noise from Mardoff.

On Friday, walking into the clinic, Gail called to me but did not look up. Her face was inscrutable. "Marty, Mardoff has scheduled you for a supervisory at four."

I sighed. So he had waited until the final hour of the final day of the week, probably wanting to increase my anxiety. I wondered if he had told Gail what was going on. She offered no clue and I was afraid to ask. Going into my office I sat at the desk and stared off into space, listening to my ticking watch.

* * *

Mardoff began our meeting as if nothing had happened between us. He was his cool, self-assured self. "Mr. Obler," he said, "it has become clear to me," he stopped and took a sip of water from the pitcher on his desk. He watched me intently. My heart quickened, beating like a drum. He smiled and stared as if he knew and wanted my torment to go on for as long as possible.

"Yes, it is quite clear," he toyed with the glass, "that Moira's case has been detrimental to your training." He allowed his voice to take on an edge and stared at me, almost inviting me to take exception. I bit my lip hard and said nothing. He continued, "Of course, the ideal thing would be your reassignment." Again he paused and watched me. A smile played at the corners of his mouth. He was baiting me, waiting for me to snap at the proffered tidbit so he could pounce.

Using all the self-control I possessed, I kept quiet.

He nodded. "Reassignment is, of course, out of the question given the length of time already spent in treatment." My patience and resolve were ebbing. I knew, however, I could not let go. I searched for a spot on the wall behind him and concentrated on finding it.

Mardoff poured some water from the pitcher slowly into a glass. I wondered playfully if he was planning the water torture. "Instead," he said almost casually, "I propose two concurrent solutions." I kept my eyes on the imaginary spot. "First, I will assign some interesting new cases to you."

Shocked, I stared at him. I could not help the look of surprise which spread across my face.

Mardoff added, "Thus your overinvestment in Moira will diminish naturally." I swallowed hard. The gurgling sound I made was audible. For a moment there was a pause. Then deliberately Mardoff took a pencil from the pile in front of him. Watching me, he broke it between his fingers with a snap. Then he went on. His voice icy. "The second solution has to do with clinic policy. In this last year of your training, you will become involved with the group therapy process. I feel the combination of the two will do the trick."

I sensed that this was a critical moment for Mardoff and for me. If I objected, he would destroy my future with few qualms. After all, I had been forewarned.

"That sounds very good," I said.

There was a silence. In it, despite my placating words, my mind raced back and forth. I was not fooled by his decision to enlarge the scope of my practice. It was a subterfuge to divert me from exposing what he had done. Still, I recognized that I had to accept his words at face value. I had no choice in the matter, not if I wanted to be a psychologist. I made my choice. "I'm flattered." The words tripped from my tongue. Only I knew the bitter aftertaste I swallowed. I had no way to oppose him. Not at this point. I had to wait for my opportunity.

I also felt relief. The fact that he was not transferring Moira to a new therapist was the most important thing, at least for the present. For now I would have to do as he said. I swore to myself at the same time that I would never rest until I found out the truth and exposed it.

Mardoff assigned me the task of forming a therapy group. I was to select the group participants from both my new assignments and my previous caseload. Neither of us raised the issue of whether or not to include Moira in the group.

The group was to start in November. I would be supervised by a specialist in group therapy, Dr. Robert Marcuse. In the interim, Mardoff directed me to concentrate my studies on psychoanalytic group therapy theory. I was also to observe a number of ongoing group therapy sessions at the clinic and attend training seminars at the postgraduate center for mental health.

During our supervision sessions in September and October, Mardoff and I focused on the significance of Moira's mental state at my last meeting with her. "I am very interested," he said, "in what has happened, especially the way she has fragmented. It is most unusual for an hysteric." Briefly, I deluded myself that I had been mistaken that Mardoff and Moira were not really involved and he might be coming around to my way of thinking.

I was still very curious and suspicious of Moira's activities during her absence. She, however, was not interested in talking about this and remained vague in her responses. She seemed intent on not revealing any further details of her whereabouts. She also refused to discuss any further her strange sexual fantasy about the older man.

In general, she seemed withdrawn during therapy. My impression was that the events had been effectively screened from her consciousness. Was she hiding from me or herself?

At first I gave only an edited version of Moira's session to Mardoff. Mardoff interpreted her behavior at our last meeting as a form of regression. He said forcefully, "It is an ego function provoked by the rearousal of her oedipal attractions to the two of us."

Round and round my mind went. I tried to bring my thoughts back to the present to focus on what Mardoff was saying.

"The primary reason I have given you new patients," he said, "is to help you shift countertransference attention to other patients. This is a common technique used by therapists when an overinvolvement with one patient occurs. Group therapy is also an experience that can help foster recognition and interest in many types of disorders. Therapists, as well as patients, must learn that this is a professional relationship. It is transitory by definition. Successful completion of the therapeutic process requires both parties to grow to a point where they are emotionally neutral to each other."

I did not respond.

"Well, Obler, we shall see." Mardoff informed me, "In November, you will be taking on a new patient named Lori.

Like Moira, Lori is an hysteric borderline patient. At the core of Lori's syndrome, however, is a latent depression. The central etiology in Moira's case is a victim mentality. Even though the roots of the two disorders differ, the manifestations in behavior are exactly the same." His eyes never left my face. His intense gaze invited comment. I was determined not to be provoked.

He stuck the zapper in. "I believe that you will find it interesting working with two different hysterical women. It may also help you to resolve your personal weakness and attraction to women who are hysterical."

I made no comment.

I recognized the emphasis he was placing on developing psychological distance between Moira and me. Therefore, during supervision, I tried to create the impression that I had greatly diminished my emotional investment in Moira. Of course, this was not true. However, during this period, I felt that my sessions with her were going nowhere. Still I knew I had to be patient to watch and wait for the right climate in which to explore the truth about her past and present and expose Mardoff.

By the beginning of the new year, I was heavily enmeshed with the dynamics of group therapy. My sessions with Moira had taken on a very formal analytic tone. We rehashed material from her past that had little emotional significance. She tried to impress me by declaring that her libido was very active since the masturbatory incident at the office. She felt liberated sexually. When I asked her to explore more specifics about her liberation, she offered no details.

I felt completely frustrated. Until she was ready, the best I could offer Moira was to listen passively to her monologues. I wondered how long my emotional distancing from her would last. When would she tell or remember the past or talk about her relationship with Mardoff?

As time passed, I found myself becoming angry and impatient with her. In my personal analysis, I brought up the issue of my sudden distaste for Moira. Jill, my analyst, offered an interpretation. She suggested that perhaps on a subconscious level I was reacting to a sexually provocative experience in my past, one that threatened me. "Perhaps," she speculated, "you are defending against an impulse of rage at Moira possibly becoming involved or at least wanting to with an older man—a father figure. Wasn't this similar to the way you retreated emotionally as a young child in your relationship with your mother?"

I did not reply. While all this sounded good, it did not ring true to me. The reason I felt I was angry and frustrated with Moira was more elemental. Survival. Moira held the answer to our escape from imprisonment in Mardoff's web. We both dangled there, unable to cry out, unable to move, awaiting her breakthrough.

By December, however, that breakthrough seemed even farther away.

Moira suddenly stopped talking about her sexual awakening. She began talking about the past. What was new in her analysis was not the content of these examinations but the meanings she now assigned to the events. Although it was not the information I needed to free us from Mardoff, she had found a way to reengage me.

I felt her past was the key to the present. Many of the events and experiences from her past were too painful for Moira to examine. There were so many gaps and lapses of memory. At times, Moira felt that it might be impossible to piece together what had actually taken place in her family. While she recognized that she was unconsciously screening out the unbearable memories, the large gaps of time that she could not account for frightened her.

Moira would try hard to recapture events successfully blocked from awareness, but nothing came back. Only in her dreams, particularly nightmares, were there glimpses of what had really occurred. Once she dreamed of hiding in the basement of her parent's house. She was with her younger brother. All she saw were large boots descending the staircase toward her. While Moira knew that something like that had actually happened, she could not remember any details or substance, only feelings of fear.

Moira's one memory jog had to do with her relationship to her younger brother Bill. She now remembered Bill as someone who would help and protect her. She reported that even as a very young child, she depended on Bill to clue her in on what was happening around her—to connect her to reality.

Moira could not remember a time when she hadn't experienced memory lapses and gaps. She had always felt separate from other people because of this lost-time ordeal. She remembered feeling frequently confused, unsafe, and alone.

Her fear of "being crazy" had increased with the passage of years. It had become particularly acute when her brother became a teenager. Psychologically, he had moved away from her and toward an inner world of his own creation. Moira felt that her only way out of these unremembered times, lost days, unaccounted time, was to "have the eyes of others." She said that it served as a vehicle to retain the memories of her blank time.

I was uncertain what exactly Moira meant by "having the eyes of other people." Did it mean that Moira had tried to feel out other people's impressions of events to define or assure her reality, or was it her way of describing a form of dissociation, permitting another part of herself to retain the memory of painful events?

Therapy had become a means for her not only to recapture the past, but also to assign it meaning. At first, I thought that she was remembering events that had been previously hidden from her view. But as her probing exploration continued and she uncovered more and more new insights, I realized that in many cases she was in fact interpreting events that had always been assessable to her but that she had not had the words or tools to understand.

When she talked of her past just as the present, however, it became clear that only pieces and fragments were recalled. Typically these were disconnected fragments mixed together with threads of remembered dreams and fantasies. Our task was to form a whole picture from the fragments.

It reminded me of putting together giant jigsaw puzzles. Not infrequently, pieces had been misplaced or lost. In Moira's case, I felt the missing pieces were the critical connecting links or patterns that would help us see what the larger picture looked like. The only consistent themes were feelings of continuous panic and terror, memories of recurring physical and psychological abuse, and a sense of an unexplained sexual climate.

I began to realize that the family history we had explored the year before was not information Moira had gathered through her own observations of her family or through general discussions of family folklore. When I questioned Moira more closely, it turned out that the majority of it came from a diary of her maternal grandmother. Moira had accidentally come across the diary and had kept it as a keepsake.

The endeavor of extracting actual rather than reinterpreted memories of events is one of the primary tasks in therapy. Moira's difficulties were but an extreme example of what usually goes on in typical psychotherapy. Most of what really happens during the formative years of our childhood is not remembered. It is only through secondary materials like dreams, slips of the tongue, and fantasies that we are able to reconstruct some of the events that actually occur. Moira's reconstructions were made much more complicated by the large gaps in her memory because of the dissociation process.

During our next session Moira jumped from thought to thought. "My father's gun stood for power, omnipotence, and control. I was always really attracted to it," she began our last meeting before the Christmas vacation. "He always had it with him, even carried it around the house. He wore it with great pride."

She signed heavily, "I realize that my father used the gun as a kind of displacement. He used it to compensate for feeling fragile and helpless much of the time. When I became a cop, I probably used my gun in the same way, as a concrete symbol or reminder of my acquired power." Her eyes sought mine.

"Go on Moira," I said acceptingly.

"I remember longing to be a boy. This was when I was very young. I remember thinking that then I would have the strength to hit my sister Janice and my mother. I would fantasize about going to get my father's gun and shooting them.

"I also began to half-pretend, half-hope that my father would protect me from my mother and sister. Is that why I turned to him for attention? That wasn't very smart of me. I guess I just couldn't accept that he was just as weak as I was."

I tried to focus her attention. "Do you actually remember turning to him for affection?" I asked Moira.

"I recall constantly wishing he would give it to me," she stroked her forehead. "But actually, I'm not sure if these are actual memories or things I have been told about how I was. My memories are like dreams. I guess no one is ever really sure if they are dreaming.

"But I think I realized early on what the power hierarchy in our house was really like. It became clear my father had relinquished all control to my mother. His gun became his only remaining source of pride and power. I think we were very much alike in some ways. We both had this fear of taking control of our own lives."

"That must have been frightening," I said quietly.

She nodded. "I often wondered why I didn't become a raving lunatic. With all the repressed rage I have, and as a cop, I could shoot people. I've seen lots of cops that way. As long as it's not too many or too obvious, they can get away with it. Why didn't my father go crazy? Why didn't he develop separate personalities like I did? He was just as abused, repressed, and fragmented as I am."

"No he wasn't," I responded. "When he drank, he would blow up and get his anger out. He also had the chance to develop into an integrated person. Moreover, he had a different set of experiences as a child.

"You suppressed most of your anger and only expressed strong emotion through the fragmented disconnected parts of yourself like the British personality. Your power was sublimated into the fragmented personae of your hidden personalities and never allowed into you awareness.

"Instead you rechanneled the anger back into your body. That is what brought about the severe pain in your back. In other words, Moira," I said gently, "the back pain is a psychosomatic symptom due to displaced hostility."

"Then it's all tied up with anger?" she asked.

"In your case, I believe so," I said.

She seemed to understand what I was getting at. "Being a cop gave me an outlet to express the aggressive part of myself. That part only comes out when I'm pressed against the wall, I think. I'll only get rid of my back pains if and when I let out my anger toward my husband and family. They deserve it for making me a scapegoat all these years."

"If you can get away from them for a while and live a life of your own, maybe you won't need to dissociate anymore," I suggested. "Let me validate your perceptions: Your family is crazy. They are abusive people. And effectively, if you remain, you are colluding with them. It would be difficult not to remain a victim. They're not going to accept your independence. That includes your husband, parents, siblings, and children."

"Where does my religious background fit in?" she asked. I saw this as a strong sign of her growing and healthy thirst for additional analytic exploration.

"It is not your religion but your fanaticism that fits perfectly," I offered. "For the repressed masochist, doesn't it offer a clear rationale for accepting victimization? I believe that feeling like you were a martyr gave you a much needed explanation for your miserable life.

"When you heard the priests and nuns at school talking about obedience, it gave you the framework for accepting the guilt you felt. Guilt was a safe way of covering up the rage and anger you felt that you needed to contain.

"Moira," I said, trying to reassure her, "a strong alliance has been forged between us. It might take a few years and it will certainly take a lot of work, but there is little doubt in my mind that you have the capacity to fuse your separate personalities."

My work with Moira had become satisfying again. Still, there were so many unanswered questions, especially concerning Mardoff. I had been considering proposing to him that Moira join my therapy group, but since my suspicions of him always lurked in the back of my mind beneath the surface, I was concerned with how to do it. Yet Moira seemed ready. She could also use some group confrontation —maybe it could jar her short-term memory. The idea of trying group therapy with Moira excited me.

Cautiously I spoke with Mardoff concerning Moira entering the group. He wouldn't give me a definitive answer. "I need to consider it more carefully," he said slowly. I didn't press. I didn't want to take the chance of opening our defenses and having him destroy them.

My patience paid off. A few weeks later, Mardoff agreed to allow Moira into the group. "I want you to wait until spring, however, so as not to disrupt the others," he added. He suggested that a weekend experience might be an interesting time to introduce Moira into the group. With the additional time available during a weekend, the group might have an easier time adjusting to a histrionic woman.

I readily agreed. I didn't want him to suspect I was weighing his every word. "Perhaps I shall come, too," Mardoff said. "I am interested in how group marathons work, their theoretical and scientific efficacy, and the connection to psychoanalytically oriented group therapy."

I had done substantial reading on the subject in preparation for this meeting. In addition, my group supervisor and I had spent hours discussing the ins and outs of the practical side. I kept our conversation focused on making a valid case for the intensive group experience of a marathon.

But even as we spoke, my thoughts focused on whether Mardoff was using the scene as an excuse for being with Moira. I hoped that by bringing out the past again, I could find out. By facilitating her joining the group, I was preparing to introduce Moira to a repressed part of her upbringing.

Eleven

Setting the Stage

That Tuesday, I suggested to Moira that she might benefit by group psychotherapy. Though noncommittal, she agreed to try it, but said, "I have to wait until spring." Mardoff's words echoed in my mind. Had he given her the same directive he'd given me?

"Why?" I asked.

"I have to, that's all," she insisted. I let it go.

Then in early spring she did a disheartening about-face, announcing that she was strongly opposed to the idea and had no wish to work with "other fucked-up people."

I had begun to believe, by this point, that group therapy could produce beneficial change. My group therapy instructor, an able and pleasant person, was allowing me to lead our group rather than just participate. Until then, I had emphasized that treatment should be focused primarily on problems and conflicts that had been transferred from childhood to adult life—transferred, that is, to the one-on-one process with a therapist. Certainly, transference and countertransference had been central to my work with Moira, but the dynamics of group therapy showed me that some people found it easier to relate to members of a group, rather than just one-on-one.

During discussion by our group of the possibility of a weekend marathon in May—with Mardoff's approval—I suggested taking in a new member. I was thinking of Moira, of course, and I talked of her. The group offered no objection to Moira joining us. They suggested she enter during the planned marathon.

I sounded Moira out at our next session. "Why should I consider being a part of a group you run?" she snapped. "You've been avoiding me for months. I'm not even sure I want to continue therapy at this point."

Once again, Moira had me on the defensive. "What do you mean? I haven't been avoiding you!"

She sat up ramrod straight. Her face changed expressions. "Stop the bullshit, Obler," she flashed angrily. "You know what I'm talking about. You haven't been in this room for months—your mind has been somewhere else. Probably with those young bitches in your group. I'm getting fed up with your indifference to me. Maybe you get a charge out of erotic behavior in female patients, but I don't. If you aren't serious about helping me, transfer me to another therapist." She drilled me with her eyes and snarled, "Can you deny you've felt withdrawn from me as a patient since you started working with the group?"

I answered as earnestly as I could. "That's simply not true, Moira. I'm just as committed to you now as before I joined the group, but I have told you I think the group could be beneficial to you." Her aggressiveness had shaken me. I let my anger show. "Moira, if you're too anxious to begin therapy with a group, okay. But don't hand me that nonsense about my withdrawing from you, which I haven't been, just to avoid facing your own anxieties about opening yourself to other people."

My anger sobered her. She gazed at me pensively.

"You may not want to let yourself see that you can handle other people much better now," I continued. "I've been mentioning group therapy to you for some time, because you might get a lot out of it at this point."

Again, I watched enthralled as Moira changed personae. "Shove it up your ass, you fuckin' bloomin' faggot," she shouted. Her British accent assaulted me. Then she quieted. "Steady on, Obler, just kidding. I think group therapy might be a good idea. I can hang out with other neurotics. Who knows, maybe I'll find a sucker I can mess around with. When do I start?"

I stammered, "Probably in a few weeks. We're planning a marathon weekend. You could start then, if Mardoff approves your case for group therapy."

It was the combative Moira who answered, "Why do you insist on calling me a case?"

"What do you prefer I call you?" I countered rather clumsily.

"How about acquaintance, or friend, human being? Any of them would do fine, you asshole. I swear, you're getting as dumb as that pussy-licking Mardoff. Well, maybe not as dumb, but as pretentious, certainly. That professional tone doesn't suit you any better than it does Mardoff. Why not take off that mask and be a real person?"

"Why are you so hostile to Mardoff?" I inquired. "You haven't had much contact with him."

"How do you know who I've had contact with over the last year?" Playful expression. "Don't you want to ask me about that older lover I described to you six months ago? Aren't you curious about who he is? You should be." Her green eyes swept over me. "Have those new group therapy cases made you lose interest in me as a female? Maybe your marriage is on the rocks like Mardoff's and my being female scares you. What do you think, Martin?"

I looked at her searchingly. How did she know

whether or not Mardoff's marriage was in trouble? Why did she want me to ask who her lover was? I didn't want to push her too far and chance another fragmentation or breakdown at the marathon. I tried an innocuous question: "That's the first time you've ever called me by my first name. What do you make of it?"

She batted my query back, "What do *you* make of it?"

Trying to soothe her obvious agitation, I said quietly, "I think it means you want to recreate the closeness we once had. As far as group therapy is concerned, I think we should make a decision so we can get endorsements from the group and the supervisor. I'll have to talk to the group about your joining us and tell them about your reaction to my invitation. That's the usual procedure before someone new enters the group."

Crossing her legs provocatively, Moira answered, "Who gives a fuck! Let's get on with it, my formal, frightened, intern 'shrink'—or should I just call you 'friend'?" She stood up and the meeting was over.

I was glad to walk outside. The air was crisp and cool. Spring had come. I decided to bring up Moira entering the group with Mardoff at my next session with him. Since it was the date he had suggested, I was sure he would go along with it. I would say that introducing her to the group at the marathon seemed appropriate. In that way I would be able to get final permission for both at the same time. The idea of conducting a marathon had become more and more attractive to me.

Marathons had been popularized in California by a young group of mental health professionals who termed themselves Gestalt Psychotherapists. They believed by and large that analysis by itself could not create a climate for genuine change. Attitudes and values that had become neurotically entrenched in an individual, they maintained, had to be confronted and attacked in a group setting if the patient was to gain emotional health. So these young therapists had conceived a blend of psychoanalytic techniques that focused on early personal fixations, with a new methodology concentrating on examining daily experience in which the patient's fixations conflicted with each other. These innovators were introducing their ideas and techniques at workshops. I attended a number of them.

Although the marathons were popular on the West Coast, East Coast therapists were conservative and resisted experimenting with new innovations in analytic technique. They believed that these short-term encounter experiences would provide only superficial releases and could not deliver the depth and insight of conventional therapies. Mardoff himself, I knew, disapproved of diverging from traditional therapy techniques. But in my training I had been exposed to these new ideas and had been sufficiently impressed with them to want to be the first member of my graduate training program to try them out.

I was disappointed in his response. Although Mardoff had said Moira could enter the group in the spring, he now seemed to oppose not only her entering the group, but even the idea of our conducting a marathon weekend. I argued with him, pointing out that though the West Coast techniques were in their infancy, research already suggested their effectiveness. I mentioned several people prominent in psychotherapy who felt the new approaches had promise—Fritz Perls and Carl Rogers among them. Then I played my strongest card. I told Mardoff that a Dr. Widofsky from my graduate program had approved people under his supervision to experiment with weekend encounter groups. That did it. Widofsky's reputation as a pioneer in psychiatric research was world-wide. Mardoff considered him a rival for renown, and if Widofsky was allowing weekend encounters, Mardoff was not going to be caught hanging back. He approved the marathon. Nothing like waving a competitive flag, I chuckled to myself.

One of our accountants located a country house we could rent inexpensively. Now all that remained was to get Mardoff to approve Moira's participation. During our next meeting he declared to me that his approval of her joining depended on whether she had grown mature enough to handle the experience productively.

A few days later he strode into my office. "I've decided to approve Moira for both the group and the weekend. Unfortunately, I can't come as I had hoped." But as though to keep the whip hand, he stipulated, "My colleague Dr. Marcuse must be in full charge of the weekend, and Obler, everything that happens will be reviewed in supervision."

The day for the marathon finally arrived. We were on our way! I couldn't believe it! Up Route 17, a beautiful old country road leading to the Catskills. Three cars carrying Dr. Marcuse, Moira, seven group members, and me. In the group were Lori, Inez, Gregory, Elsie, Grace, Peter, and John. I had travelled this route many times as a youth. Gazing at the mountains now, I reminisced to myself about my summers in the Catskills as a young man.

The rest of the group chattered; Moira was silent as we drove along. At last we arrived. The setting was lovely: Verdant green fields and small clear-watered streams crossed the property leading to a large creek. The main house was a quaint renovated barn fitted out for comfortable living.

As we settled in, the surroundings seemed to invigorate everyone. We dashed through the green fields, enjoying the tall grass brushing our legs. Inez, Peter, and John playfully rolled in it. Grace chatted with Moira, trying to make her feel welcome. Lori and Elsie debated the relative beauty of New York State versus Ohio and California. Only Gregory remained aloof, walking off and distancing himself from the others as he often did during sessions. Dr. Marcuse and I unloaded the car.

Clinic policy did not allow interns to conduct group therapy without psychiatric supervision. Marcuse was in charge, but I would be allowed to conduct the Gestalt exercises. Marcuse had a city-wide reputation of being an expert and experienced analyst. I respected him but somehow felt I would be the real leader this weekend.

After dinner, Peter, a tall, dark, athletic-looking guy in his late twenties, talked to me out of the hearing of the others. "Are you aware, Mr. Obler," he said so formally that I winced, feeling for the moment the weight of being an authority figure, "that some of the other group members and I have learned of a tragic circumstance about Marcuse." I shook my head. "His family were killed by the Nazis, after which Marcuse was imprisoned in a concentration camp." I suffered a moment of nausea and despair. Another Nazi nightmare. Would they ever end?

I recovered and reassured Peter, "He'll be alright, Peter, but thank you for telling me."

Peter walked back to the group. I stood thinking about what he'd said about Marcuse and mentally crossed my fingers.

Psychologists, psychiatrists, and others dedicated to helping troubled human beings toward emotional health learn to live with a fair degree of uncertainty in their practices. Much is known about how the human psyche works, but emotions are complex, subtle, and unpredictable. It's often difficult to foresee what may occur at various stages and phases of our efforts to help people help themselves.

After coffee, Marcuse and I decided to start things off by having each person in turn describe why he or she had chosen to undergo psychotherapy. Each responded well, talking with an openness achieved only after months of sessions. At this point we refrained from calling on Moira—she needed time to feel at ease. Marcuse worked brilliantly with the group, drawing the members out and volunteering helpful points for each to consider.

Then I guided them through an exercise I had learned in a Gestalt workshop. Participants lay on the floor, forming a large circle with their feet touching. Each placed a hand on the face of the person next to them. Their eyes remained closed throughout the exercise. I got them to breathe deeply and regularly, mediation-style, and instructed them in muscle relaxation. They cooperated gratifyingly.

After all reported feeling relaxed, I started them on a fantasy exercise I had adapted from one of the Gestalt workshops:

"Imagine you are sitting all alone in a bird cage, on a tiny stool. The door of the cage is open and you may leave anytime you wish. Now, then, try to decide what you would like to do. You can go outside the cage. You can stay where you are. You may decide to let someone in the group join you in the cage if you trust them enough. If you can't trust them, you stay alone. Remember your feelings through all this. How are you going about deciding whether to have anyone join you or not? Is the choice difficult? In what ways? Try to remember any images that come to you."

The exercise brought out many emotions and conflicts. Touching the faces of those next to them during the exercise produced strong feelings of closeness in the group members.

After the exercise, I asked them to share what they remembered. Peter said softly, "I felt trapped in the cage with no one available to help me."

John, normally self-confident, said, "I felt intense fear venturing by myself from the cage into the world."

Most of the group selected someone to be with. With

the exception of Elsie and Moira, all felt great relief when the person they selected joined them. Moira shyly said, "In my fantasy no one wanted to be with me."

Elsie's experience fit into her view of the world: "I feel fine, and can't think of anyone I trust enough to invite in." This wasn't a surprise, because in childhood she had learned to keep her disturbed family at a distance to protect herself. Her mother was psychotic and her brother schizophrenic.

Moira would only say, "I feel trapped. There is no way out of the cage, whether the door is open or shut. I can't even get myself to rise from my seat on the chair! I feel alone," she added softly, "as I have all my life."

As we retired that night, I felt satisfied at the results of our marathon so far. Even Moira admitted that sharing and closeness had taken place.

TWELVE

The Hot Seat

After breakfast the next morning, I announced, "We're going to do a nonverbal exercise in which we touch each other in loving ways to help overcome distrust. I'd like you all to circle the room until each of you has a partner he or she wants to work with. Each in turn will then blindfold the other, turn his back, and fall backwards into the arms of his partner, trusting to be caught." I watched each of the group try the exercise. Moira was not able to trust letting herself fall.

Later that morning Marcuse confided in me, "I've gained confidence in the exercises you are trying." His comments were gratifying, and I felt good. The group's mood was good—Moira was breaking out of her aloofness by making friends with Lori. Before lunch, we took a break. I was somewhat apprehensive about the evening exercise I had planned, the "hot seat."

In this Gestalt procedure one person is seated, surrounded by the group. He or she then talks of personal troubles and problems, after which the rest, with no holds barred, comments on what they might see as the person's self-deceptions, delusionary viewpoints, and anything else they can pick on. The hoped-for result is that the person in the hot seat sees himself stripped away by the confrontations of the group. An honest give and take becomes possible, during which the hot seat person sees himself as others see him—in ways that he had sheltered himself from to defend against frightening feeling. Hopefully then, beneficial growth and change occurs.

During lunch a convivial feeling arose. Peter and John jocosely threw food at each other. I was glad to see Peter finally relaxed, as well as John, whose rigid upbringing customarily forbade such rowdiness. After lunch, as though someone had sounded a signal, the marathoners ran out of the house and in a childlike way rolled on the grass, hugging and roughhousing with each other. I was startled by this unexpected spontaneity, from which only Elsie and Moira held back. It seemed that the therapeutic work we had done so far might have lowered inhibitions. I wondered whether if in childhood we had seen grownups behaving like that—loving and childlike—we might have avoided many inhibitions that arrive with adulthood.

Though I attributed this unabashed jollity to the effect of the previous exercises we had done, I was still uncertain as to how it had arisen. During weekly sessions the patients tended to be much more guarded with each other, but now these people had allowed the repressed child in them to surface. I could not underestimate the significance of this. As people of normal mental health grow to adulthood, they are taught to be "grownup," and they largely suppress the childhood spontaneity they had as children.

With Moira, however, and others similarly beleaguered as children, the burying of the "child" may be extremely damaging. Her spontaneity went into hiding early in life, in retreat from unbearable family situations she was unequipped to handle. Eventually, as she grew older, the wall-ing off of feeling outlived its usefulness. The impulses turned against her, making her sick. She withdrew into a world of emotional illness. To find Moira's child in its hiding place and coax it into the sunlight was the first stop, I believed, toward helping her toward health. I was elated to see this release of childhood joy among the other marathoners and hoped it would rub off on Moira.

However, my mood tuned pensive at dinner. After an attempt to be friendly with Lori, Moira had withdrawn into herself and was sitting alone in a corner. Marcuse and others tried to chat with her, but she didn't respond.

The Saturday evening session was due to start at nine. After dinner the group appeared tired. I wasn't sure I should launch the powerful "hot seat" exercise at this point. More than anything else I worried about how Moira would handle being under fire. She had held up pretty well so far, but being strongly "encountered" might make her fall apart. I decided to postpone the hot seat exercise, at least for the time being.

As we sat around sipping coffee I observed, "We all seem tired." Murmurs of agreement rumbled. I nodded. "Let's forget about the activity I had planned," I suggested, "and just talk about feelings anyone has from what's happened so far. Who wants to get the ball rolling?"

No one spoke. I said slowly, thoughtfully, "I'm not sure how to read this silence. I thought it might be a good idea if everyone gave us some idea of what they're feeling or thinking."

Not a whisper or a word. Ten minutes passed. I stayed calm outwardly but felt tense over the lack of response. Then Inez spoke, staring first at Marcuse and then me. "You both want us to open up and look at our past shit. How about you two? Why don't therapists ever reveal anything about themselves?"

I was startled. What had happened to the warm loving feelings from earlier in the day? Then came more surprises. The others backed Inez's position, challenging Marcuse and me to talk about ourselves and our feelings about the group.

At first I reacted angrily. "That's not what you came to therapy for. We're treating you and not the other way around. I think it's important to go back to the experiences we had during sessions last night and today. Some of you didn't have a chance to talk. Moira and Grace haven't said anything. And what about the playfulness you all felt at dinner and outside? Why do you think that happened?"

As though he hadn't heard a word I said, Peter addressed Marcuse. "What about you? I heard you were in a concentration camp before you came to the United States and trained as a psychotherapist. That must have been a huge experience—why don't you tell us about it? We've all been in sessions with you for over a year, and we often discuss our experience among ourselves. I don't know about anyone else, but I'd like to hear what it meant to you."

I watched Marcuse's face darken. He looked uncomfortable. Peter went on, "I understand your family was killed by the Germans while you were in hiding. They caught you and put you in a concentration camp. What a horrible experience! What was it like? How did you overcome it?"

The group pressured Marcuse. He answered in a quiet, calm voice. "As your supervisor, it would be inappropriate for me to discuss personal issues of my own." There were mumbles of disagreement. Marcuse looked around apprehensively, then he went on. "If you wish I will discuss it after the marathon," he paused, "if people are still interested." Again the mumbles. "I've undergone psychotherapy for many years to help me recover from the experience. I would appreciate it if the group respects my privacy during the marathon setting," he said gently. I thought he handled the situation very capably, compared to my angry reaction. But then, to my surprise, he added, "To tell you the truth, I've blocked out most of what happened."

Then John volunteered, "Maybe we can help you get in contact with some of those blocked memories." I felt a bit dizzy. What was going on here? The patients were becoming the therapists! What Marcuse had been through was none of their business, but his having said that his memories were hidden opened him to further questioning.

John continued: "Perhaps those techniques Obler used on us might help bring your memories back."

Gregory challenged John, "What are you talking about? Hypnosis?"

"No," said Elsie, "he means the exercise in the cage."

I could tell from the uncomfortable way Marcuse shifted in his chair that he was uneasy. He looked to me for help. "I'm not sure you want the group's attention focused on me, do you, Mr. Obler?" he asked.

It was legitimate for Marcuse to turn to me as a cotherapist for help and to bail him out, but I hesitated. For one thing, he was supposed to be the supervisor and not the other way around.

"I don't see us as having to stick rigidly to one program," I answered, "and I'll go along with any decision you make." A mistake. I could feel it immediately. I should have supported Marcuse unconditionally at that point. He was already in a tight spot, and by throwing the choice to him, I weakened the control he and I as a team were supposed to be exercising. Two impulses prompted my response. One was that I wanted to keep Moira off the hot seat, and the other was that I, like the others, was curious about his war experience.

But my alliance with Marcuse came first, I realized, and I tried to get things back on track by supporting his position. "I believe it's most important at this point," I suggested, "to hear from the people who have shared so little. I don't think it would do any of us any good to take time on Dr. Marcuse's personal life when we all agreed at the beginning that our focus should be on the experience of group members."

Gregory jumped in. "Maybe then the best pursuit at this point would be to look at what each of us hopes to gain from group therapy. We have been together for a year," he pointed out wisely. "It's time to talk about our goals and how they might have changed. The entrance of a new member," he added, "heightens the value of reevaluation for ourselves and for her."

I breathed a sigh of relief when the group seemed to accept this suggestion. "It might take us beyond what has already come out in the marathon sessions," Inez offered. It was decided that all should take part. We went ahead.

Peter volunteered first. "I've always had trouble developing satisfying, rewarding relationships with men. I have no close male friends. Mostly I've spent time seeking sex with women to try to make up for a childhood during which my mother was unable to give me the nurturing I needed. I fantasize having sex with women who resemble my mother. I want to find out why I have trouble being closer to men—I think it will balance my life, help me to resist obsessively chasing women and escaping so much into fantasy." He was silent.

Elsie began to speak. "I want more intimate relationships with both men *and* women—people like me—but I tend to feel I'm a freak, and I can't shake the feeling. Part of the reason I feel that way is that my mother was really sick, and at one point she and I had sex. I've felt like a pervert ever since. Only in this group have I felt, for the first time in my life, accepted and not judged."

Gregory chimed in. "I used to think I was a social wart. During my adolescence I couldn't make friends with anyone—could barely talk to people my own age. I wanted a haven where I could learn to be with people in an easy and friendly way, without feeling I was a total weirdo. I can appear confident because I talk well and I get good grades. I'm on my way to completing a Ph.D., but I often freeze up when I have to be in a social situation like a party. I shake inside. Ever since I joined this group I found a place where I can be myself. If I feel I'm being an oddball I can check it out with you people. You've helped me to see I don't come across as freaky as I thought!"

"I need friendships with women," Inez volunteered, "that's why Moira bugs me. She's like a lot of women—too female-focused. Women have a lot more going for them than worrying about how attractive they are to men or if they'll be good wives and mothers. I came to group because I felt rotten inside a lot of the time. I lacked self-confidence: I thought I was a failure because I couldn't compete with men professionally. Group has helped me realize that a lot of my bad feelings come from the inferior status women suffer. I finally got angry at being given second-class citizenship just because I was a woman. I need sympathetic women friends who know what I'm talking about—strong women I can have good friendships with. I don't think men have real friendships—hanging out and talking sports doesn't add up to satisfying relating—but I prefer not to spend group time on women like Moira who have been abused by men. I'm sorry they went through that, but I need healthy women friendships. So, I can identify with Peter wanting to bond with other men."

John shook his head. "Can someone tell me what this male bonding bullshit is supposed to be? It sounds like Peter's scared of dealing with mature women. I can't connect to what he's trying to do—I'm trying to use group to augment my private therapy. I have difficulties with people, and I want to get over them. I don't mind people trying to escape their loneliness, but that's not my problem. Why pay to have your social problems analyzed? You should be able to handle them yourself."

Grace broke in. "You know, John, you've always gotten on my nerves, but I never understood why. Now I do. So you don't see group as having social value for you, you nerd? Listen here—you're more of a misfit than any of us. I never get the feeling you're interested in listening to anyone else's problems but your own. Your narcissism comes through everything you do or say."

John flushed and quickly retorted, "Fuck off, you little bitch. All I've heard from you since you came to group was the terrible suffering you went through at the hands of your awful Southern parents. You don't think I connect to anything going on here? As far as I'm concerned, your level of empathy is zilch!"

I was about to step in when Gregory said, "Things appear to be getting out of hand. What I'm hearing is that we all joined group for similar reasons: friendship, meeting people, listening to others and being listened to, male and female bonding, and getting the best feedback we can. I think we all have more in common than we realize."

Inez grimaced. "Gregory, good heaven's sakes! You're a natural diplomat! Why waste your time getting a Ph.D.? But you turn me off, because you're so scared of conflict—you try to calm things down when they get hot. I'm sick of it. We relate on different levels, all of us, and we don't need a half-assed negotiator. Do you have any idea what I'm saying?"

Moira, who had been quiet all this time, now broke in. "Wait a minute, I think Gregory has a point. And do you have to curse to be heard?"

Inez, who seemed to have been waiting for this, pounced on her. "Oh, dear, we're hearing from the prima donna! I can't believe it—she's finally decided to get involved. Let me tell you something: John is a sexist pig, and his condescending male attitude is typical. Men refer to women as narcissists, but what's really going on is they're afraid to deal with us as equals, as human beings."

Peter kept his voice quiet and unperturbed. "Let's get back to what we were talking about."

Sarcastically, Gregory said, "What's that?"

Ignoring the sarcasm, Peter answered, "If you'll remember, it's why we're all in group."

Lori backed him up. "I think it's important to put the good of the group ahead of the interests of any individual.

That's what brought me here. I was sick of the California individualism of my husband and his friends. They were totally self-centered and justified it with jargon about the freedom of 'doing you own thing'."

John raised his eyebrows and said, "Well, that sounds socialistic, maybe communistic. This happens to be group therapy, not some bullshit retreat where sickies hang out for sympathy because they can't get into real relationships in the world."

Peter answered impatiently, "You know, you're getting on my nerves. You haven't heard one word anyone has said. I'm not sure I want to be in the same room group with you. I believe we're here to help people—Moira, for example—and not just shovel out our bigoted anger toward each other. You don't want to face the fact that you take your misery out on minorities in the name of venting your rage and anger."

Marcuse, who had been avidly watching now stepped in. "There's plenty of room in group therapy for differences between people. I don't think you have to pressure John to feel guilty because he expresses his genuine feelings."

Inez nodded. "Every time I leave group I feel agitated about the effect John has on me. He's a sexist animal and I'm fighting with him continually about control and manipulation. As if that weren't enough, I also contend with his intolerant Catholic views on homosexuality, sex, and abortion. He's too argumentative—polarizes us. His stupid religious proselytizing just disguises a busybody housewife mentality. Peter may be an obsessive mother fucker, Gregory's an uptight asshole, Elsie's kind of a weird, contented loner—but they're tolerable as humans. I'm not sure I can say as much for you, John."

Lori grumbled, "I have news for you, Inez, everything you point out about John goes double for you! You're just as guilty as he is in continuously pushing people's buttons. That feminist bullshit you hand out is just as bigoted and biased as his. You're a very bitter and hostile lady. I think you need to get laid—that's what I think!"

There was an uneasy pause. Then Grace retorted, "I've about had it with you, Lori. Why are you defending John? He's a male chauvinist bastard, period. You don't fool me one bit. Neither does Inez, with her maneuvering and manipulation to seduce that repressed little bitch!" Pointing to Moira, she said, "I'm not fooled by your constantly taking the men's side—you want to fuck them, too. When it comes to the 'me' mentality, you take the cake. This isn't California, where every self-involved freak can do just what he wants to do. I know you can be very perceptive, but I've noticed when the focus gets off you, you fall asleep."

Gregory interjected, "Maybe her symbolic dreams supply the information for her perceptions!"

Elsie couldn't let the remark pass. "That's right, Greg, crack a joke whenever you can't deal with strong feelings." Such angry exchanges were typical of most group sessions. As they continued, Moira suddenly stood up and pointed a finger at me.

"Is this the purpose of group therapy?" she screamed.

Peter interjected, "Calm down, Moira, what do you mean?"

Inez retorted. "Yes, I'd like to know, too. We haven't heard a peep out of you all weekend, and now you're going to criticize this process?"

Everyone turned toward Moira, waiting for her answer, but she fell silent. "Moira," I said gently, "why don't you tell us what's on your mind." She took a deep breath, pushed a back lock of blond hair that had fallen in her eyes, appeared to be struggling with herself, and then let it out:

"I mean," she said slowly, "that feelings we can't deal with in our outside lives are coming out in group. All this anger comes from somewhere else—a deep dark place in our souls that we can't touch. We attack each other because we're afraid of our need for each other! I think group therapy reflects our family horror, the only difference being we can express it here, but we can't there."

I looked at her, startled. Moira was more aware of her family than I had thought and more sensitive to its conflicts.

I was about to say something when Inez broke the silence. "The young novice finally speaks up! Two days and she's got our family histories down to the last detail. I don't know what happened with you, baby, but I got along fine with my family. I happen to like my mother and father. We had our little battles—who doesn't?—but I can't remember fights and rotten feelings like I have with these shitheads!"

Lori backed Inez up. "My advice to you, Moira, is that you concentrate on figuring out what you want from group therapy. You're very repressed and displacing your crap on our warfare here. Something very heavy must have happened to you in childhood to make you so passive and repressed."

Lori had hit a chord in Moira, who sat quietly, apparently in shock. We all felt sympathetic to her, but to help her was contrary to the usual practice of letting members open up when they were ready to and not form group pressure. Moira began to cry. Peter got up to embrace her comfortingly.

As I tried to decide how best to react, I heard a moan from the back of the room. We turned to see what was going on. It was Marcuse. He was taking deep, gasping breaths and moaning. Tears flowed from his eyes and he stretched his arms toward Moira. Both seemed joined by a bond of such pain and sadness that they had become unaware of their surroundings.

The group's anger had fled; Marcuse's behavior shocked us into silence. I was immobilized, as were the others, by what we were seeing.

As though sleepwalking, Marcuse moved toward Moira. Her arms were locked about her and she was rocking back and forth. The room was dimly lit, but we could make out Marcuse with his arms around Moira's hunched body as it continued the rocking motion.

He began to mutter. My background in Yiddish helped me to recognize that he was speaking a combination of Yiddish and German:

"Cume tsoo meih, my yingeleh, my shaine maidel, du bist meine kleine tuchter, meine yunger schvester."

The group members who understood Yiddish whispered to the others that Marcuse was asking his younger daughter—and then his sister—to come to him. Moira grew frightened by the grip of Marcuse's powerful arms, strengthened by years of hard labor in the concentration camp, and by the impassioned flow of Yiddish and German. She struggled unavailingly, then broke partially free and leaned back against the plasterboard wall.

Spasms of terror racked her. She shouted at the top of her voice: "No, Daddy! Please don't touch me! I'm a good girl! Yes, Mommy, I promise I won't tell anyone what you've done—don't hurt me with the broom—I know I've been a silly girl—but I'll be better from now on—just don't hurt me!"

"Du bist a tatteleh, a kleine butt a gutt kinde," Marcuse screamed. They seemed in an eerie way to be talking to each other, but not to each other—rather, to figures and events in their pasts.

Marcuse persisted. "Let me hold you, tatteleh—you'll feel better, meine sheinemkeit. The schveinhunts will not take you away from daddy again. You've been a good little girl. Daddy and mommy will not let them hurt you and things will be better."

"Daddy! Why do you do this to me?" Staring into Marcuse's eyes, Moira was talking to a memory.

I could feel confusion in the group as they watched these powerful exchanges. My mind raced. Was I witnessing psychotic episodes unearthing deep horrors from Marcuse and Moira's pasts? Had Moira split into one of her detached selves or launched the sort of convincing performance that hysterics like herself were capable of?

I couldn't account for Marcuse's dramatics, unless extreme fatigue brought on by our lack of sleep had caused an aberration in him. What puzzled me was that until now his manner had been poised and admirably professional. I wondered if he'd been seized by a temporary psychosis.

Now Moira lunged toward Marcuse and shrieked, "Stay away from me, you bastard—I *hate* you. I won't let you fuck me any more! You pretend to love me, but I'm not fooled by you or that other fuckin' pig!"

Marcuse grabbed her. She pounded her fists against his chest. In a flash I understood what was happening. She was in a state of dissociation, and the split-off part was bringing up the first evidence I'd had that she'd been sexually abused. I glanced at the others—they could not know what was happening, and I didn't want them trying to intervene. Fortunately they stayed rooted by what we were seeing.

Something nudged the back of my mind and I had a second illumination. Marcuse, without realizing it consciously, must have picked up that horrendous sexual memory in her, and it triggered in him a memory of what might have happened to his own daughter at the concentration camp. This was his painful attempt to connect to his lost daughter—killed with the rest of his family by the Nazis prior to Marcuse's being imprisoned. It was his daughter to whom he was muttering in German-Yiddish.

Moira's remembered sexual abuse by her father was not surprising in view of how close they were and how troubled he had been. This had been made clear in her psychotherapy, but now she was recalling another abuser, "that other fuckin' pig." Who did she mean? Was it sexual play with her brother? Probably not, because she held rage toward this unknown person that she did not feel toward her brother.

Another puzzle: How had Marcuse and Moira taken on a hypnotized state without being hypnotized by a third person? It could have happened through what was called "vicarious induction." I had seen something like this occur in a training class for hypnosis I had attended a year before. An observer had fallen into trance by just watching a hypnotist work on a colleague. Perhaps the hypnotic effect of the "cage" exercise had affected them similarly so that they were sharing a delusion in which they relived separate personal memories. For a few minutes I continued meditating. Then with a jolt I came back to the present. Marcuse was continuing to embrace Moira as she rocked back and forth moaning. Eventually I'd have to bring them out of it. But how? Moira offered a solution by falling asleep. Leaning over Marcuse, I was about to awaken him when, loudly and forcefully, he began to shout commands at the group in German.

I couldn't understand what he was saying. He seemed to be hallucinating as a Nazi officer shouting at camp inmates and then at me. Shocked, I stepped back.

I watched as he gently placed Moira on the floor. He now marched back and forth in cadence—a soldier on parade. Bringing himself to a halt, he grabbed up an imaginary shovel and started to shovel dirt into an imaginary hole in the wooden floor. Then he picked up the sleeping Moira and carefully put her in the "hole" and muttered distractedly, "Meine grandpapa and meine mutter, meine schvester and meine tatelleh, meine friends and de gontze welt. . . ."

Before I could contain myself, I burst into uncontrollable sobs. I'd comprehended that I was watching a broken human being walking in circles around the graves of his slaughtered family.

As he continued his tragic pacing, I realized that the group deserved an explanation of this spectacle. My voice hoarse, I said, "When people undergo fatigue, as we all have, hallucination can occur." I added, "Moira and Marcuse must have built up great inner pressure during the weekend exercises that has somehow been converted to altered states of consciousness in which powerful and shocking events from their pasts have come to the surface." I tried to speak calmly with professional assurance, but I was only making an educated guess. Actually, I was unsure of myself and at that point wouldn't have minded getting the hell out of there.

"Let's take a break," I suggested to the stunned group. "We've just been through a very draining experience." Just then Moira awoke, and Marcuse retreated, with sleepwalking movements, to a corner. He began to sob quietly. Moira looked around, tossed her blond hair seductively, and acted as though nothing had happened. Marcuse, on the other hand, was highly disturbed, and I had the feeling he was aware of what he and Moira had been through.

I struggled with two sets of reactions. The first had to do with Moira. What had happened to her was understandable in light of her severe disturbances. Clearly she had fallen prey to a multiple personality regression: a part of her that was separated from other parts had encountered savage memories of childhood abuse. It was predictable that, having gone through them so painfully, she would now repress them again. Hence, she had no memory of what had happened. I decided that because she was my patient and my responsibility, I would work with her privately on the occurrence as soon as I could.

Marcuse was another story. Although I was sympathetic to the agonized feelings he had revived, I could not avoid being appalled at an experienced psychotherapist losing control of himself to the degree he had. It was his responsibility to monitor his own unresolved conflicts, not relive them here where that very process could seriously disturb our patients. I didn't want to get him in trouble, so I decided to talk to him privately about getting help. Meanwhile I concentrated on our patients. "We've all been through a lot," I suggested. "Let's call it a night, get some sleep, and start again at 6:30 A.M." All agreed, with relief.

THIRTEEN

Acting Out

It was evident, as we assembled the next morning, that we were still fatigued from what we'd been through. All except Moira! Peppy and upbeat, she volunteered to speak first at the morning session. Her good spirits, I guessed, were due to her having gotten a lot of negative emotions out of her system during her exchange with Marcuse. Although she didn't remember what had happened, the cathartic effect of her outbursts had given her some relief.

I watched her intently but was unprepared when she said, "My name is Marcia"—I took a deep breath as she continued—"and I want to tell you about my life with Moira." Was this a joke? No, it quickly grew clear to me that Marcia was going to speak for her.

Marcia continued, "Moira is a pussy and gives it to anyone who asks for it." She giggled. "But she likes to pretend she's being forced. What a crock that is. She loves it!"

Murmurs rose as the group stared at me. I rubbed my forehead. Was total confusion going to start the day? I knew I'd better let them in on Moira being a multiple personality. So far, no one had referred to what had happened the night before. The members were treating Marcuse and Moira gently.

Before I could decide how to do it, Marcia continued:

"The whole mess started with the men in Moira's family. Incest is common in demented families, isn't it? The first time her father asked her for sex, Moira, she took him right up on it. So why shouldn't he fuck the little wimp?" she continued bitingly. "His black gun rammed right into her. She acted as though she was going through something horrible, but she was enjoying every minute of it." Inez and Grace gasped. Marcia glared at them. "What's bugging you girls? I'll tell you what it is. You're both uptight, sexually repressed assholes, that's what. But that doesn't give you the right to judge Moira. You act so horrified about childhood molestation, but I've got news for you: It happens a lot. You've wanted to have sex with your parents, and you know it very well. But you don't have the guts to admit it. Neither does Moira, and that's where I come in. I had to show the little nymph what fucking was all about. How to forget that Catholic guilt and enjoy a big dick sliding in and out. Just ask Obler. I told him all this in a session some time back, and can you believe it? He thought he was talking to that putrid little Moira."

We were riveted. Though I welcomed Moira's alternate personality revealing itself to me more forcefully and candidly than it ever had, I was worried about its effect on the others; it was a mesmerizing experience.

During a pause in Marcia's ranting I talked to the group about Moira's multiple personality problem. I tried to get it all across to them of how it had come about and what my experience of it was. They listened, but it was coming too fast for them. They weren't really accepting it. I could see by their skeptical expressions that they thought she was faking—trying to play-act her way out of the embarrassment of her behaviors with Marcuse by diverting them with "Marcia."

As I raced mentally to keep up, it occurred to me that in a way it was better not to try to convince them they were wrong about Moira's carrying on: If they accepted that she was indeed a multiple, they might question why I had brought such a complicated person into the group.

I took Marcuse aside and brought up his behavior the night before. "I admit," he said, "it was a mistake. But I wasn't fully conscious of what was going on. When Moira's suffering burst out," he said slowly, "I lost all awareness. I really lived that concentration camp again.

"You never get over that sort of thing," Marcuse continued. "Whenever I'm faced by someone suffering as a victim I tend to revive the camp experience. It happened often when I was in psychotherapy. After psychotherapy had helped me I found I could usually resist the regression, but the extent of poor Moira's suffering was too much for me and it all came back."

"I'm terribly sympathetic to all you must have been through," I said earnestly, "but I have to think of our patients, and your unprofessional conduct could seriously affect them." I was confronting him with my convictions about what had happened, because in my view he was rationalizing excuses for himself and not taking sufficient responsibility for what he had done. I pressed him: "What you did was totally unacceptable under any guideline governing psychotherapists' ethical responsibility. Perhaps I should have moved more effectively to stop your and Moira's psychodrama, but I'm the student under your supervision. I'm supposed to go along with your decisions. When our roles were reversed, I naturally became hesitant about taking action."

"I have no problem with your letting us play it out," Marcuse replied. "You were doing the best you could. Why don't we schedule a conference with Mardoff about the whole matter? That should get us back to normal."

I had more to say. "I think that what we were seeing in Moira last night was fragmentation of a multiple personality. If you back me in this interpretation with Mardoff I'll forget about your irresponsible behavior. I won't say a thing about it. Mardoff has rejected my diagnosis, but I'm more and more convinced I'm right. She's a multiple. I'm sure of it. I think last night was a step forward for her in that regression to the dissociative state brought out repressed material hidden until now."

Marcuse and I agreed that we would discourage any further dissociation in Moira for the balance of the marathon, and take up the questions of his actions when we got back to the clinic.

We walked back to the group, where Marcia was talking again. Suddenly she stopped. After Marcia's aggressive declarations ended she closed her eyes, was quiet for a few minutes, then opened them again as Moira. Her first remarks were to Marcuse. "At least I had a family," she shouted angrily at him. "They didn't abandon me as you abandoned your family. You fucking coward!"

Marcuse maintained composure, but I sensed tension mounting in him once more. "I think you were treated very badly as you grew up," he said to Moira. "And it hurt. If the others will let me, I'd like to help you."

Moira mimicked Marcuse bitingly: "I would like to help you! I would like to help you! Let me tell you something, buddy. You need a lot more help than I do. You're the fucking wimp that hid to save your ass, just like my father did."

I cocked my ears. Was I hearing Marcia again? She continued, "You think I don't know that therapists hide behind their professional facades? I happen to know that most of you are as messed up as your patients—maybe more so. You just put on an act of having your lives together and your relationships in good shape. It's horse shit, that whole scam."

Marcuse had concluded that Marcia was back, and he said gently, "I realize, Marcia, that you're trying to protect Moira as you always do."

"Does the name 'wimpo' ring a bell, Marcuse?" Moira/Marcia shot back. "Because that's what your name should be. You can't even remember the names of the people you're supposed to be treating."

"But I thought," Marcuse ventured, "that Marcia was

the way you introduced yourself. Isn't that what you want to be called? Which is it, Moira or Marcia?"

Now Moira was her shy self again. "Who is this person Marcia you're talking about?" she asked, clearly puzzled.

Marcuse and I looked at each other in amazement, but we had agreed not to speak of dissociation in Moira's presence, so we held our tongues.

Grasping for diversion, I said, "It's time for our next session, but I think we all need a break." We all welcomed this suggestion and shortly found ourselves walking through the nearby woods and meadows. Moira and Marcuse stayed behind. Absorbed in reflection, we walked along in silence. I was struggling with guilt. It seemed to me that the course I had set for the group, which included the difficulty of fitting in Moira's special needs, may have steered us away from giving them fullest benefit. I wondered whether we should call the weekend off at that point.

When we got back from our short walk, Moira and Marcuse were in the living room, chatting like old friends. I sensed that all of us were trying to relax after what we'd been through.

I had planned a psychodrama before lunch, but decided against it—too much emotion had already been expended. We all took seats on the living room floor and it seemed to be accepted, without anyone explicitly saying so, that we were going to talk about whether we should go on or not, and if we continued, what we should do. Marcuse and Moira sat comfortably with the rest of the group.

Elsie suggested, "I think in the little time we have left, we should let anyone who hasn't had a chance work on whatever issues they want to."

Inez and Grace agreed, pointing out that Moira had taken up quite a bit of time. Lori vehemently shook her head when the subject of Moira came up. "I can't believe you fools have fallen for Moira's play-acting routine. Talk about Bette Davis dramatics! Moira's just pulling the fashionable number of seeing a schizy woman who's been sexually molested."

"Lori's got a point," agreed Gregory. "We're all playing the game of 'sicker-than-thou.' It's a status contest."

"Wait a minute," chimed in Peter. "Are you suggesting that she put on the Marcia personality just to get attention?"

"You have figured it out all by yourself, my boy!" replied Gregory sarcastically.

The ensuing debate lasted through lunch and into the early afternoon: Was Moira faking or not? Along with Mardoff, the members couldn't accept that multiple personalities existed. It was easier to write it off as malingering. I wasn't surprised at how hard the group found it to believe how disturbed Moira really was. My family's reluctance to acknowledge how mentally ill my sister was arose from the same fears of mental illness. I let the discussion run on, because I didn't know what else to do.

All through the talk Moira sat unperturbed, holding Marcuse's hand and ignoring the debate.

At one point John outlined Freud's conviction that personality fragmentation occurred in hysterical women like Moira. "Freud encountered such disorders frequently," John said. "Would you discuss that, Mr. Obler?"

"In the repressive times during which he was formulating his theories and practicing," I replied, "his view was that when 'unacceptable' sexual impulses arose in a straitlaced woman, her super-ego, which was in charge of her sense of whether or not she was behaving correctly, defended against the forbidden impulses by 'depersonalizing' them—creating separate parts of the personality unacquainted with each other, much as Moira's splitting apart happened. This unbearable sexual guilt was stored away in these unaware sections of the self, safely out of sight. Being emotional energy, however, the impulses could not be destroyed and might burst out in disturbed physical and emotional symptoms. The entire blockage was in fact what made women 'hysterical.' The word *hysteria*, interestingly enough, is from the Greek *hysteria*, the womb. The sexual tie-in is evident. Popularly, of course, so-called hysterical behavior comes from rising feelings that are difficult to cope with and thus causing extreme disturbance."

The group began an extended talk on psychoanalytic theory much like discussions the group often had during regular sessions.

But the weekend was ending, and I was troubled. I didn't want us to close in a flurry of intellectual discourse. I had hoped that the group members would agree the experience was valuable and that they would be willing to accept Moira.

I broke into the debate. "It's time to try another exercise. Will everyone please stretch out comfortably on the living room rug." When all were settled, I explained and set up a psychodrama. "Could I have volunteers to present an imaginary scene in which you are having a conflict with your family. Others can take on the roles of the embattled family members and act out the conflicts as you interpret them." This, I felt, should get everyone away from the topic of multiples. But no one volunteered!

I explained carefully, as I had at the beginning of the exercise, how psychodrama worked and how valuable it had proved in other marathons. No response. I felt discouraged. Then, Moira came to the rescue again—this time as Moira, not Marcia.

She talked of her family difficulties, especially the pressures on her as her mother and husband tried to retain control over her. She told of her wish to divorce her husband but not of her decision to stay with him because of her responsibility to her children. She revealed that her sex life was perfunctory and unexciting—but that she'd decided to deal with that frustration by having affairs with other men. I realized she was going over ground she and I had covered before. As nearly as I could tell, we were hearing from the same Moira who had begun the weekend with us. There was no evidence she was aware of the events with Marcuse and Marcia.

Inez then grilled Moira on details of her sex life with her husband. Had she had orgasms? Had she ever liked sex? Moira said that she enjoyed orgasms during masturbation but not during intercourse. Elsie suggested we act on these conflicts.

Gregory protested, "When you consider the awful molestation stuff Marcia came out with, Moira would probably flip out if we roleplayed her sexuality."

"Wait a minute! What do you mean? What sexual molestation?" challenged Moira, unable, of course, to recall Marcia or what she had talked about.

"Let's not get into the game again, Moira," John shouted.

"That's what I say, too," joined in Inez. "If you're going into the phony Marcia routine again I'm going to drop out of the exercise. Just own up to your shit, as we all do."

Moira was baffled. "I'm not playing. Who are you calling Marcia? She was my friend long ago. What's this about childhood molestation?"

"When you were in kind of a trance yesterday," continued Inez, "you said you were Marcia, and you were going to tell us about your friend Moira. Marcia said that you, as Moira, fucked your father. Some other man was also involved. Who that was, we never found out. It looked to me you were trying to do a 'Three Faces of Eve' number on us just to get attention. Well, that isn't going to work anymore."

"But I'm not trying to fool anyone," Moira pleaded. "I've had memory lapses since I was a kid. I don't understand them. I've tried to work on them in therapy. Ask Obler."

"It's true," I said to the group. "Moira often goes into what we call a 'fugue' state and blocks out large parts of her memory. *Fugue* is from the Latin meaning 'flight.' I was trying to explain that to you earlier today. It's different from amnesia in that she never remembers what she has blocked out. She simply transfers it to Marcia or one of her other selves."

Peter burst in excitedly: "You mean she wasn't putting us on with that Marcia character and those awful stories from her childhood?"

"No, she wasn't putting us on, Pete," I said. "We call what she does dissociation, and more and more of us shrinks are accepting that it really happens in some people."

"Then why didn't you tell us about it before we started the weekend?" Elsie angrily asked.

"And I could have avoided kicking the crap out of this woman," commented Peter.

"I've got to be honest," I said, "I'm not sure why I didn't tell you. Let's just say there's a lot of disagreement at the clinic as to what precisely is wrong with Moira. I just thought she might benefit by being with us."

"Disagreements between who?" Gregory asked.

"The therapists who work with Moira can't agree on an acceptable clinical category to put her in," I said slowly.

"I thought she was having sessions just with you," John said.

"That's true," I replied. "But don't forget I'm under supervision myself. My supervisor disagrees with my assessment of Moira as a multiple personality." I didn't want to discuss Mardoff any further. That was a dangerous subject both for Moira and for me. "I suggest we get back to our psychodrama, to get the most out of the time left. We can discuss Moira's situation another time."

All agreed, and John, out of his widened knowledge about Moira, suggested, "Let's set up a love scene in which Moira would make love to a man who cared about her." The others thought this a fine idea—possibly motivated by guilt that they had attacked Moira when she revealed having been molested as a child. They appeared to have the idea that a healthy sexual involvement with a man could overcome the effects of Moira's molestation. This was a naive speculation: While allowing connection with any person would be beneficial for Moira, much more would have to occur therapeutically to heal the effects of what she'd been through. The effects might never be erased totally, but much could be done to mend her and bring her the wholeness and peace she had never known.

Though I wasn't sure that this love-making exercise was a good idea, I decided to go along with it, and the group selected Grace as Moira's alter ego and Gregory as Moira's lover. Lori, we decided, would play the part of a liberated friend of Moira's who advocated extramarital affairs with loving males for her. John and Elsie would play a priest and nun from her local parish. Moira's first reaction to the proposed scenario was that she would have a lot of trouble simulating sexual love with someone she cared for, because she never had that sort of love and had never had an orgasm with another person. I was surprised! I'd never heard Moira talk about herself in such a grownup way. She sounded like a well-balanced adult who had solved most of her underlying sexual conflicts and knew what she wanted from a man. She sounded so integrated and mature that I decided to go ahead with the experiment.

At first all went well. Grace, as her alter ego, mirrored Moira's fears in an interaction with a man. She helped Moira express feelings she could not easily reveal to a man to whom she was attracted. Grace urged her to imagine a sexual interlude with Gregory and not worry about guilt. John then took over as a priest, rebuking her for breaking religious rules about sex. Gregory and Moira convincingly played the role of warm and caring lovers getting to know each other. The rest represented her family, criticizing the affair. Moira handled this disapproval well, pointing out that she had needs of her own that needed attention and that her family members would have to learn to take care of themselves.

If we had stopped at this point it might indeed have been a healing experience, but Peter suggested we help Moira get over her orgasm problem by simulating sex with her new lover. Marcuse and I looked at each other uncertainly. Was this a good idea? We weren't sure. I recalled reading accounts by Gestalt therapists who had tried similar experiments with some success. Still, there was another consideration: At the time of the marathon, open displays of sex were frowned on as a rule. Before I could decide on a course of action, Gregory, pretending to be her lover, mounted Moira.

"How's this?" I laughed nervously. "We shrinks will try anything to help our patients."

Positioned on Moira, Greg plaintively bleated, "I'm not sure what I'm supposed to do!"

"You're a big boy—do what comes naturally," chuckled Peter.

Gregory launched the immemorial thrusting, Moira arched her back. She appeared accepting of the role playing, but I felt a tingle of apprehension.

Watching with visible distaste, Grace exclaimed, "This is very boring and idiotic."

Lori agreed. "I don't enjoy being a voyeur. Watching other people have sex is not exactly a thrill."

Inez was firmly with her sisters: "You might get your rocks off watching people do it, Obler, but it does nothing for me."

I felt it was time to end the exercise. At that instant Moira's behavior changed: She started to foam at the mouth and tremble as though in the grip of a Grand Mal epilepsy seizure. I grabbed Marcuse's arm to enlist his help, but he was again immobilized. John pushed Gregory off Moira, and Peter, with admirable skill and speed, forced a rolled-up handkerchief into Moira's mouth to prevent her from biting her tongue. I placed her head gently in my lap. She spit the handkerchief out of her mouth and before we could replace it began to utter cries like those of a child in distress.

"What the hell is she saying now?" yelped Grace nervously.

"Shut up, Grace," said John.

The words became clearer. The voice of a child murmured, "It hurts. Please, stop—whoever you are. Don't hurt me!" Once again, as we had heard during the weekend, we were hearing a detached part of Moira cry out from some canyon of despair.

Then Moira sat up, pulled her hair away from her face and began to twirl in her hand what looked like an imaginary key attached to a chain. I gasped when she spoke in the same voice that I had heard from her on the session after her three-week absence: a sophisticated man's voice, deep and harsh. "Just another minute, I'm coming . . . I'm coming! All over your face, your beautiful face, you lovely little thing." Her voice got louder. "That's right, lick the sticky goo from your face, my dear. It tastes good—like candy."

Horrified, we stared wordlessly at each other.

Sitting beside me on the trip home, Moira sobbed quietly. When we dropped her off at home, she left us without a word.

Fourteen

Illusion or Love?

After several of the group had been dropped off at their homes, I suggested to Marcuse and those remaining that we get a bite to eat in Brooklyn. We needed nourishment after such a brutal marathon, and I had much to think about. I was terribly worried. Moira's wordless leave-taking suggested to me that perhaps we had pushed her too far too fast. Yet, I also wanted us to try to recapture the closeness and camaraderie we had felt early in this weekend.

For many in the group the marathon had been a good experience. Most had dug out much deeper feelings and insights than they usually did at weekly sessions. They'd been more honest, more open, and more intimate with each other than ever before. They had accomplished that feat so difficult for humans: They had taken each other into their inner lives, those hidden places inside in front of which most people display "no trespassing" signs. As always happens when people manage to connect so significantly, we would forever after be a little closer to each other as we endured the aloneness that is the inescapable companion of each human being through life.

As I settled at a table across from Marcuse, I realized we would have to provide a summary of the weekend to Mardoff that would satisfy his clinical requirements. We must present a report that would also, I decided, keep Marcuse's unprofessional behavior a secret.

Our waiter, in the immemorial manner of Jewish waiters from the Catskills to Brooklyn—and everywhere else—was the soul of impertinence. He let us know that we were "nebbishes" to order so skimpily.

His comforting abusiveness, as he slung our sandwiches and beer in front of us, called up in me poignant sensations of being a child in these neighborhoods. What had happened to my childhood friends? A scary thought! These days I had few friends. The passing of my childhood had left me alone and lonely.

The marathon had been a significant experience. Those around the table—Marcuse, Peter, John, Gregory, Grace, and I—had much to talk about, the funny events of the weekend as well as the tragic. Gregory observed, "People who are abused as children often in adulthood become abusers themselves."

"Yes Gregory, I agree." His comment struck a spark in me. I was sure by now, especially after what Moira had expressed during the marathon, that she had been abused as a child, but she had not abused her own children! To me this conveyed a strength that could be used to support her work and move her toward healing. And, come to think of it, she normally kept her deeper troubles so well hidden that if the marathon hadn't brought them out of her, it might have been a long time before I discovered what had happened to her. My next thoughts were that because she was stronger than I had first believed—in not having abused her children—and had revealed material while in a deep level of unawareness, she was clearly a good patient to treat using deep psychoanalytic techniques. This treatment could, little by little, join together and mend divided sections of her torn-apart self. At length, I believed, her present pathetic state could be replaced by sound emotional health. But I worried that the long process might prove too costly financially and emotionally for her.

The other possibility was cognitive therapy, which was often used to help battered women. Cognitive therapy, simply put, is administered on the conscious level, rather than the unconscious, where deeper analysis is administered. With cognitive therapy, the patient examines and "works through" troubled ways in which she experiences herself. As she pursues this process, she takes into account her characteristics, her memories, and her habits of thinking, put in the light of what happened to her and how she feels about it. At length she is able to arrive at a healthier, more positive but realistic view of herself. This approach is often valuable for battered women, allowing them to rebuild their damaged egos so they can make peace with, and resolve as much as possible, the effect of the shock of events they have lived through.

Greg broke into my reverie. "What are you thinking about?" Avoiding the subject of Moira, I told him I was considering that I'd chosen an interesting period in which to become a psychologist.

"Why?" queried Peter and Marcuse. This gave me a chance to tell them some recent thoughts I'd had about the profession and its connection to the times we were living through.

"These are fascinating times. Take the Freudian viewpoint. In spite of the great insights Freud developed, he still related to women as a male chauvinist, particularly to his wife and daughter.

"Overall, the intellectuals who lectured me about change in the coffee houses of Greenwich Village when I was a teenager were armchair philosophers. They talked a good game of changing economic and social life, but they conducted their personal relationships in the same way their parents had. Especially their relationships with women. *That's* the hypocritical bullshit I'm talking about."

I paused for a breath and Gregory charged in. "I love it. How you psychologists delude yourselves that you're so much more honest and equal with people than anyone else.

From what I hear, psychologists conduct their lives pretty much like the rest of us poor plebeians."

"Cut it out, Gregory," protested Grace. "I'm interested in what Obler has to say."

"Yeah, let him talk," supported John.

The beer I'd been drinking, along with my fatigue, had begun to fog me out. Did I want to keep this up? I didn't want to come across like a soap-box orator. But I also felt the need to pour out my pent-up energy from the weekend, so I continued.

"Despite the uproar over civil rights and the progress that has been made, most of America is still made up of segregated neighborhoods still racially and ethnically divided. There's an illusion of peace between minority groups and the whites, but believe me, it's only an illusion. The reality is, the lid is still tightly in place because whites have very little to do with minorities. Both sides of this dividing line believe the boundaries are going to be in place forever. And that's the great delusion handed down to us from the past.

"Change is on the way, even though at this moment intellectuals are preaching to non-white minorities the same equality and humanism bullshit they always have, even as they practice prejudice and bigotry themselves. But blacks and Hispanics are getting wise to it, and watch out! The cities will explode.

"The revolution I'm talking about is more than just a racial and class struggle. It's more a revolution of ideas than a battle for equality. The battle is being joined between the older and younger generation of therapists. If you could be a fly on the wall at our staff meetings at the clinic, you would hear these issues being discussed.

"In those meetings there's a tug-of-war going on between the interns and the established therapists. The younger people are always pushing for change and for our advocacy for the disadvantaged population we serve. We want to defend clients' legal, moral, and financial rights along with attending to their psychological needs.

"Today's therapists believe America must confront a hard reality: That social forces act on the oppressed, making them nonfunctional and powerless. This is the real threat to our national fabric. Women, Hispanics, blacks, and poor whites are all fettered by second-class status. To ignore these truths is like sitting on the San Andreas Fault and claiming there's no such thing as an earthquake.

"My peers and I are not accepting Freud's dogmas uncritically any more. There's no question, of course, that for some people neurosis and other psychopathologies can come about from physical abuse, emotional deprivation, shocks of other kinds, and vulnerabilities traceable even to the womb. But for a large part of our disenfranchised populations, including women, severe emotional damages are inflicted at base by underlying social and economical inferiority. My supervisors are as much victims of these deceptions in our value systems as are their parents.

"And I don't think I'm contradicting myself when I say that America was a more honest country before the Depression. For a while, we were great! People could get ahead if they worked at it. The family was nurturing and supportive. Communities were places of pride and safety—you knew everyone, everyone knew you. We watched out for each other.

"Food was plentiful, we were better educated, healthier, and we were living longer. We had a sense of responsibility for the planet!"

I paused for breath, but not for long. I was possessed by what I was saying. "Then the unravelling started. The atomic and hydrogen bombs obliterated forever the notion that life could keep on getting better for all of us. Suddenly we could obliterate all life on earth. Humans became insignificant. If we could unleash such cataclysm, how could a strong family or nation protect us? And if we did not cooperate, find larger identifications that could allow us to live peaceably internationally, we were doomed.

"When ghetto kids watched TV they must have sensed what was lacking in their lives. To them, 'Little House on the Prairie' with kids running through a meadow was like looking at life on Mars. It was foreign to them. This prepared the way for them to be aware of social inequities when they become adults. By then they were fully and bitterly aware of the imbalances in this country. Instant gratification became the ghetto way. Get what you could when you could. Enjoy it now.

"Let me talk about another whole area of our lives, the corporations. Corporate America. We've developed a new exploited class—corporate executives. These guys let themselves be conditioned to give more to their companies than to themselves or their families. In becoming successful they've neglected their own needs and those of their families. They are rootless, and their success in business has not brought them a balanced, nourished life. I can't think of a male in this culture who has friends, feels connected to other people, and is contented."

I paused, took a big stretch, gulped some beer. "I've really been holding forth here. I guess the point I've been trying to make is that humans have to find a way to love and care about each other if we're going to make it on this planet. And that's my quarrel with the psychotherapy counseling service we work for—they're still handing out the line that what matters is climbing the corporate ladder to a successful private practice. No different from anywhere else in the business world. Dog eat dog. Get those patients into your waiting room.

"What we saw this weekend sums up what my peers and I in psychology believe we should do. We encountered a woman whose personal horror was much greater than anything we could have imagined. For a moment we were forced to transcend our own narcissism, materialism, and concern for the trivial. We suddenly experienced another human being in a larger, realer way. That's the sort of concern I and others hope to dedicate our lives to if we can escape the pressures of becoming successful income producers." I paused and sighed. "Thanks for hearing me out."

Marcuse raised his glass and toasted me and what I

had said. The others joined him. I had gotten my convictions over to them, and I felt satisfied. In these minutes we were not doctors and patients, only people who, by sharing what was deep down inside of us, had converted into affirmation painful feelings we'd felt all weekend. We laughed, we joked, we were affectionate. I thought that if I could teach Moira to play and have fun the way we were right now, she might get through her nightmare as a whole person.

It was time to go, but no one wanted to. We began to talk of Moira's plight. She had been cruelly abused and made mentally ill by the accident of being born in a home in which very sick people took out their problems on her. We had been touched by her and felt we had to help her. I sensed that everyone around the table felt the same way. After all, our lives had not been very different from hers. Perhaps we'd had stronger defenses against the calamities we'd endured. Most parents gave their children support and reassurance, but Moira had no one. There was little prospect that her family and her husband would change for the better. Her only hope lay in finding a place where people cared about each other.

I saw parallels between how my friends and I wanted to start real change in our profession and the challenge facing Moira. We felt we could no longer accept the realities of a selfish world of personal gain. Moira, similarly, could not accept or try to adjust to the insane realities of her family—and now, some of the very people treating her.

My contribution as a psychologist, I believed, was to try to bring about truths I believed in. I could not accept psychotherapy and psychoanalysis that avoided seeking a higher prospect for mankind. I could not accept Freud's pessimistic view of man's capacity to change for the better. Life must be lived as though the human species had only a brief time remaining.

I wanted to help create a new way of guiding people by means of psychology. A way that would focus on humanizing man's experience on this planet, not just accepting the harsh realities dictated by the deteriorating quality of the environment and humans' negative traits. There had to be ways of developing treatment methods to improve human standards—first in our clinic and then, with luck, around the world.

If I was going to pursue these noble goals, above all I must as a psychologist be involved in the real problems of society. To start with, I would have to find a way to keep working with Moira, rather than bow to wrongheaded clinical policies. I felt the marathon had changed me. I was letting go the pragmatic approach to my work and my life in which I had felt secure. I had mounted Rosinante, couched Don Quixote's lance, and was preparing to charge the windmills. I felt I had no other choice.

I mused about Freud. A true genius. I had no doubt that history would revere him as a central illuminator of the human psyche. The giant who carried on his shoulders as pygmies other psychology greats who followed him and who owed to his work many of their contributions. But his tradition was increasingly unconnected to the swirling changes in values and behaviors raging through modern life. Intrapsychic analysis was necessary but not sufficient if we as psychologists were to help patients help themselves in genuinely effective ways.

Freud had responded to his times. The women he treated had been rendered hysterical by the repressions of their era, and men were pressured to constantly prove themselves by excelling in their professions. This sort of demand often produces an obsessive-compulsive neurosis, and it was these problems in men and women that Freud addressed.

But now, other malaises were afflicting people. They had become self-preoccupied and hedonistic. Those two major dysfunctions arose from a declining capacity in humans to contact and experience that in themselves which was loving and nourishingly connected to others. These conditions, so different from the emotional disturbances of Freud's time, told us an important truth: Sigmund Freud's theories had been revolutionary in 1895. But now, they had become archaic.

More accurately, it was classical and outmoded ways of interpreting and applying Freud's theories that had become archaic. Freud's central discoveries, such as the significance of dreams, the existence of the unconscious, and the revealing character of free association, will be part of the makeup of humans as long as they are humans. But rather than utilizing these tools in a manner suited to Freud's world in the last century, as those practicing classical analysis have persisted in doing, we must confront a challenge: to adapt Freud's enduring truths as building blocks of relevant helping techniques, methods that can illuminate and alter for the better human beings and their ever-evolving ways of living on this planet.

Conversation wound to a halt. We stretched. It was close to dawn. Our daily lives beckoned; I would meet patients at the clinic in a few hours, then attend classes. I toasted my comrades for the last time.

For one moment we had glimpsed a brighter future, and the weekend had allowed us this glimpse. Perhaps we could enlist our hearts and minds in the cause of making this future a reality.

That night, after therapy and classes, I got home at last and learned that my father would never know the world for which we hoped. He had departed it.

Before the marathon weekend, my father, Harry, had prostate surgery and seemed to be recovering well. On my return, I learned that he had developed internal bleeding due to what I eventually found out was botched-up surgery. My father would never know a better world, because the world in which he lived routinely deprived the poor of competent medical attention. An intern of substandard capability attended him because my father couldn't pay. Like Moira, his station in life brought him undeserved suffering and, in this case, death.

Fifteen

Confrontations

After my father's funeral, my family observed the Jewish custom of sitting Shiva for seven days. So it was almost two weeks later that I found myself back with Mardoff for supervision. He'd gotten wind of what had happened during the marathon and decided to sock it to me about what he felt were my misjudgments.

"It is not the role of the therapist, Mr. Obler, to encourage acting out by patients with neurotic sexual problems during treatment of any sort. Even in group therapy, a therapist should use extreme caution in encouraging a patient to discuss his or her sex life. It's too easy to fall prey to voyeurism. Discussing sexuality with a patient should occur only when it is absolutely organic to the exchanges going on. I thought this had been made clear to you. The only role —and I emphasize the *only* role—of the therapist is to stay neutral and not encourage transference issues. To encourage the patient to express feelings about their sexuality complicates the process; it becomes next to impossible to differentiate between what happened in a patient's past and what he expresses as a result of being in therapy. That's the damn problem with those experimental treatment techniques you used this weekend. They just stimulate disturbed patients to express their sicknesses. As a result, the transfer process is complicated. Freud pointed out over sixty years ago the value of manifesting healthy sexuality in one's love and work. Our patients should resolve their neuroses so that in their daily lives they can sublimate their lustful impulses through healthy emotional connections."

I stared at him, wishing he could see what was in my mind. Who the hell was he to lecture me on healthy emotional connections? But he was talking, of course, from the standpoint of classical analytical theory. From that viewpoint he was correct. I had to try to defend myself, though. Too much was at stake, in terms of Moira's plight.

I started cautiously. "I thought Freud also pointed out that repression is one of the major mechanisms in the formation of neurosis." I paused. What strategy should I adopt now? I knew it was futile to try and convince him that other sets of assumptions about psychotherapy had been arrived at. Could I outflank him by referring to literature that refuted the underlying hypotheses of orthodox psychoanalytic theory and practice? But that issue, I was aware, had little to do with the power struggle going on between Mardoff and me. I decided to continue trying to persuade him that my approach might best help Moira.

I cleared my throat, crossed my fingers, and said, "Dr. Mardoff, helping our patients learn to be sexually passionate seems to me one of the essential ways to help lift repression. An active libido leads to a healthy psyche; a jammed-up libido blocks the psyche. We didn't actively zero in on Moira's sexual problems. They came out organically, triggered by the exercises, by the emotional climate of the marathon, and by what was happening inside her. The group and I guessed that Moira was probably fantasizing or engaging in some type of sexuality outside the marriage." I paused, and stared at him intently. His face whitened but he met my gaze. I went on, "And we thought that perhaps learning to enjoy it could help her. It seemed appropriate to work on her orgasmic dysfunction and not avoid it. Moira is in an oppressive marriage with an abusive husband. Might it not be healthy for her to simulate fulfillment in a group therapy setting that is not at the moment possible for her in her real world?"

"You're either being contradictory in your analysis or Marcuse distorted his report of Moira," Mardoff shot back. "I understand from both of you that Moira fragmented at the introduction of sexual abuse in her childhood. At that point she had reproduced the state of being a very sick child. Then you proceeded at the very next session to treat her like an integrated adult. You introduced her to sophisticated lust exercises to deal with a serious sexual dysfunction. Make up your mind! Are you dealing with a mature and sophisticated adult who manifests healthy sexuality, or a sexually disabled individual still suffering from her original abuse?"

Answering him was a no-win proposition, but I continued: "Perhaps we're dealing with both! On Saturday night she certainly was an abused, victimized child. In the next session I was confronted by a sophisticated woman who understood the nature of her sexual frustrations with her husband. I was not alone in making these evaluations. Marcuse witnessed her rapid transformation from molested child to integrated adult. We all saw the same thing happen. No mistaking it, I was dealing with two different people. If you'll let me tell you about the weekend in detail, you'll see that we probably are dealing with a multiple personality. I've always told you this is the case."

Mardoff stared off into space. He shifted nervously in his chair, summoned a wan smile. Then surprised me by apparently shifting ground. "Complicated cases like Moira are difficult." He looked at me. Gone was the reproving manner. As the silence lengthened, I wondered if by a miracle my argument for using different techniques to treat separate parts of Moira's fragmentations had impressed him after all.

I should have known better. Suddenly his expression turned vindictive and he barked at me. "We'll probably let the issue of your competency on the weekend be decided by your peers. We've set aside the next staff meeting to review the events of the weekend."

I sighed. I hadn't sold him on anything, and now he wanted to humiliate me by questioning my competency in front of my colleagues, while his own professional conduct went undetected. I gritted my teeth and waited to see what was next. He went on to review the weekend as it had been described to him by Marcuse, and he asked me if the report was accurate. I nodded.

Then he dropped a new bombshell: "I think, Mr. Obler, we should talk about your tenure at the clinic. Your term as an intern will end soon. Since you persist in believing Moira is a multiple personality, we should decide whether it is advisable for you to continue as her therapist. It will take years of specialized treatment to cure her." His eyes narrowed. "Any thoughts about this?"

It wasn't easy, but I remained respectful. "I've been wanting to discuss with you letting her continue with me in private practice after I finish my internship. I know it's an unusual request, but I believe in this case there are mitigating conditions that warrant serious consideration for what I was suggesting."

"And what might those be?" he inquired sarcastically. I felt frustration mounting in me as I realized he was holding all the cards. I bit back a desire to spit in his face, then pulled myself together.

"I know clinic policy opposes the transfer of patients to private practice. But I also know that exceptions are sometimes made under special conditions. There's no question, too, that I need your supervision to ensure a successful outcome for Moira, so I would like to pay you independently for continued supervision of Moira and a number of other patients. I'm certain she would reject transfer to another psychotherapist and would drop out of therapy. Without your continued guidance she would fall apart."

I was certain Mardoff wouldn't buy this obvious maneuver, but I had to convince him during this session that I would abide by whatever decisions he made. If he or anyone else in supervision at the clinic found out I hoped to try to transfer Moira to my private practice later on, my professional career would be terminated.

His response was short and firm. "My decision is to switch Moira to a new therapist within the clinic as soon as you prepare her to make the change."

I blew up. "How do I know she is emotionally ready for this, coach?" I asked. "Why don't you just select a Mardoff clone from among your clinic pals? That way you can continue supervision and everything else you're doing for her," I added bitterly. "How about that for a solution?" As soon as I had spoken I regretted it. Regardless of the pressure on me, what I had said was stupid and immature. Before he could say a word I apologized.

Upon which he shifted gears again. Mardoff said in a glibly empathetic voice, "Look, I'm not trying to offend you or hurt your professional development. But I believe it is in your and Moira's best interests that she start working with a more experienced therapist. I just don't agree with your multiple personality hypothesis. But there's no rush. I want to discuss this with you, work with you. We want what's best for the patient, and timing is crucial." He fingered his Phi Beta Kappa key for a moment and then smiled at me.

The bastard had me by the balls. It was true that I was overinvested emotionally in Moira, more so than was appropriate for most patient-therapist alliances. But if I was wrong, so was he, and in a much more reprehensible way. If, and it was a sizeable if, we could get someone trained to work with her complicated case, it would probably be better to switch her therapist's supervisor as well as her therapist. I was convinced that no one associated with Mardoff's clinic was more qualified than I to work with her. Very little was known about treating her condition.

To me, the real battle between Mardoff and me had to do with what was really going on between Mardoff and Moira and my tendency not to accept his evasions and to think for myself. That I was opposed to his actions and views about Moira was a threat to his position and, perhaps, his confidence in his own skills and knowledge. I wasn't sure if he even had someone in mind to take over Moira's work. After all, she was hardly a wealthy socialite from Park Avenue.

Nevertheless, Mardoff had on his side a legal consideration: If a patient was transferred to an outside private therapist and something went awry leading to a malpractice suit, the clinic could be held accountable in the suit for having transferred her. Sometimes this rule was set aside and a patient was allowed this transfer, but only if it had been determined that the problem was a simple neurosis and the patient was clearly no threat to him- or herself or others. Moira's illness, of course, was much more complex, and not transferring her was certainly warranted from the standpoint of clinical policy.

Suddenly I remembered that a similar rule applied to transfers of patients *within* the clinic. If a patient was transferred from one therapist to another within the clinic and problems arose as a result of the transfer, the clinic could also be brought to account.

I now had a line of attack. The opening gun would be to remind Mardoff of that second legality. Then I would try to convince him that I wanted to cooperate with him in whatever way we worked out. Maybe this way I could somehow keep alive the possibility of keeping Moira with me.

Taking a deep breath, I started cautiously. "I want to apologize again for anything I've said that offended you. I think I felt insulted by suggestions of my incompetence at the marathon, and my ego got in the way. I'm grateful for all you've done for me, and your analysis sounds accurate. Moira and some of my other patients do need a better-trained therapist. And their transfer to that therapist should be timed in their best interests.

"It's also occurred to me that we are responsible to the police department—they referred Moira to us. We let them know the original diagnosis—hysteria—and after two years of psychoanalytically oriented therapy we told them recently that her therapy was going well and should be concluded within a year. But now we're going to tell them we're transferring her to another therapist. I need your sound advice to help them understand the need for this transfer." I said this almost respectfully.

I'd reminded Mardoff of some important concerns about Moira—his face had turned grim and wary. He stared off into a corner. Then he said, as if I was on his side, "Let's move slowly. First, you should work with her on getting her to understand that you feel the transfer is important in effectively continuing her therapy. But don't tell her about the transfer at first. Start with explaining your time limitations as an intern, then suggest that one option could be a transfer in the fall. Tell the police department what you're doing —about your time limitations and the need for transfer—in your monthly reports to them. Now, if Moira brings up the possibility of continuing with you in private practice, tell her you'll discuss it in supervision, but suggest that probably the best thing for her would be to transfer to another therapist at the clinic eventually."

Inside I fumed. However, I responded, "Sounds good to me." I was relieved. For the moment I had calmed our conflict—a conflict that could have ended my quest for a Ph.D. in psychology. I had to own up to my own conscience, that for the moment I had conveniently discarded my idealism in the course of all this maneuvering. But for the time being I had breathing space to think about how I could continue my career and help Moira at the same time.

Before I left him, Mardoff and I were actually acting friendly again, although for us both I knew it was only a mask.

Standing up, I raised one more issue. "What if Moira doesn't want to make the switch and threatens to leave therapy altogether?" His reply shocked me. "At this clinic, we don't force patients to do anything against their will." Repulsed, I looked away for a moment. Though what he said sounded correct, to me it suggested a callous dismissal of both our troubled patients and our responsibility to them.

As I seethed about that, another thought came to me—

we hadn't decided whether or not Moira should continue in the group. I asked Mardoff how he felt about that.

"Definitely not," he barked. "It's clear you made a big mistake introducing her to the group at all. The weekend was a fiasco, and I'll have to find a way to insulate you from being attacked by your colleagues because of your misjudgments."

I stared at Mardoff. What a hypocrite he was, and now, in a strange way, he was supporting me against paying a price for my weekend "mistakes!" I said nothing as I walked out of the room. Again my idealism had taken a back seat to my need to survive professionally.

The next day Moira had an appointment scheduled. I hadn't met with her since the end of the marathon—over two weeks past. I was met by a thoughtful person who had obviously been deeply affected by the experience.

She had a lot on her mind. "Why do I have to suffer more than other people to become normal?" she challenged. "Since the marathon I've been talking with a lot of women on the force, and it seems that sexual child abuse is pretty common. Little girls are routinely molested by their fathers, brothers, cousins. It's not as exceptional as the group told me it was. They're touched improperly, slyly. Someone runs a hand up their leg or touches their genitals while helping them on or off a swing. They feel their fathers' erections while sitting on his lap. Often the molester is drunk. And how about this: One woman on the force told me her father put small sticks in her vagina as some vile form of 'control' so she wouldn't touch herself!

"We were in a bad situation. What could we do about it? We got the message, one way or the other, not to tell anyone what was going on or we'd be sorry. I'm sure my mother knew what was happening, but she just ignored it. And turned her back on what my father was doing to me."

Tensely, she rubbed her forehead, moving her fingers

back and forth. "But I get the picture now. My mother hated me. Having me chained her to my father. And when I got old enough to replace her as his sexual partner she must not only have ignored what was going on, she must have been pleased about it. Why not? It got him off her back! She hated sex with the bastard. If I had gone to her for help she would have smacked me around and threatened to ship me off to a foster home."

She stared off into space for a few moments then went on. "When I try to remember what went on, one of the first things that comes back is that my father was so nice when he was sober. I can remember happy times with him, like when he'd buy me an ice cream cone or take me to feed the ducks in the lake in Prospect Park. And only vaguely do I remember the abuse itself. When I try to bring it back I get dream images of a beautiful countryside, while I feel something penetrating my vagina."

Her voice dropped to a whisper. "I can't believe he wanted to hurt me. But does it matter if he wanted to or not? The fact is he did. And I try to sugar-coat it with my guilt. I've found out a lot of women do that. It made us keep it to ourselves. The shame and humiliation of it, which made us feel undeserved guilt, may have kept millions of women from telling what happened to them. But if I start talking, maybe others will."

Now I faced a tough one—exploring the possibility that she might have imagined the whole thing. That was Freud's hypothesis, that his women patients who complained of sexual molestation had only imagined it, perhaps out of a wish that it had happened! Eventually, though, Freud had to revise his views. He found out that by and large if a patient recalled being molested as a child they actually had been. I said in a tactful tone of voice to Moira, "You know, we've discovered in psychotherapy that a lot of men and women recall being abused as kids. But in the face of analytical scrutiny we often find that people confuse a fantasized wish with reality."

I continued, "One of your central problems has been a

confused memory, because in your mind and feelings you were trying to get away from so many awful things. People suffering from that sort of dissociation problem have to, in effect, rewrite their history to block out unbearable memories. Now, you've often recounted violent behavior by your father but never anything about sexual contact with him. I'm not saying it didn't happen, but we have to be careful. It might be that since you were so dreadfully needy you might have imagined it out of a wish to get some kind of emotional touching from him other than violence, even if it was abusively sexual. We want to work toward finding out if your fragmentations had their root in your father's sexually abusing you, and to do this we must make sure they really happened."

As I talked, Moira grew restless. "What's this fragmenting you're always talking about?" she burst out. "What does it have to do with my multiple personalities?"

I was about to answer, but paused. I was distracted by the sweater she had flung over the chair near her. It was of beautiful hand-woven wool. The dress she wore was a white cotton print with yellow flower designs. As never before, I noticed Moira's loveliness. Usually she dressed somberly; this bright dress flattered her, hugging her attractive figure. Growing healthier through therapy had ignited a glow—I was in the presence of a beautiful woman! No wonder Mardoff had been attracted to her. Still there was no excuse for going to bed with a patient. I glanced at her breasts straining against the dress and felt my face redden.

"What are you blushing about?" demanded Moira.

I tried to explain my blushing by murmuring, "I'm flushed because it's hot in here." Then I pulled myself together and found confidence in answering her question. "Fragmentation . . . is when one part of your personality becomes disconnected from the other parts. You're not aware much of the time that the disconnected part even exists. But it's there, a disturbed piece of you that has carried part of the horror you've been through away from the rest of you into hiding. Under certain conditions it will emerge and become dominant, and while it is dominant, the other parts of you will disappear into hiding." I paused for breath.

"Don't stop now," encouraged Moira. "For once, you're describing something in plain English so I can understand it. Just keep it simple." God, she was lovely. I gulped and held onto my professional manner with difficulty.

Then I continued, "What psychologists call dissociation or a disassociative state means a state of mind you get into in which your brain waves are a different frequency from what they are normally. You know, don't you, that the brain emits tiny waves of electricity? That's what's measured on electroencephalograph machines." Moira nodded. "Each of your selves has its own electric frequency.

"Now, that splitting-off part of you in its mild state is like at parties when we're high and feel spaced out, as though someone else is doing the talking. Like we're not quite there. In your case, though, the dissociation is much more extreme. During the weekend you were dividing into separate parts like crazy without our being able to tell what was setting you off. You created altered states with whole new personalities who functioned independently and knew nothing about each other—a sort of amnesia. And as I've explained, each of these split-offs were made up by you to carry a portion of the horror you underwent as a child. The splitting off happens again as an adult when you remember what happened to you as a child that started the smash-up in the first place."

"Did I do that on the weekend?"

"Don't you remember?" I was puzzled. How could she remember being sexually abused if she hadn't remembered becoming Marcia, who had recalled the sexual abuse?

With a graceful gesture, Moira placed her palm on her forehead. Then her face tightened; her voice was a tense monotone. "I've been getting glimpses of memories that may have happened during my blackout periods. Until now, I've depended on other people to tell me what happened during those blackouts. That's what happened over the weekend. I got through my amnesia and remembered that my brother had told me I was molested as a child." I nodded—that would explain the mysterious third person she had mentioned. "Through other people I've put together what happened over a lot of lost time. All my life I've been forgetting things that I had to find out about through other people. Here's a good example: The other day on patrol in Brooklyn Heights I walked by the Hotel St. George. I pass it all the time on my beat, but I don't remember ever being inside. But this time, as I stared at the hotel, it came to me that I knew the décor of the lobby, how the halls and elevators looked, and the layout of the rooms. The impression was dreamlike but vivid, though as I say I can't remember ever being inside. A couple of days later I had a frightening dream about a room like the ones in the St. George—I was there and with me was a man. Didn't you say that in my fantasy at the marathon I was being sexually abused by an older man?"

"Yes! And you might have been fragmenting on patrol, bringing back the experience. Perhaps you were in that room with that same man."

"There's a way we could find out," Moira suggested hesitantly.

"How?"

She swallowed, then straightened her shoulders resolutely, as though coming to a decision. "We could meet at the hotel for our next session. I'll bet somehow or other we can find out if I had been there!"

I was intrigued. I'd never heard of a therapist meeting a patient outside the office for this kind of reality-testing. Orthodoxy forbade it—having contact with a patient outside the office was held to be counterproductive to the transference bond. But I badly wanted to fill in the missing pieces about Moira; I couldn't resist the idea.

"Well, it's an unusual idea," I answered cautiously, concealing for the moment my fascination with the prospect. "I think before I decide one way or the other, I'd like to hear the dream you had about being about being with that man."

Moira recalled the dream:

"I was sitting in a large room with many people. Seems to me it was my family, but they looked different. The room looked a little like what I imagine the lobby of the St. George looks like. But it's also shaped like my mother's living room. I felt sad, apathetic. The people, including myself, were sitting in a circle with our backs turned to the center of the circle, and each was looking out a separate window.

"The scene changed and now I was looking at a little girl sitting in a sandbox and playing with a pail and shovel. It was a warm, sunny day, but the little girl was shivering with cold. A woman approached her and put a fur coat across her shoulders.

"Now the scene shifted to a large orange room with huge columns, like a sports stadium in ancient Rome, or maybe Greece. For some reason I couldn't understand I felt terror, and I tried to scream. But I had no voice.

"I think the last part of the dream was in a hospital or mental institution. I may have been there for a long time, but I wasn't sure. A bunch of teenagers were hanging around. After this the dream gets confused, but I had the sense that all the people in the dream were very important to me. Once more I flashed to the large ornate room with the marble floor. It seemed so empty, isolated. Along the walls and on a second floor balcony were rows of confessionals like in our local church. Then I sensed who two of the teenagers were in the institution—my brother and me! I grew very upset as I realized we were both murmuring weird fragments of words and sentences that sounded crazy. I ran into a confessional booth, fell to the floor and grabbed a chair with one hand as I dug the nails of the other hand into the wall. A priest showed up, peered at me through the opening in the booth, and screamed at me that I was innocent of any wrongdoing. I banged my hands against the walls in a frenzy, then hugged myself as I lay on the floor and rocked back and forth in fetal position.

"That's the dream," Moira concluded. Then she asked plaintively, "What do you think it means?"

I had the good sense to admit my uncertainty. "I'm not sure, but it seems to suggest a lot about people being isolated from each other and very strong feelings of loneliness in you."

"What do you make of the institution setting with the marble floors at the end of the dream?" she shyly asked.

"Does it remind you in any way, or do you associate it in any way, with the hotel room?" I asked.

"It seems more like the lobby of the St. George."

"Any other associations?"

"Not that I can think of."

I speculated: "It sounds like a typical room in a mental hospital—not a modern hospital, but a house on an estate that might have been converted to such an institution. My interpretation at this point is that you are choosing the image of a mental hospital to reflect your fear that isolation from your family will lead to constant loneliness. And you might find yourself in such a place."

"But how does it tie into the hotel room?"

"I don't know."

Earnestly, Moira said, "I'm going back to that hotel, with or without you."

Should I go with her? In that dream and in that hotel might lie the key to final certainty that she had been abused in childhood. If it turned out that her recollection of childhood abuse grew out of reality rather than fantasy, I should finally be able to convince Mardoff of the validity of my multiple personality diagnosis.

"I'd really like to go to the hotel with you to help us both find out what if anything happened there," I said slowly. "Let me talk to some of the other therapists at the clinic and think about it some more."

SIXTEEN

Theories and Reality

Well, I'd painted myself into a corner! I could hardly imagine Mardoff approving Moira and me wandering around Brooklyn trying to find out whether Moira's memories were fantasy or reality. Nevertheless, I was excited at the thought of breaking new ground as a psychotherapist. There was another consideration: Without fully realizing it did I want to meet her at the hotel in order to get to know her better? I found her attractive—that was for sure. The thought stopped me in my tracks. I had to be very careful. I didn't want to step over the line as I believed Mardoff had done, in my opinion. It is crucially important to keep precise boundaries between patient and psychotherapist. A therapist must be constantly aware of his position of power and must conduct the treatment well within the bounds of that position. This was particularly true of some deeply troubled borderline patients—people such as Moira whose hold on reality was often as tenuous as smoke. Their craving, out of desperate need, to blend their egos with their therapists and get the love and closeness they lacked their entire lives. To maintain a healthy separation between a therapist and a patient requires vigilance but, in my opinion, is critically necessary.

I vowed to keep my relationship with Moira strictly

professional. With that in mind, I decided to push ahead. We made an appointment to meet near the Hotel St. George for our next session.

During the next two days I grilled my fellow interns on their views of the limitations of traditional psychotherapy. We talked of H. J. Eyesenck's book on the efficacy of therapy, *The Effects of Psychotherapy*. I asked my colleagues their opinions on the work of R. D. Laing and Martin Shepard. Both these radical therapists advocated that patient and therapist live in the same environment for the treatment of schizophrenia and other severe psychotic conditions. They viewed these illnesses as originating in substantial measure from social and environmental factors, combining with intrapsychic conflicts afflicting the patient. To my surprise, Shepard went so far as to recommend sex between therapist and patient as an effective way to resolve society's repression of natural healthy instincts. I wondered if Mardoff had read him.

I kept an eagle eye on my motivations throughout these inquiries. I was aware that as a scientist and human being I was irresistibly drawn to this effort, because I wanted to unearth the truth about Moira. The fact, however, that we were going to meet in session outside my office transgressed, I knew, all accepted therapy guidelines. If called to account, I wanted to defend myself with all the ammunition I could gather.

We decided to meet at a subway entrance close to the hotel. We made our appointment for early evening, after my day was over. Moira had set her patrol schedule to be able to meet me. As she came out of the subway I saw that she was in police uniform. In contrast to the lovely dress she had worn at out last session, the uniform concealed her womanly curves. We walked along together. She seemed cheerful, but I felt agitated. Meeting her outside the therapy room made me uneasy. Moira pranced along like a teenager on her first date. "I'm really sorry for the uniform," she said, "I'm still on duty." It struck me that her official role might help us gain information from the hotel staff.

Across the East River, the sun set behind the towers of Manhattan. Moira chatted away. Her job. Her boring home life. Her intention to leave the therapy group because "I made a fool of myself during the marathon. Anyway, I can make faster progress working with you privately." Finally we came to the hotel entrance. We looked at each other tensely, and I saw that under Moira's cheer lay panic. We walked into the lobby and sank onto a worn, old-fashioned couch.

As we tried to relax, I thought of Walt Whitman sitting on these couches sipping coffee—he had lived here before the turn of the century. I thought of his robust and passionate lyricism. What a giant, burning with life from head to toe. My eyes wandered around the now dilapidated lobby. The scarred coffee tables plastered with polish, the frayed velvet chairs with springs showing, reflected their surroundings. On the walls were paintings of sailboats on the Hudson in seasick bilious green. Old people and mental patients sat around the lobby gazing listlessly at nothing. As though sensing my thoughts, Moira exchanged a glance with me and laughed. Not exactly a lobby for a wild affair!

Moira said softly, "How should we get the information we need?"

I replied, "What about asking the manager which clerk was on duty the day you thought you were here?"

Moira replied, "I've another idea. As a police person I could pose as searching for a suspect. This would allow us to scan the register over a period of months. So I can try to spot names I recognize." She added, "We might also wander the halls and stick our heads into a room now and then. To see if I remember anything."

"Agreed," I said. We started by talking with the manager, a white-haired, rotund man who stood behind the counter.

He was a friendly person who pointed out, "Two or three different clerks work different shifts each day, and high employee turnover makes it nearly impossible to find out who was on duty at any particular time. You can have this though." He passed us the registry book. Moira leafed through the pages.

She shook her head as she finished it the first time. "No names are recognizable."

"Try it again, more slowly." I suggested.

The second time through, though, she motioned to me and pointed to the registry. "Here's my last name, but look here." I bent over the book. The name "Marcia" jumped out as a first name to Moira's last name along with a date that was just before Moira's three-week absence from therapy early in the year. Moira whispered to me tensely, "It's not my writing." Her hands were shaking. It obviously made her fearful. A notation next to the entry showed that a single person had taken the room.

Returning the register, we thanked the manager. Trying to appear casual, we asked and got a pass key to the room Marcia had taken. We trudged up to the seventh floor and walked down the hall. Moira's cheerfulness was gone. I could feel tension building in her, and not wanting to exacerbate the problem, I didn't speak.

We walked into the room and Moira seated herself on the bed. She sat quietly for a few minutes, then began to take deep, hurried breaths. I moved closer to calm her down, but she waved me away and began bouncing rhythmically up and down on the mattress. A strange smile was on her face. Suddenly her face contorted; she began the heaving that precedes vomiting. Jumping off the bed she fled into the bathroom, forgetting to close the door. The air filled with the smell of vomit. Returning, she paused by the foot of the bed, her expression deeply sad. Again I started to speak. Again she motioned me to silence, then gestured that she wanted to leave. We returned to the lobby.

The manager waved goodbye as we dropped the key at the front desk.

We walked into the night. I badly wanted to find out why she was quiet, and what had gone on inside her in the room, but I gritted my teeth and waited for her to volunteer.

Though impatient, as we walked I was taken by the

mellow beauty of Brooklyn Heights. Despite the influx of money and new construction, it was still venerable and atmospheric. Emerging on the promenade we seated ourselves on a bench. Facing us was the spectacular Manhattan skyline, blazing with lights against the darkening west. It seemed a dream city. I recalled that O. Henry had termed Manhattan "Baghdad on the subway." Beside me was a person of dreams—tortured, yearning, sumptuous. A beggar drifted by. Moira got out a $10 bill. I gently took it from her, and gave the man fifty cents. I slipped the bill back in her purse.

After closing her purse she sat tensely. Then she said bitterly, "I don't want to talk about it!"

My own feelings rushed out. "But I do! What was going on with you in that room? I think I have a right to know. I compromised myself professionally by meeting you. I'm not supposed to be doing it. Now you clam up. The idea is to work together and see if we can try to find out if your memory lapses have to do with suppressing actual events or whether you were just fantasizing the whole thing. It might help us get to the root of your troubles."

Moira sighed. Staring at the Manhattan skyline, she murmured, "I don't believe it will. It was like an event that happened a long time ago. I'm not even sure it ever happened. I've told you, I'm not sure of my hold on reality. Now, I do think I was here as Marcia. But I don't remember who was with me, if anyone. Maybe I had a few drinks while I was here as Marcia and confused it with reality—yearnings for sexual contact projected from the past. I've seen men lying on pavements. Drinking in bars. Sometimes I'm attracted to one of them, and maybe I internalized them in my dreams. I'm not sure of anything. On the other hand, I might have been here with the man I've been having an affair with."

"Who the hell is he? Are you holding back on me?"

She replied primly. "Just a man I've had an affair with recently. It's really none of your business, but I may have been bringing back my affair with him in my hotel dream. It began on a spring afternoon. We'd been drinking. Now, don't judge me. He was one of you, and you psychologists advocate sexual freedom, releasing super ego constrictions, all that—but underneath you're as conventional as everyone else."

We fell silent for a few moments. Moira asked me, "Have you had extramarital affairs?" I knew what she was up to: get me on that subject and she could get away from those hotel room memories.

"Now look, Moira," I said. "You're not going to get me off track. I want to help you. What was going on with you when you threw up? Stop this avoidance crap and tell me!"

"Get off that subject," she snapped. "I don't want to talk about it!"

I couldn't give up. Too much was at stake. "Moira, I'm not leaving until I get some answers. I can't help you unless I do. Now, c'mon. Why are you hiding your memories? Why was the ledger signed Marcia? Was that so no one would know you were there? Or was it that Marcia had taken over, as you suggested? God damn it, tell me!"

I couldn't crack her. She rose. "I can't talk about these things now," she said forcefully, then stalked away. I knew there was no point running after her.

At our next session I pressed her for answers as soon as she arrived. I hadn't seen her for days, and it was crucially important that I find out why she didn't want to talk.

After I asked her once more about the hotel room experience, she was silent for a moment. Then, her face looking down at her lap, her voice just audible, she said, "I've been thinking I was around four when I was first touched sexually. But I've come to think it was closer to age nine or maybe eleven. I remember that I had pubic hair and breast buds. It's all vague in my mind. Sometimes I wonder if it really happened."

She continued, "When Gregory was lying on me at the

marathon when we were doing that role playing, I did have some frightening memories. My father was lying on me, smelling of alcohol, forcing his way into me. But I'm not sure that it wasn't a dream. My memory in the hotel room of being a child was much sharper. I'm sure I remember my uncle—my mother's brother. I saw him approach me, slobber all over me. That was when I got sick and vomited. I remember the taste of his sperm in my mouth." She bowed her head as if seeing it all again.

I mused for a moment. Then, "You never mentioned an uncle before. You think he raped you when you were nine?"

Moira pushed her blond hair away from her eyes. "I think so. I never saw much of him when I was a kid. He kept to himself and didn't come around very often. He started to take an interest in me when I had my period. He took me swimming at the hotel swimming pool. I was tall and very developed for my age. It must have been during one of those visits that it happened. He took me into a hotel room and forced me. I can't remember any details, though."

She burst into tears. I gave her a kleenex and took her hand. We had a moment of sympathy and closeness.

After she calmed down I said, "Did you know him very well? Why would he have to attack a young girl?"

"No, I didn't know him well. Why did he attack me? Who knows? What I remember of him is that he was a fat, sloppy, Irishman who drank too much. Boasted he was an IRA member. He and my father were disasters, inept alcoholic Irishmen who lived repressed and isolated lives. I heard that he beat the prostitutes he paid for sex. He and my father hung around a certain bar with drunks like themselves who spent their time reminiscing about the 'old days,' whatever the hell they were.

"But I have to tell you, Obler, I'm not even sure my uncle *did* attack me. Or my father. I'm not sure I was having an affair. I'm not sure where I was for two weeks when I didn't come to see you. Above all, I'm not sure I want to know the truth, whatever it is."

"From a psychological standpoint, that's understandable," I said. "Most people would feel the way you do and blot out whatever happened."

"It's as though you know what's happening but you have to insulate yourself from it. You get into a half-awake, half-asleep state. Don't you call that a hypnagogic state?"

"That's what it sounds like," I replied, surprised and pleased that she recalled that term from my mentioning it in our sessions. For a moment it was a relief to lecture. "Hypnagogic is when a person starts to enter that level of sleep when his eyelids flutter. That's called rapid eye movement, or REM, sleep. It's a light sleep. But in a hypnagogic state, one is also awake and conscious. We call the awake state the 'beta' state. That's the term for the brain frequencies the brain emits during our active daytime hours. So hypnagogic is REM sleep combined with beta awakeness. A relaxed, hypnotic, but aware condition." We fell silent. I knew we were touching on unknown areas that eventually might yield fascinating truths about the human mind, such as connections between hypnagogic states and the multiple personality phenomenon. And why each personality in a multiple emitted specific brain wave patterns, different from those of the other personalities in the same person. I also wondered whether a particular personality in a multiple disorder might be electrically alive—as evidenced by its individual frequency—but not be experiencing awareness. But another part of the brain might receive and store shocking and dangerous stimulation that the "asleep" personality had been created to handle but avoided at this point because the event was too shocking. Then when the unaware personality sensed that the dangerous event had become less threatening, as, perhaps, it receded into the past, it would "awaken" and become aware of its recollection of the event. This could explain why multiples block out certain experiences, apparently forgetting them entirely, yet recall them fully at another time.

"Do you believe all that stuff I seem to remember really happened to me?" Moira asked.

"It's your daydream," I responded. "You wrote the whole thing. Directed it and acted it. It sounds real. Doesn't it sound real to you? I suppose you might have concocted the whole thing as a reaction in a sick household to the rising of your adolescent sexuality. I'm not one hundred percent sure of anything at this point. But it might help if you could tell me everything that came back to you in the hotel room. What else, that you can remember?"

"Well, when I was in the bathroom I had an image of Marcia having sex with an older man. The guy I had an affair with. It was somewhere in New York. As I watch, Marcia goes home after the sex to clean sperm off her clothes, same as I did. And, you know, it wasn't Marcia as I remember her. It was her, but it was also part me, part Moira. Acting sensuous and sexy. And I was aware that in my fantasy Marcia had an orgasm with the man. Unlike me —most of the time I'm frigid. I don't have orgasms except when I masturbate. I enjoyed my fling with the man, but I did not climax. Yet in my dream of her, Marcia did!"

I left the clinic that day, my head spinning. Reality was a lot more incredible than anything people could make up. At least that was the way it was seeming to me. As a person undergoing psychological training, I was certain that the unconscious mind existed—that there was too much indication of it to doubt that it did. I knew that repression was a defense by which the human being protected himself emotionally, but that a person could be as out of touch with themselves as Moira appeared to be seemed hard to grasp. She was saying to me that a profound and powerful memory was reporting to her that she had both had and had not had an orgasm at the same time! To regress because the ego could not handle some place of reality was commonplace. To go back in time inside oneself and become two different interior people with no relation to each other seemed incomprehensible. I understood theoretically what being a multiple was about and why it happened. Meeting Moira, who had fragmented to this extreme degree, took my breath away.

However, my time to ponder this mystery was running out. I had to either keep Moira with me or terminate her therapy. One clinical student had told me how he was going to continue treating his patients after leaving the clinic. He would simply ask them to continue to see him and enlist their help in not letting the clinic know he was doing it. I decided on a similar plan. I would suggest to Moira that she temporarily transfer to a new therapist for a short time, then contact me in private practice after I had established myself somewhere. Timing was critical. I had to act quickly and carefully.

Three months remained before the end of the school year and my completion of my internship. My first priority was to handle my buddy Mardoff with kid gloves to ensure a smooth transition for Moira to a new therapist. Mardoff had to think I was going along with his plan; I could not allow him to guess what my real intent was. I was also hoping to get his permission to continue with the group in my private practice—this would give me a group of patients with which to start my private work, an important concern for fledgling therapists.

There was a flagrant double standard in the mental health profession these days: psychiatrists were allowed to continue working with clinic patients in private practice after they had qualified, but psychologists were not allowed to do so. I decided I had to fight this standard—but not with Mardoff. To oppose him over that issue could complicate my effort to help Moira and other patients.

That evening I told my wife what had happened at the hotel with Moira. I was trying as hard as I could to make my marriage work—it had been seven months since I'd broken with my last lover outside my marriage. I had done that for my kids' sake, I reasoned. I thought a responsible therapist should at least maintain a facade of a sound marriage.

My wife and my friends strongly urged me not to go ahead with my plan for continuing with Moira. They believed it would jeopardize my career.

Moira's dream, I concluded, told me she was preparing to confront deeply repressed material from her childhood. I got three impressions from the dream. The first was that she clearly saw herself unconnected to everyone around her: each person, while sharing the same room, was staring out a separate window. Second, at this point in our work she deeply yearned for therapeutic support and friendship to help her overcome her childhood terrors, but she feared it wouldn't happen. So she imagined herself in a sandbox wishing for a woman to place a fur coat on her to protect her from the world. In the third and last part of the dream, Moira feared that the abuse she received as a child, emotionally and physically, would cause a mental breakdown and she would be placed in a mental institute.

It seemed to me that our visit to the hotel had been daring and successful. It opened up sexually repressed material central to her dysfunction.

I wondered how wise it would be to open up new material in Moira at this point, however. I would soon be leaving the clinic and would not be able to follow up properly anything new that came up in her. Maybe it would be better to allow her to integrate the new strength she had developed and wait for further exploration of her childhood memories when we resumed therapy in my private practice.

I also had to be careful about stalling Mardoff. He was starting to ask when I was going to terminate Moira. If he was unsatisfied about what was happening, he could delay evaluating me as an intern and hold up a recommendation critical to my finding a job. He could even hold up my completing my doctorate. I didn't want to transfer Moira to a new therapist too soon. The therapeutic alliance between her and me, especially since our visit to the hotel, had strengthened. I was walking a tightrope, but I was determined to do things my way.

I'd been reading about new techniques that had been developed for the healing method called fusion, which was used to treat dissociative disorders such as Moira's. These new applications for the technique included using hypnosis or altered states of consciousness. Preliminary results had led to the first reported successful treatment of a multiple personality, but the literature I was reading cautioned that these methods were still in the experimental stage. It also said that the type of disorder Moira suffered from was extremely rare.

These reports reminded me that Mardoff's view of a wide range of dissociative disorders, including Moira's, was that they were of a hysterical character and should be treated as such. For a few moments I dwelled on the fact that I had no answers, but this was the conventional wisdom of the time and it was a large roadblock for me. I was convinced Moira's condition was that of a genuine multiple, but the odds were stacked high against my proceeding as I wished to in helping Moira. It was a very difficult predicament for a young intern completing his training.

June was showdown time for the five remaining interns who had managed to stand up under the tough evaluation process of a doctorate program. Qualifying doctoral exams were scheduled at the same time that interviewing started for fall jobs. A tricky part of getting a job was that it had to involve patients for treatment work that would be material for a doctoral dissertation. Some interns, such as myself, also had to get well-enough paying jobs to support families and pay off loans. Faculty recommendations had to be acquired, clinic evaluations held, termination discussions completed, and a master's thesis finished by June. I couldn't imagine a worse time to try to put my rescue plan for Moira into action.

Moreover, money was a big problem for me. For three years I had supported a wife and two children on scholarships and loans while pursuing full-time graduate work. All along I had been undergoing my own analysis, four sessions a week. Although I paid a moderate student fee, I had been making only partial payments and had run up a debt of several thousand dollars, and my analyst told me at this point she would have to increase my fee.

To begin reducing my debt, I got a job at a children's camp for the summer. Then I sought further work at the clinic, which would help me financially and allow me to continue to work with a number of my patients, including Moira, until the last possible moment. In addition, I applied for a part-time job with two clinic administrators. They accepted me, as long as Mardoff approved the patients who would be assigned to me. They were getting a bargain in me —though still new to the profession, I had become a skilled clinician and would work for minimum pay.

The clinic was maintained by charging moderate fees to lower-middle-class clients who would be reimbursed by their insurance companies. The therapists treating them were paid very little. Although the clinic was officially a not-for-profit institution, it paid high salaries to Mardoff and the clinic administrators. Also on staff were the chief medical psychiatrist and two clinical psychologists. These people, too, took fat salaries for themselves, to which they added fees from their private practices. Their position allowed them to select highly motivated and interesting patients who had the best chance to recover for their private caseloads. This made their work more rewarding than those of us who treated individuals with a less hopeful diagnosis.

What all this amounted to was that our type of private, not-for-profit neighborhood organization was a lucrative kickback system enabling those in positions of power to enlarge their private practices. They chose people to add to their practice from the choicer cases who entered the clinic. Thus, a self-serving arrangement was masked by the facade of a not-for-profit mental health facility.

For them, psychotherapy was a lucrative profession. As interns we seldom if ever talked of the money to be made in the field, but all of us were very much aware of the income potential from a successful practice. We felt we deserved it —we had worked hard through tough economic circumstances. Now we wanted to be paid back. Despite the idealism I had voiced after the marathon, we fledglings all looked up to the big-money shrinks. Still, to be fair to myself, I had an equally strong, if not stronger, drive to work toward the goals for therapy I believed in.

Despite that fact I felt the strength and growth evident in Moira and my patients would impress any supervisor with my increasing competence—so much so that he would allow me to take the part-time job in the clinic and to continue to work with my people through the end of the year. I felt that Mardoff had his own reasons for getting me away from Moira. Still, it seemed to me that a persuasive case could be made that Moira and I should not terminate at this time. She had made a great deal of progress with me, and so I plunged ahead, naively optimistic and unaware of the painful and difficult obstacles I would encounter.

SEVENTEEN

The Nature of an Illusion

Halfway through the summer I got the first indication that my plans would not go as smoothly as I had hoped. A letter from the clinical internship program at my university told me that I was being put on probation because of a supervisory evaluation that had assessed my performance as mediocre. I knew immediately from where it had come. But then another problem developed: I had received a less than satisfactory grade on the cognitive section of my comprehensive exams. I was told the clinic would grant me a master's degree, but I would have to postpone my doctoral dissertation preparation until I had taken additional courses in supervision and psychodynamic theory. These could be taken during the fall and spring semesters while I continued outpatient clinical training.

Within a short time word got around that I'd been put on probation. It unnerved me, though it often happened that second-year interns were put on probation for one reason or another. In my case the big problem was that during probation I would not be able to take outside employment for money I so badly needed.

At first what had happened dismayed me—it aroused memories from my childhood. I recalled feeling humiliated when my father trundled his pushcart around the neighborhoods. I remembered praying that my friends wouldn't recognize him! For years I had avoided asking my friends to my house—I was ashamed that we were poor and on welfare.

My first response to the probation letter was to hide it. I wanted to keep people from finding out what had happened. I wondered how I could have done such a mediocre job on that one part of the comprehensives. I thought I had done well. Did I also owe this setback to Mardoff or perhaps to the clinical placement coordinator?

I brooded for a day. Then the very memories of the past that had given birth to my first frightened response strengthened me. A new strategy occurred to me: I would transfer to a completely new doctoral program at another university! If I did it right, I could, as with my past, turn a setback into a triumph.

My plan was based on my well-known reputation around the clinic as a complainer. Almost from the start, I had outspokenly criticized the program's inflexible theoretical approach and the poor quality of several of the instructors. When I started having trouble with Mardoff's supervision I announced to everyone who would listen, and even those who wouldn't, that all academic clinicians were "uptight assholes." At one point during a student and faculty meeting at the university I became so outraged at the lack of openness being conveyed by our faculty that I announced my intention of transferring to a new doctoral program.

There was no shutting me up. I openly advocated broadening the options for selecting a doctoral thesis. With what I'll admit was annoying persistence, I condemned psychoanalytic methodology as outdated and lacking in effectiveness. Our program strongly emphasized Freudian psychoanalysis as the treatment method of choice. I screamed that fresh air in the form of later methodologies was long overdue.

Well, my big mouth, which had so often gotten me into difficulties, now opened the way for a new beginning. It figured that a prominent malcontent such as myself might be expected to jump ship and swim off in a new direction. So I proposed to do just that.

Another advantage of changing programs might be that in a new situation I could find employment on the side to give me the income I needed. I sent out inquiries to a number of different clinical programs in the Northeast, asking to be accepted on a probationary basis because I was applying so late. I asked full credit for the courses I had completed and acceptance for my master's degree in psychology.

To my surprise, I got back four acceptances, along with offers of substantial financial assistance! I would be taken on probation, as I had requested, and probation would end when I had completed certain courses I had not taken in my present program. One school even offered me private laboratory space for my thesis research. Best of all, that school assured me I could work full time while completing my Ph.D.

I put on my most potent thinking cap, sat down, and tried to work out a strategy for Mardoff.

To start with, I would agree to transfer my patients to other therapists early in the fall—as we had discussed—if he would agree to continue to be my supervisor in the new part-time position I had applied for at the clinic. The problem was that I felt it was he who had given me the mediocre evaluation. If he thought so little of me, would he want to continue supervising me? I wasn't sure, but I needed him to supervise me if I was to continue with Moira, at least while I was finishing up at this clinic.

I decided I could influence him by appealing to his ego. The institutions that had accepted me, providing I continued under his supervision, were more highly esteemed than our college and clinic. Hence, to be affiliated with them through his supervision of me would add lustre to his reputation as a prominent psychiatrist.

Out of those offered me, I decided to apply for a position at the Wilson School for Boys. The clinical program there was considered to be the best in the New York City area. I knew Mardoff would personally benefit from being associated with it. I'd be able to take another long step toward my Ph.D. One "if" hung disturbingly in the air: I wasn't sure I had sufficient training and qualifications to meet their high standards, but they had asked me to interview. With trepidation I prepared to meet with them.

The Wilson School for Boys was a halfway house for young male offenders who had done a term at an upstate treatment center. Wilson was a transition stage for them, after which it was hoped that they could return to society.

At the upstate center, these youngsters, mostly from the lower classes, had undergone treatment for a variety of psychological disorders. The legal justification for their being held at the treatment center was to protect them from parental abuse or because they behaved uncontrollably in school. My job at the halfway house would be to try to prepare them psychologically for re-entry into the world.

Wilson, an old brownstone in a row of turn-of-the-century three-story houses, was on the East Side of Manhattan. The tree-lined street was peaceful and serene on the morning I arrived for my interview. Despite my nervousness, I noted the attractive neighborhood with approval. It looked like a wonderful environment to work in. As I climbed the stone staircase to the door, I was greeted by a small sign above the door: "A Home Away From Home."

The interview was conducted by Robert Lowe Harris, a family systems therapist well known in the therapeutic community. The chance to work with him had been among the attractions for me of taking a position at Wilson. He was young and gifted, and his reputation for an approach to treating these young people, which varied from the traditional, impressed me.

The good-looking, dark-haired clinician and five other staff members waited in the conference room to interview me. They discussed for my benefit the overall treatment approach at the school and the role each played. Looming over the gathering was a hugely fat, copper-skinned woman named Dolly Rollins. Her enormous presence appeared to arouse respect. Next to her, constantly fidgeting, was Dr. Richard Babcock, acting chief psychiatrist in charge of medical supervision. Beside him was Charles Hanson, a tall, powerfully built black man with penetrating black eyes. I learned later that he was a unit director. The other two present were two psychotherapists from other units of Wilson.

After talking of the school operation, Harris and the others went to work on me, hammering away in an apparent effort to locate weak areas in my qualifications, my experience, my motivations. I had heard through the grapevine that they felt a white psychotherapist would be too soft for this tough environment and that a nonwhite person would be better equipped. Combatively, they let me know of their conviction that psychoanalytic approaches to these emotionally bruised, streetwise kids would be ineffective—this came out with a roar of laughter when I asked if any of the young people suffered oedipal problems with their parents. I had pretty well expected this reaction and had posed the question to uncover their attitudes. They lost no time in telling me that they felt confrontational, rigorous discipline of these kids was what was needed, not Freudian probings.

I took their pounding well. I was no stranger to rugged confrontation—I'd had plenty of it growing up and during my early struggles toward my profession. I knew how to give as good as I got and I hit back strongly at each thrust.

After about an hour, they eased off. For one thing, they were impressed that I'd grown up in poverty, struggling with my family on welfare. They also seemed impressed by my ability to handle their hostile attacks. I felt confident that I would get the job.

There was one disappointment for me: Harris told me he would soon leave to take a distinguished position with a training institute. He was an important reason for my wanting to work at Wilson!

I kept my disappointment to myself and explained that if they offered me the job I would have to get the approval of my new graduate program and would use my Wilson patients to provide material for my dissertation. They readily agreed to this. The atmosphere relaxed. Someone mentioned that Hanson had been a left tackle at a Southern college. Something about the friendliness with which I was told this signaled to me that the job was mine. I asked them whether I could fit sessions with my private patients in with my work at the school. All appeared to approve of this request except Babcock. "I don't think it is a good idea," he said disagreeably. I asked why and was greeted with another roar of laughter.

"You'll find out soon enough," Harris said smiling.

I left feeling confident. I still had to pin down the possibility of working with private patients, but overall I had much to feel hopeful about. It seemed to me that Mardoff could pose no objections to my Wilson appointment; he had to approve it if he wanted to benefit by his association with me.

On my way home, replaying the interview in memory, I recalled noting that Babcock's hands and body quivered as we said goodbye, and that he had fidgeted throughout the meeting. I wondered what he would be like to work with.

As I entered Mardoff's office the next day for a supervisory session, I was still glowing from the welcome I'd gotten at Wilson. If Mardoff approved my request, I could keep working at least for a while with Moira and the group. Then I could begin my position at Wilson and complete my doctorate. After a shaky interval, my career seemed back on course.

To add to my upbeat mood, I was further uplifted, if somewhat taken aback, when Mardoff greeted me warmly. We chatted for awhile, swapping summer gossip. Things were looking better by the moment.

I took a deep breath, leaned forward and told him why I had decided to switch schools. I implied that the change could benefit both me and our clinic through his continued association with me as my supervisor. Surprisingly, Mardoff was very supportive and agreed to all my recommendations. His only reservation was in approving me to continue to see Moira and my patients after the end of the year. "Clinic policy is clear," he said forcefully. "Patients are assigned for a maximum period of two years with our interns. Exceptions have been made to allow them to continue in therapy beyond the two years, but only if that is unmistakably justified. I'm not sure it is justified in the case of Moira and your other people. And your schedule next year will be so demanding that I can't see how you could do justice to working intensely with advanced patients. You'd also have to undergo additional postgraduate training analysis," he continued, "before launching into intensive analysis with advanced patients. Moira and your other group therapy patients will become the responsibility of Marcuse and the new therapist we will assign to the group."

As though to sweeten the disappointment he was handing me, he added, "But, as I say, there's no objection to your working part-time at the clinic." I looked quizzically at him but said nothing. Still, I wondered if he was doing this to keep an eye on me. "And you can use your new therapy clients as subjects toward your doctorate. We'd have to get administration and school approval, of course."

I gave him my best shot: "What about Moira's situation, though? I've done everything you told me to do to prepare to transfer her to a new therapist, but it's extremely doubtful that a more experienced therapist could work with her more effectively than I am. We've reported to police officials that both she and we are deeply committed to her continuing therapy with me. My investment with her over the past twenty months makes it evident that she should continue with me rather than someone else. I know her. I can feel her moving toward health. Slowly, but she's getting there. However, she's hostile to any suggestion of a new therapist. Couldn't you make an exception this time for her as well as for my other patients? I don't want to see our progress go for nothing."

"No exceptions!" was his maddening reply. "This approach has been shown to be best. It's similar to the issue of whether an intern's patients should be transferred to his private practice. It simply goes against what's best for the patient!"

He drove his dogmatic points home. "A trainee is contractually bound to patients for two years. Period. We can only extend their relationship under very unusual conditions, and those conditions do not exist in this case. There's a therapeutic issue involved here. To change policy without its truly being warranted is like giving the patient a message that contracts can be changed arbitrarily. That's not what we've been teaching them. Setting a contract aside too easily is like breaking a commitment—any responsible person knows this just isn't done. We've moved carefully in this case, and now it's time for the hysteric to move over."

What had he said? Hysteric? I wondered if it was a Freudian slip of some sort.

Mardoff continued, "I don't see that continuing with you is justified in Moira's case, or with any of your other patients."

"What would you consider adequate justification?"

"As I say, if it's in the best interests of the patient to continue. And in your case it is not."

As I had more times than I could remember with this character, I fought back my anger. "All I'm suggesting," I said, "is that you offer them the option of continuing with me. I'm not trying to force myself on anyone." As persuasively as I could, I tried to convince him of my viewpoint. I emphasized that consistency in treatment—staying with the person who was helping progress to be made—outweighed any expertise or experience that might be offered from another person.

"Why is that?" Mardoff asked.

"Because they all had pathological relationships with pathological parents. No trust. No emotional security. And if we transfer them without their being ready for it, they could interpret it as a parental rejection, become hostile, and express the hostility by leaving therapy!"

"We'll have to take that chance. Have you discussed the matter with your patients?"

"No. Since you gave me a few months extension I took it for granted I wouldn't have to raise it with them until the fall. It gives me a chance to work out the best approach in each case. I'm going to bring it up to them in two weeks. Will I then start a part-time caseload with completely new patients?"

"John," he replied. "One of your new patients will be John."

"Why?" I was amazed at his answer.

"He's the only nonanalytical candidate in your caseload. Your other patients, including Moira, are psychoanalytic candidates, and I've told you, Obler, several times: you haven't been trained in specialized analytical techniques." His face darkened, then he went on.

"But before we go into that, I want to change the subject and make something else crystal clear to you: I'm not going to be duped by any maverick intern trying to take on patients illegally in a private practice. And that's what you're planning to do, isn't it? You know it, and I know it." He paused, with a "now I've got you" look on his face.

I settled back in my chair and gazed at this man. God, how I hated him. He was a slimy excuse for a human being. He enjoyed making people squirm and loved power. The fact that he had probably misused it with Moira didn't stop his pompous attitude. That alone disgusted me, but he also represented a struggle that had long existed in the ranks of professional psychologists and psychiatrists. As aging professionals clung to older treatment techniques, they were increasingly challenged by new, younger interns pressing for reevaluation of approaches to the art.

Was Mardoff confronting professional mortality? Setting aside his relationship with Moira, might that in part explain his adversarial stance toward me? I knew, for one thing, that after writing and publishing some highly regarded work in his career, he had published nothing for years. Whatever was going on, he and I had been at swords' points from the day we met. He seemed bent on either bending me to his will or booting me out of psychology.

I drifted out of my reverie. Mardoff asked my reaction to what he had said. And I told him my thoughts—except for my suspicions about him and Moira. He rubbed his chin thoughtfully for a moment, then smiled. "I believe, Obler, you are avoiding coming to terms with the truth that you aren't as important to your patients, especially one of them, as you had hoped you were."

EIGHTEEN

Unsettling Confrontations

I had no choice. In my next session with Moira I explained, "For the time being at least, clinical policy requires me to end our therapy connection and help transfer you to another therapist." She was clearly unhappy with the prospect and said little. I rushed on: "Moira, I'm really hoping that in about six months you and I can start working again. You can phone me at Wilson, where I'll be working, and set up an appointment. I'll have a private practice there. No one has to know, and you have a right to the therapy you need. We can investigate insurance coverage to help you pay."

Not angrily, but pensively, Moira asked, "It's interesting. During a year and a half of therapy you tell me to be my own person, but the moment you run into bureaucratic nonsense you cave in. I've really worked with you—I've gone back to my past even when it was horrifying to do it. I've suffered, I've had pain, but I hung in there. Why can't you practice what you preach? Tell them to shove it! It's a ridiculous policy—is it applied to all clinic patients?"

"Most," I answered.

"What about the group? Are you continuing the group?"

"Probably, but I'll be working with a new therapist who'll be in charge."

"I can't believe you're going along with all this. Is it because you're afraid they won't qualify you?"

I sighed. "It's true that I have to watch out for myself, Moira. I'd be a fool not to, but I think I'm handling this in a good way, if it works out. Their policy here is that after two years of psychoanalytically oriented psychotherapy the clinic believes patients should be transferred to a more experienced therapist for their more advanced work. Generally this policy makes sense, but these are unusual circumstances. What I want to do is transfer to my private practice you and several other people who are getting particular benefit from working with me. This all has to be done carefully. Psychoanalysis is a specialized and unusual skill."

I paused, realizing that what I was saying—aside from my plan to transfer patients to my private practice—was familiar.

I said musingly both to Moira and myself, "You know, except for what I said about transferring you people to me, I've been repeating every word Mardoff fed me."

Now Moira was angry. "You got it! You're getting just like the assholes who run this place."

I stared at her. I had never seen her so angry and yet so in control of herself. This was a far different person from the Moira whose split-off selves used to behave so violently in sessions. She seemed focused, healthy, intact. I was hearing legitimate adult anger, not the shrieking of a disturbed child—and she had a point. I was being hypocritical, trying to justify clinical policy on the one hand and surreptitiously transferring patients to my private practice on the other.

She socked it to me: "What does our relationship, which we've built out of all these horrendous sessions, have to do with stupid bureaucratic rules? It reminds me of my mother. My brothers and my father never questioned her sick rules—we obeyed them, or else. Something like that is going on here. You and I are being tyrannized by this clinic and you're just giving in to it and betraying what we've built up between us. What's really going on with you, Obler? Has this whole relationship with you been about your ego and your professional advancement? Have we been living a lie? It seems to me the clinic wants to transfer us patients back and forth like cattle. But we're not cattle, we're human beings—in case you hadn't noticed."

Moira took deep quivering breaths. "You can't *do* it. I've felt a bonding with you that's like nothing I've ever felt in my life. You don't just end the connection because some rule or law dictates it. But I've made up my mind not to accept a transfer. I don't give a fuck what you or anyone else in this rotten facility decides. If you go along with them, even though you want to see me later again, I may decide I don't want anything more to do with you, either. I'm going to make up my own mind who I want to see, and if you or they think you can tell me what to do you can kiss my little ass goodbye."

She had guts—more than I did. She was right, but I was doing my best to help her and to save my career. I had to go along with the clinic.

"I think you're overreacting," I lamely suggested. "You're not going to be used by anyone. At this point your therapy has been successful—you're starting to knit together. Can't you feel it? You're much more focused and grownup. I'm just trying to make sure that we continue, and once I'm out of here they can't tell me what to do. You gotta understand I'm not abandoning you. We'll work together for awhile longer, transfer you temporarily to someone else, then you and I will get together for sessions at my private practice. I'll have to set up a new office; I'm transferring to another doctoral training institution. But our work will hardly be interrupted. It might even do you good to work with someone else for awhile—you might get new perspectives. Why don't we stop fighting each other? I'm your friend."

Moira was silent. Then she said softly, "When I went to school I longed for the other kids to accept me. But the more popular kids didn't, and I got stuck with the misfits. It was like the inferiority I felt in my family. They treated me badly, so I treated myself badly. I was attractive, but I looked at myself with disgust. Seeing myself in the mirror, I thought I looked gawky; I was too tall for my age. So I decided my body was what was wrong with me and why I wasn't accepted by other kids. When I developed breasts and hips I saw them as fat that had to come off. I believed if I was thin I would be loved and have friends. Marcia, my friend, was taller than me, beautiful and quite slim. That had to be why she was popular and I wasn't.

"What I'm getting at is that I had no sense of having my own personality. I was anorexic, at least for a time. The more aggressive boys, I learned later, used to draw lots to see who had to dance with me at dance classes in the gym. Another thing that happened, I now realize, was that to try to make it up to myself for being such a loser, which was the way I saw myself, I began to imagine another girl who lived inside my mind. She was the most beautiful girl in the class—a real princess. She was everything I wanted to be. And *that* was the woman who brazenly showed her genitals that day in session. Now, let me tell you what all this has to do with your wanting to transfer me. I'd appreciate that."

She ground out her next words from between clenched teeth: "I've just decided that I don't want to be passed around anymore between men like my husband, you, and Mardoff who control me."

We finished the session, leaving the matter of her transfer up in the air, but I knew our relationship would never be the same again. I felt I had to ensure my own survival. On the one hand, I decided that Moira might have been a bit more charitable toward me. Though still disturbed, she had acquired enough mature judgement to understand—or so it seemed to me—that I was doing everything I could to help her, but if my career evaporated her chances for full recovery would be postponed and perhaps ended.

On the other hand I saw how similar Moira and I were. Having undergone harrowing childhoods, we had both concluded that self-survival came above all else. It was hard for us, as adults, to truly trust. Our drive was to avoid reliving the pain of our early lives. Moira did it through repression, I by trying to control everything around me. I believed that every moment counted and had to be utilized fully; she had the conviction that no moment mattered.

That evening I received in the mail an offer from Wilson. I was thrilled and excited. My first paid position in psychotherapy! For a moment I was tempted to cut my ties to the clinic, take the new job, and see Moira when and how I pleased. However, I knew that wouldn't be wise. I needed Mardoff's signature to obtain continuing insurance from the police department to pay for Moira's treatment, and it had occurred to me that if I treated Moira without charging her I could offer Mardoff money from the insurance. That might make him easier to deal with all around.

I awoke the next morning feeling the world was at my feet. I was due to meet with Dr. Babcock, my new supervisor at 10:00 A.M.

I hurried over to Wilson. As I approached and entered the building, feeling more confident this time than when I had first visited for my application interview, I was struck again by the quiet beauty of the neighborhood and the venerable quaintness of the turn-of-the-century buildings that had once housed the very rich. The entrance to Wilson itself was graced with hand-carved wooden doorways and an old wrought-iron railing down which the kids slid.

As I approached Dr. Babcock's office, I was greeted by Dolly, who, I learned, was female administrator of Wilson. Fixing me with an imperious eye, she pointed to Babcock's door and declared, "Go to it, white boy! He's awaiting your esteemed professional presence." As she said that, I noted several black teenagers sitting nearby paying attention to what was happening. I realized that they were waiting to see how I would answer Dolly, and would measure me by my reply. I'd have to come up with something pretty sharp. Staring back at Dolly, I flipped my right hand in the air in a careless gesture and said, "I'd sho' appreciate y'all tellin' me where I can find the man, honey!" She and the boys roared with laughter. The boys slapped each others' palms in a "gimme five" salute, and I was in!

Babcock's office looked like the waiting room of a cheap bordello—red, velvet-flocked wallpaper, red carpet, and a bar with a marble counter top. Offering me a glass of sherry, he motioned to me to sit in a large, velvet-piled chair. For a few moments I stared at his gray hair and pale, triangular face. Startled, I realized he looked a bit like Mardoff. However, his conservative, charcoal-grey suit lent him a strangely funereal air. In contrast to Mardoff's calm, deliberate demeanor, however, Babcock broadcast extreme anxiety. His thick hands were constantly in motion, straightening his tie compulsively, fiddling with objects on his desk. Most notable of all was a severe tic twitching at the outer corner of his left eye. Waxing and waning with the flow of his anxieties, it was disconcerting.

Shifting nervously in his chair, he asked me a lot of questions, mainly about my graduate school experience. He seemed disinterested in my clinic experience and my work with patients. Each time I tried to answer a question in some depth, his eye-twitch increased alarmingly. It was almost as though he were interviewing me for a position, rather than talking about a job for which I'd already been hired. Despite my efforts to control it, my eye began now and then to twitch in response to his twitching. I had to chuckle inwardly. Here we were, two professionals dedicated to fostering emotional health in others, punctuating our deliberations with lunatic blinking at each other.

After a time I broke into his questioning. "Could you give me some idea of what I will be doing as the school psychotherapist?" He seemed puzzled by my question. Had he been looking at someone else's resume? He made an uncomfortable start at describing the difficulty of working psychologically with what he termed the "hoodlums" at Wilson. I leaned forward—this was what I wanted to hear. After his brief start, though, he fell silent. He seemed to feel uncomfortable sitting with me. The silence stretched into minutes. What sort of a character was I dealing with here? I had asked him to tell me about my job—what was wrong with that? Somehow he seemed like a scared parent being harassed by an overly inquisitive child.

After a while, and with several energetic eye-twitches, he launched into a description of his participation in a nightly radio program popular at the time. "The program focuses on informing an educated layperson audience about psychological topics." Babcock kept referring to the high esteem the program's host felt for Babcock's expertise in the field of psychotherapy. As he elaborated on his unique importance in the world of therapy, an ego trip clearly designed to intimidate me, I wondered with a shudder if I would become like him if I worked at Wilson too long. Then another bell in my head: what he was saying sounded familiar!

Then I remembered. This buffoon was reciting to me, word for word, a talk he'd given more than once on the psychology radio program. Claude Brown had written a book called *Manchild in the Promised Land* describing his experiences at a school similar to Wilson. On the air, I had heard Babcock read excerpts from it and deliver the spiel he was now laying on me. I felt my stomach tighten with the same sort of aversion I had experienced with Mardoff's intransigencies.

I couldn't stand it. I broke in: "Dr. Babcock, can you give me an idea of when I'll start to work here?" Babcock's eye launched a series of mad leaps, signalling I should not have interrupted. I thought it important to appear not to notice his twitch, so I pressed on. "And who my supervisor will be?"

"I'm your supervisor," he replied icily. "At Wilson there is only one supervisor—me. All the rest are purely social work 'bonkies'."

I fought to keep my brain clear. "Bonkies?" What the hell was that? "Blinkies" I could understand, if he was talking about himself.

He harumphed and said, "I keep a schedule of seeing those little basta— . . . I mean clients, between one and three each afternoon. You can see me during the hours of five and seven."

Wait a minute. The kids were in school until three. And supervision, I had been told, happened during morning hours. What was he talking about?

"Are you on duty during the afternoon?" I asked.

"No, just the morning hours."

Feeling like Alice in Wonderland, I burst out, "Then how can you supervise from five to seven?"

Again he didn't answer.

For the moment, I gave up. I decided to sit quietly. After a few more minutes of silence he began to give me the first concrete guidelines about my job he'd volunteered.

"The important thing to remember is to discourage the kids getting overdependent on us. You know about father figure transference. Try to nip that in the bud. Teach them independence—that's what I'm after. Give them their medication and teach them independence."

I waited for more. Nothing. He glanced at his watch, "Do you have anything further you want to speak about?" I shook my head. With the end of our meeting in sight, he appeared vastly relieved. I said nothing, and he reached for his phone. He told whoever was on the other end of the line to give me my patient assignment and appropriate dosages of medication. Then he nodded as though our business was concluded. I left his office. As I walked away I heard him burst into a peal of wild laughter, as disturbing as anything I'd ever heard from a human being.

I roamed the building. The kids I encountered, walking the halls, playing in recreation rooms, seemed happy enough. However, I sensed their emotional scars. It seemed ironic that these young people, after receiving treatment at the upstate facility, should be on their way back to the squalid conditions that had contributed to their problems in the first place.

When I arrived at Dolly's desk, she winked at me, as though commiserating with what I'd just been through with Babcock. This signalled a camaraderie between us that I welcomed. She directed me to my next stop, the office of Janet Carter, the head social worker. She wasn't there, so I took a seat to wait for her.

I reviewed in my mind my interview with Babcock, which brought me to a dead standstill. The whole experience had been too bizarre to try to deal with it at this point. Time passed. No Janet. I'd been waiting twenty minutes wondering what I'd gotten myself into. I heard running and shouting in the hall.

I stood up and walked into the hall. Five lively youngsters rushed past me, one shouting at the rest: "You guys better watch out! Big Chuckie'll kick our asses!" Down the hall behind them strode Charles Hanson, the huge fellow I had met at my first interview.

He greeted me with a grin. "Hey, there! You the new therapist on my floor?"

"I guess so," I replied tentatively. "All I know at the moment is I've been hired to work here."

Protectively, he threw an arm around my shoulders. "Let's go down to my office. You can relax and we'll try to make some sense out of things for you." On the way to the office, we waded through kids of various sizes, mostly in their early teens, darting and jumping around us like monkeys. One wiry Puerto Rican boy tried to throw a rope he'd found somewhere around Chuckie's neck, cowboy style. The big man scooped the kid up, gave him a smack on the seat, set him down, and the boy ran off cackling with laughter. Another boy climbed on Chuck's back, arms around his neck, and rode pickaback for awhile. I could see that they loved him. He was strong, warm, and protective, but he brooked no nonsense.

Seated in his office, I poured out to him the weird story of my time with Babcock. He roared with laughter, then said, "Confidentially, Babcock isn't taken very seriously by the staff. The work of the agency gets done more in spite of Babcock than because of him." Then Janet arrived. She was a lively and attractive brunette in her late twenties. The three of us got down to the business of figuring out what my job would be. As our conversation moved along, it became clear that Janet was an important person at Wilson. She was down-to-earth and interested in finding practical ways to help the children. She was also cynically hardened to the world of delinquency, the court system, and the failure of professionals in the so-called helping disciplines to effectively treat the emotional problems of the poor.

Chuck suggested, "With these young people, go easy on the psychoanalytically oriented therapy in which you've been trained."

Janet broke in, "For sure."

The major approaches at Wilson were a combination of work that tried to identify problems in the family systems of the kids, group encounter techniques, and "milieu" therapy. "Milieu" therapy was used with family techniques and tried to create an environment in which the child could learn to deal with and control his impulsive and compulsive behavior. I was deeply impressed by Janet and Chuck's dedication to helping the young delinquents, so different from the attitudes of therapists and interns at the clinic, who seemed to promote dealing with their troubled clients only in terms of controlling them and getting them to adjust to their troubled surroundings.

After I left Chuck and Janet, I headed for the Battery Park waterfront at the south end of Manhattan.

I sat on a bench there reflecting peacefully. The visit to Wilson had drained me. I had strong doubts as to how well I could help these young people. What I had learned at the clinic would have to be left behind. This was a new ball game. As I gazed out at the harbor toward Ellis Island and the Statue of Liberty, bathed by late-afternoon sunshine, I recalled that my father had been an immigrant. How must he have felt, embarking on an adventure in this strange new country? I, too, was heading into unexplored territory and would have to find ways to cope with what I would find and learn to deal effectively with the tumultuous world of Wilson.

When I got back to the clinic I was met by good news.

The directors had granted me an extension of two to three months to handle the termination of my current patients. I was also given a part-time job at the clinic with a caseload of six new patients, or clients, as we were to call them. One stipulation for my taking the part-time job was that the people at Wilson approve the arrangement, and I was told that they had already done so.

I felt elated. It was only a month since I'd gotten the letter announcing my being put on probation. At that point I'd feared that my career as a psychologist was about to end before it had begun. Now I'd managed to change things for the better, and even improve them a little. Best of all, I had breathing space to work toward transferring Moira to my private practice.

As always, though, I had to move cautiously with Moira. She had been very angry at the prospect of being transferred. She'd gotten a lot stronger emotionally but was still extremely disturbed. I had to make sure she could hold together during her temporary transfer to a new therapist before I could treat her again.

I also had to notify my other patients about my taking the position at Wilson, and I could not discuss with them the possibility of transferring to me. Any of my patients might, of course, raise the possibility themselves. That would be permissible, but it had to be their idea.

Moreover, I had to brace myself to hold down two jobs in psychotherapy, one full time and one part time. My own private practice must be initiated, my doctoral work pursued. I'd been encouraged by the clinic's cooperation with me, though. For the first time in months I faced the future with a buoyant heart.

NINETEEN

Transfer and Transference

My first assignment at Wilson was to treat a group of boys ranging in age from seven to fourteen. And quite a group they were.

Five were Puerto Ricans, six were Afro-Americans and one was a white child named Lionel. The Puerto Ricans were led by Angel, a powerfully built psychopathic teenager who was suspected of causing another boy's drowning at the upstate treatment facility just before he was transferred to Wilson. Angel radiated rage and violence; none of the other kids dared challenge him. Second to Angel in command over the Hispanics was Hector. Though slight of build and mild-mannered, Hector wielded power by acting as lieutenant to toughies like Angel.

Hector had a fascination for fire, and when he didn't get his way or was otherwise upset he now and then tried to set Wilson ablaze. To try to keep this urge in Hector under control, Babcock had had him heavily dosed with Thorazine. As a result, the boy walked around much of the time half asleep. The other three Puerto Rican boys were shy, lost youngsters who had no idea what they were doing at Wilson. They had been sent there by the courts because their families had come apart.

The black children in my group were similarly lost and

confused, except for Hermit and Jasslow, two youngsters who maintained a bizarre relationship that ultimately helped me solve a major riddle in my work with Moira.

I fell in love with Hermit from the moment I saw him staring through the door of Chuck's office. His dark eyes were sparkling and penetrating; his body was frail and about the size of an eight-year-old's, though he was thirteen. His skin was a deep, lustrous coal black, and his year-round garb, whatever the weather, was a white T-shirt and worn jeans. His thumb rarely left his mouth. I sometimes got the impression that he felt he might vanish if his pacifier left its lodging.

Jasslow I found unappealing. Tending toward schizophrenia, he was mentally retarded and tremendously strong, often hurting other children without meaning to. He was being kept at Wilson so that he wouldn't have to be placed in a state institution, where the care he would receive would be substandard at best.

Jasslow's only friend at Wilson was Hermit. They had arrived together five years before at the age of eight and had been comrades ever since. They watched out for each other, and in this way compensated somewhat for the deep abandonment fears they both shared—fears many times assailing kids from deprived backgrounds. Freud once talked of what he called his "most significant relationship"—that with a male cousin. Freud was three at the time. The cousin was stronger and older than little Sigmund, who benefited both by closeness with this relative and by the strength he himself had to develop to hold his own in the comradeship. Hermit and Jasslow reminded me of Freud's experience. Hermit was the weaker of the two, but he had the fortitude to hold his own in the face of Jasslow's greater physical strength. Coping with Jasslow could prepare Hermit for the rigors of life.

As I got more deeply acquainted with Jasslow and Hermit, their connection suddenly became significant to my work with Moira. She and I had been talking about her possible transfer to a new psychotherapist. Since her declaration to me that she would not accept a transfer, based on her decision not to let men push her around, she had softened her stand. She was now willing to discuss the possibility. As she did so, she revived childhood memories of her relationship to her schizophrenic brother, Ray. And although I realized I might have been reading into it more than was there, it struck me that Moira and her brother's connection was uncannily similar to that of Jasslow and Hermit. It was based on symbioses in the family constellation. Moira, in Hermit's role, sought protection by making an ally of Ray, who was stronger physically than she was. Jasslow and Ray, though powerful physically, were emotionally stunted and needed someone strong psychologically to nurture them on a "feeling" level. To assure this emotional shield for themselves they bartered their brute strength. I decided to describe the two boys' relationship to Moira at our next session and ask her whether she thought there was a likeness to her relationship with her brother.

When we met, I cautiously felt my way toward the question. "How are you currently feeling about transferring to a new therapist?"

"Depressed and repulsed," Moira responded.

"Why?" I asked.

"Do you really care?" she shot back. "It strikes me that my feelings are irrelevant in the transfer, as they were from the beginning. I told you I wasn't going to be pushed around by men anymore, and I meant it. Nevertheless, I have to be realistic. To start with, I thought of registering some kind of formal complaint to the clinic administration, but what good would it do? So I've decided to go along with a transfer, for now. For one thing, I am rather curious about what it would be like to work with a new therapist. But I'm still not sure about switching back to you once you're in your private practice." She said, irritation plain in her voice, "If I don't like the new therapist, I might consider it. That's all I want to say right now."

I then described Jasslow, Hermit, and their relationship, and I asked Moira if she saw any similarities to the bond between her and her brother.

Moira ran her fingers through her long hair and leaned her head back against the chair. "Well, I'll start with some memories I've had recently of Ray. Until we started to talk about him in session I didn't remember much about him when we were kids. But now a lot is coming back. These memories were before my sexual encounters with my father and my uncle. By the time Ray was three he was amazingly strong and aggressive for his age. I was five, and kids were starting to pick on me. I realized I could use him to defend me—he was tough. So we made a pact: he would defend me if I was attacked, and in return I would let him hug me, and I would hug him, when he felt lonely or needed to be embraced. It worked out fine. He really clobbered the kids bothering me and I gave him affection. It was weird to have a defender I would rock to sleep at night. So I guess we were like Hermit and Jasslow."

"Your babyhood and childhood were complex and horrifying," I said. "To start with, you were not given minimum basic care as a child. Then you were sexually molested, a horrendous and frightening experience."

"I'm really not sure just what happened and what I imagine, and I hate the uncertainty. It drives me nuts." Moira's voice shook.

We were both shaken and needed a respite. I took a deep breath and tried to steer her to another subject. "By the way, Moira, you haven't told me about your job or social activities recently."

"I appreciate you asking," she coolly replied, "but I don't have much time left with you and I want to use the time as I see fit. Changing to a new therapist isn't helping my confidence; I'm still shaky and need all the help I can get. I'd rather work on the fact that I'm afraid I'll go back to splitting off into those other people."

"I see what you mean. Now, I still want to explore the matter of you and your brother maintaining a protective relationship with each other. But let's work on what *you* want to work on," I said, realizing we both had to deal with the emotional intensity of her real needs. "To start with, you mentioned that memories are coming back to you that you had suppressed for a long time?"

Moira grimaced. "Yeah, and they're no fun. Tough to talk about. I was lonely as a child, but what I'm realizing is that when I first came to you I hardly ever thought about sex. I couldn't imagine my body being pleasurable to me. But as we worked, sexual sensations gradually returned to me. So I certainly had sexual feelings as a child that I must have repressed. But my memories, as they emerged in a feeling way, revolved only around my father, my uncle, and my brother. Now I'm wondering if none of it happened in reality at all—they were all the wish-fulfillment fantasies of a desperately deprived child."

I mused for a minute or two. I didn't want to cut off the flow of her mental questings, but at this point the evidence was overwhelming that her uncle and father did molest her. I thought it important that she not lose sight of that fact. Our real job lay in separating fantasy from what really happened. As memories of sexual abuse come to consciousness, many people want to believe they are all fantasy; they fear that if it develops that the abuse actually happened, their relationships with the new people in their lives will be threatened and disrupted. Hence, it's simpler to deny, repress, or call the whole thing an imagining.

To start the untangling, I proceeded cautiously. "Let's back up a moment, Moira. I want to remind you of how those memories started to first come up in you. They rose up only after a lot of work. What's important is that from the first moment you got in touch with them they caused confusion in you as to what was real and what was imagined. If you had just been making them up, in a histrionic and seductive way, to get attention and sympathy from me, as some patients do with their shrinks, you wouldn't have been confused about them. You'd have known that they were imaginary but that you'd built them up to make them seem as real as possible.

"I've become convinced that you were sexually abused. It really happened. I decided that only after we had dealt with a couple of complicated issues. Here's how the issues unfolded, and how I came to my conclusion: To start with, I know that Mardoff feels your behaviors and your memories are all hysterical imaginings. However, when I worked on how your fantasies and fragmentations had developed, I began to suspect that Mardoff and I were wrong. I'm still not sure how your fantasies before the age of eight or nine resulted in the formation of separate personalities to defend you. We still have to talk that out. Nevertheless, I began to get important clues about you when we achieved a fusion of two of the personalities—Marcia and Moira. Remember how you as Marcia went to the hotel, and at that point sexual memories came out in Moira, memories that until then only the Marcia part of you had been able to tolerate. And it was after that cross-connection that you started to have other memories of abuse—as Moira. A merging of personalities was happening. And then I saw how wrong Mardoff had been. You see, if you had been a hysteric you would not have remembered the assaults in the same way. Even conscious sexual abuse memories are not orchestrated that way in a hysterical personality. So I had my answer. You were a multiple personality and molestation had actually occurred. Your memories are true—you were abused."

Frowning, Moira mulled over what I was saying.

"Some children are so neglected," I went on, "that they do not get the hugging and love that is absolutely necessary for babies if they are to develop in a healthy manner physically and emotionally. If a baby senses that he or she is not getting this nurturing, a deep craving develops for it through the child's whole body. For you this need to be touched lovingly was in fantasy during your babyhood and early childhood, but it set the stage for the rapes. The actual touching started with your brother. Later your father and uncle touched you. At first it was probably innocuously, because they appear to have been gentle men basically. Your hungry body and soul were deeply gratified by that contact. So you must have been shocked when the touching became rape."

Moira burst into wracking sobs. After awhile the tears lessened and she spoke softly, saying, "After my brother left I had no one to hold and be close to. Why did he have to leave?" she moaned quietly. "Why did he have to roam the streets as a crazy person rather than remaining?"

"It was based on no logic or common sense, Moira," I pointed out. "His illness came about from a combination of a biochemical deficiency and emotional neglect in his formative years. I'm sure that when you and he broke off your relationship he had a desperate need for closeness, but he was so sick he could not manage to turn to anyone else."

I continued, "You've described how lonely your brother's adolescence was—it had to have been as lonely as yours. Schizophrenia usually occurs in an individual after he or she has endured a lonely adolescence. A teenager with a tendency toward schizophrenia usually doesn't have adequate social skills. What with the illness coming on, and his social ineptitude, he is forced to turn in upon himself—to a terrifying world of paranoid delusions and hallucinations. Terrifying as they are, though, they have been created by him to protect himself against the threat of the world of reality, which seems even worse to him than his inner chaos. Fortunately you were not psychotic. Ray fled into psychosis and you ran into the arms of dissociated people."

Moira heaved a deep sigh, cleared her throat, blew her nose, and gazed despondently into the distance. "I'm not sure I understand everything you're saying, but it makes sense."

She crumpled in her chair and continued her sad gaze into the distance.

I was lost in thought, too, thinking of Moira. In my early view of her, I thought the harshness of her family and fanaticism helped her repress the swirling passionate feelings inside her. After the rapes actually happened, she developed a new strategy to protect herself. She psychologically fragmented into different personalities—escaping both the horrors of recognizing she had been raped and the disapproval of her harsh guilt feelings.

Those were the interpretations of Moira's illness that I had been making. Now I was beginning to question those assumptions.

The first step in this reassessment had to do with taking a new look at her childhood sexual fantasies from a much broader standpoint.

As Moira and I sat in silence for a few moments before the end of the session, I was tempted for a moment to start to talk to her about my changing thinking. I decided not to tell her about them but to try them out when next we met.

At our next session I got right to work, trying to apply my new interpretation of the development of her sickness. I was hellbent on curing her before she moved to a new therapist. I had put the final touches, at least for now, on what I believed was a more accurate theory to explain her illness. I was so eager, in my egotistical way, to show off what I had come up with that I plunged right in at the start of the session before she had a chance to say anything.

"Moira, I've come up with a revised way for us to look at your problems. Here's how it goes: You started your fantasy life as a small child to try to defend yourself against your realization that you weren't getting any of the basic care and love you needed. You felt so passive during your first year of life because of this neglect that you were in a stage of what we call marasmus, or childhood autism, in which you totally retreated into yourself as a result of not getting love from external sources. Your earliest fantasies must have had to do with being fed and touched—which you weren't being, at least emotionally. And that was the time of life when, if a baby doesn't get basic 'feeling' nutrition, it leaves deep scars and wounds on its psyche. Even in adulthood you often behave like a woman who has never been fed or touched. You're always hungry, but you've been unable to find ways to get from your adult contacts the emotional attachments you need. That happened because since you got used to being deprived as a child you don't know how to get yourself nourished as an adult."

I continued, "Eventually you turned to your brother and expressed this need with him. He had been similarly deprived, and by taking care of him you got some nourishment for yourself. You focused all this feeling on your brother. Remember the way you wanted to hug and hold him when he was a baby in the crib? You became a servant to him and to other people and this fit with your intensifying religious fanaticism. Your role was perfectly suited to your family's needs. They zeroed right in on you, using you as an outlet for the sadistic urges that grew out of their economic frustrations.

"However, you also wanted to get away from that rotten family life—from those sick, nonloving, manipulative people. So you turned to peers at school. Befriending Marcia gave you a fantasized escape from drudgery and abuse at home. Connecting to Marcia and taking on the character of that British girl in the movie helped you to be assertive, to gain control over hopelessness. It also compensated for deep feelings of isolation and loneliness. You now had friends."

I knew all this was a lot for her to absorb, but I felt it important and went on, "Your early needs were not met, and so you didn't develop in a healthy way. By eight or nine you were starting prematurely to bloom sexually. You began consciously to think about people having sex, about yourself and sex. What was it all about? you wondered. Marcia, being accepting of her feelings, got you to think about what men and women did in bed. You started to get away from just experiencing sexual fantasies inside yourself and began to connect them to other people. You thought about penetration and fellatio, as Marcia had described them to you.

These thoughts were forbidden by your fanatical religious beliefs, but your mind dwelled on them anyway.

"The stage was set for fragmentation. Until then, your sexual fantasies were about other people such as your father. These didn't frighten you or upset you. However, when you were raped by your father and your uncle, you couldn't handle it. Your guilt was overwhelming. Now, you had a gift for fantasy, and in this unbearable situation you put it to work for you. You created other people, Marcia and the British girl, to take your place in the sexual attacks. In the desperate inner world you created, it was they, not you, who had had those rape experiences. What a tremendous relief that must have been. Fragmenting became your best friend!

"Usually a multiple disorder doesn't develop as yours did—accompanied by all that guilt and fantasy. What customarily happens is that the person is sexually brutalized early in childhood and begins fragmenting by age five."

I paused and noted how intently Moira was listening. "Moira," I said gently, "I don't think your uncle and father were outright pedophiles. They were social misfits, inept in dealing with adult women. They were more comfortable with passive young girls."

"What do you mean by 'pedophile'?" Moira asked.

"Adults who are sexually attracted to young children," I explained.

"Oh my God," Moira burst out. "Is that what happened?" For the first time she was letting herself see that she had been too fragile and too young to resist the abuses of her father and uncle. With a gasp of revulsion, she exclaimed, "I was just a lonely child and they abused me. They didn't care about its effect on me, they just took advantage of me for their own needs."

"Yes, that's what happened. They sensed your guilt would not allow you to report the molestations. You might have gotten some relief telling what happened, but the fact that the nuns and priests at school suggested that suffering was ennobling stopped you from speaking out. All you could do was create a young woman who, unlike yourself, was powerful and aggressive. That rageful British girl became part of you."

"Why didn't my father and uncle pick on my older sister Janice or some of the old maid relatives I had? There were plenty of lonely women available when I was growing up."

"They knew better than to try anything with those people. Those others may have been lonely, but they were not as vulnerable or guilt-ridden as you. Abusers know their victims, and they know who not to attempt sexual contact with. Other girls or young women would have reported them instantly.

"In reality, Moira, no one loved you. You were just exploited and tossed aside. To somehow find a way to make the hurt and pain bearable and understandable, you turned to religious fanaticism. The applicable term is *masochism*, the act of interpreting painful experiences as pleasurable. In this case you saw the possibility of your sinful self being redeemed by becoming a martyr, denying yourself and serving others. And you freed Moira from guilty knowledge that she had been raped. You did it by making your first fragmentation—it became Marcia who had gone through all that, not Moira!"

Our session was over. We were both frustrated by not having time for further exploration. My main concern was to keep following this line of thought and not let Moira decide to block it out because of its painful nature.

I started right in again at the next session.

"When you were first sexually persecuted you saw the experience as a dream. Gradually it crept into your preconscious that you were being violated, and it created all sorts of problems. You had to defend yourself, and gradually you sought ways to do it. I've discovered that the damaged psyche is like an onion, with many layers, each covering and protecting the next. As I peel away one layer, a deeper one exposes itself, revealing additional information all tucked away and protected by the layers above. It was not just that you were sexually abused which shocked you and caused you to fragment. It was more like layers and layers of abuse heaped on until little was left of the original child Moira. As the years went by you relied on dissociation and fragmentation to help you cope with the terrible realities of your life.

"At this point, Moira, I believe the abuse persisted into your adolescence. It probably only stopped when they became frightened that you might finally report them.

"I know this all sounds startling, but it happens a lot. Rape victims often completely suppress any memory of the events surrounding what happened to them. In a number of cases women under hypnosis report having to psychologically disconnect from their bodies during rape to avoid becoming insane. Your creation of other people helped you prevent insanity—and it was the only control you could exercise over your life."

The emotional impact of my words made us both silent. We stared at each other. I could sense that Moira had something more on her mind. As we closed the session and walked to the door, she looked to be in deep thought. I asked gently, "What are you thinking about?"

As she looked up I saw there were tears in her eyes. "I was realizing that we won't be meeting much longer. And I'm wondering how I could ever tell a new therapist all this." I patted her back sympathetically but could say no more.

TWENTY

Further Problems

The session had taken a heavy toll on me as well as Moira. That evening at home, after resting for a while, I wrote an evaluation for my last clinical summary on Moira. In it I broadened the scope of my observations, widening my view from Moira as an individual to human beings in general.

> Human beings have always relied on complicated constructs to deal with unconscious fears of their surrounding environment—surroundings they were often helpless to control. Originally, the constructs consisted of symbols and rituals designed to ward off threats. As knowledge and awareness grew, the constructs became more complex and sophisticated. Eventually, humans grew to understand that internal fears in their unconscious that they were largely unaware of were creating the tensions that caused them to develop the constructs in the first place. To reassure themselves in the face of their aloneness in a threatening universe they produced theories about how the world was created and what the role of humans in that world should be.
>
> As time passed, two drives emerged in humans as they tried to adapt to the bewildering experience of existence. The first was to preserve psychological stability, and they developed the ability to repress, to push into forgetfulness, any realities that threatened their safety and security. The second drive, opposed to the first, was to try to uncover the

truth of things. One of these searches for truth was about ourselves—who were we, what were we, in our inner and outer natures? One of Freud's great contributions was to perceive how tumultuous were our inner struggles. By this I mean that after we had evolved rules for behavior within our families and within our social groups, any urge in us to disobey these rules made us feel we were in danger, so, as I say, we repressed those urges. An important issue of this sort would have been the taboo against having sexual intercourse with a member of one's immediate blood-related family—incest. And yet, children feel sensual attractions to both parents from the moment they are born. To repress these urges and rechannel them toward healthy development is only one of the many kinds of feelings human beings must deal with one way or another, healthily or in a disturbed way. And during the lifelong struggle to deal with, reconcile, and adjust these feelings, damage and conflict may occur in peoples' psyches.

Freud believed that many of these conflicts were impossible to resolve and could only be handled through understanding them as fully as possible. Freud termed two opposing central drives Eros (a Greek god of love) and Thanatos (from the Greek meaning the instinctual desire for death). He feared that Thanatos would eventually dominate our overall motivations.

At the present, I believe that this sums up what Moira and I are dealing with—her conflict, as she grows healthier, between experiencing more and more of her life force and her pull toward repression and pathology.

After my session today I saw that Moira's personal truth must win out to insure her psychic survival. The illusion of safety she derived from fragmenting must be shattered or she will not survive emotionally. Illusion, which had once been her good friend, had now become her enemy. As she grew toward emotional health and became stronger, her fragmenting, which had once helped her survive, was becoming unnecessary. She was now able to face the terrible truth about her childhood directly, without disguising it from herself in any way. And far from being too painful to bear, she found facing the truth a relief. This, of course, was in part because expressing or repressing the truth takes energy, and behind the hiding devices the truth still remains, exerting a disturbing and troubling effect on the entire organism. Strip away the concealing contrivances, however, and the energy needed to hold them in place is released and the person is blessed by a sense of well-being, despite the horror of the truth that has been exposed.

Moira must contact the child she was before she set up her desperate defenses—the deprived child who lay inside her, helpless and unattended. She must find this child, become acquainted with it, love it, and embrace it. In this way she will give the love to the child in her that it should have been given from her parents. She will in a sense become her own parent, loving the child that she was, so that both may find health at last.

I strongly urge Moira's new therapist to continue the work of fusion with this unusual woman. She needs to face the truth of being a multiple personality even if it means being alone—although healthy and self-supportive emotionally—for the remainder of her life.

I presented this evaluation to Mardoff at our next supervisory meeting. "I am dubious about the value of her transferring at this point to a new therapist," I said. Mardoff didn't comment on my evaluation. He appeared to be indulging a misbehaving youngster. I saw that he was glad I wasn't resisting Moira's being transferred. However, I could not let go the subject of Moira. So involved with her was I that I continued talking about her, pointing out this and that about her problems and the progress she had made.

Mardoff abruptly changed the course of the conversation. "I want to tell you," he said, "that I could help you make the transition from the clinic to full professional employment." Again, my heart sank as I realized the total lack of his genuine interest in Moira and her plight. Once more I bit my words back and said nothing.

He continued glorifying his aid to me, declaring, "Not only that, but you can continue to work with your group, and I am arranging for a higher salary for your part-time job with the clinic than you might normally expect at this stage of your experience." Gratifying as this news was to me, I felt a tinge of uneasiness. What was going on?

I sat back and studied him. As I did so my gut pushed uncomfortably against my belt. I was reminded that two full years of training, study, and working with Moira and the group were starting to tell on me. The work at Wilson was proving more stressful than I had expected, and I was eating too much of their institutional food that included a lot of carbohydrates. I had gained thirty-five pounds in four months at Wilson. My body, normally strong, active, and healthy, felt fatigued and aching. I wondered if my physical situation reflected an underlying depression, perhaps at the unremitting effort to guide Moira toward mental health.

As though he sensed what was on my mind, Mardoff interrupted himself to point out that I "looked terrible." Asking about my health, he remarked on my weight gain and aroused near hysterics in me by inquiring, "I hope I haven't said anything to upset you."

"Just working too hard," I said through gritted teeth. "My full-time job is more demanding than I thought it would be, and I haven't even started my thesis."

He frowned. "It seems to me more than that. What's going on with you? You seem despairing."

"I'm very worried about Moira," I confessed. "Would it be appropriate for me to meet the new therapist assigned to her? I'd like to tell him my experiences with her; it might help."

A jovial roar of laughter. Then he said, "You've already met him, my boy! He's sitting right in front of you!"

It was as though someone had punched me in the stomach and taken my breath away. I couldn't utter a word, and in fact had to force myself to listen to what he had to say next.

"In view of the immense problems in her case," he continued, "I felt I wanted to get the best psychotherapist available, which happens to be me. You've become quite competent yourself, but, as I've said to you, you haven't been able to avoid falling for her histrionics. She needs someone who can deal with her constant manipulations and who can make sure her medication is correct. It has to be me, because of my experience and because I've been supervising you. I'll work with our attending psychiatrist. How do you feel about this decision?"

I didn't answer. Mardoff continued, toying with me. "My knowing what's going on with her could also prevent both of you from arranging to transfer her to your private practice—you know the rule against that."

Rage erupted in me. I had to fight desperately to keep from leaping on him and choking him. Words continued to flow from his mouth. All I was aware of was the ticking of the office clock on the wall and the thumping of my heart. I felt that, like Moira, I was splitting apart. One part felt numb; the other, capable of thought, decided that he must have guessed somehow that I was planning to transfer Moira to myself, and that this arrangement was to punish me for the plan.

Then, as suddenly as it had assailed me, my agitation departed. I felt eerily calm and in control. "I can't think of a better therapist," I said duplicitously.

"I'm glad you're taking it this well," Mardoff responded, surprised.

There followed one of those inane conversations that seem to intrude into life's most calamitous episodes. We began to compliment each other on our prowess as therapists. Through the stream of phony irrelevancies, however, a deeper part of me felt I had hit bottom. I was impotent. I could afford to face the truth, because I had nothing to lose. He had all the power. He had known all along that he was going to transfer Moira to his caseload. For some reason he needed this helpless woman in his life.

At this point I retraced my thinking and questioned myself: were my speculations about Mardoff and Moira correct, or was I just projecting them out of my disturbed feelings about my own mother? Some intuition told me I was correct. I decided firmly I would not let this man engage me in an oedipal battle over poor, beleaguered Moira. She needed help, not manipulation. Somehow I had to make sure she got it.

I took another tack. In a confidential, friendly tone, I said to Mardoff, "Although you haven't mentioned it, I sense we share a lot of frustration about our marriages. Rumor has it that yours is breaking up."

He flushed with anger. "Watch what you're saying," he barked. "Remember, officially you're still a student and I can give you a negative evaluation and hold up your degree. Remember what I told you before. Don't get involved in my personal life—it's none of your business!"

"I'm not trying to upset you," I said in a tone of voice that suggested I was trying to do just that. "I just want to become more friendly with you. Be more open with my colleague and benefactor," I said.

Mardoff inclined his head. "Let's stick to the matter of transferring Moira. Is there any reason you feel it should not happen shortly? Because that's what I've decided to do."

"Why ask me? You've got it all sewn up. I'd rather get back to our marital difficulties." A tingle at the base of my spine warned, be careful! Nevertheless I couldn't stop. "We're old buddies, right? Isn't it true you've been having problems in your sex life with your wife and that you've been seeing Moira on the sly? How 'bout some of the juicy details?"

Jerking to his feet in a rage, Mardoff stalked out. I went limp. I hauled myself to my feet and headed for the rest room.

The mirror there showed me an unwelcome sight. My face was sallow and unhealthy looking. Look at all that extra weight! I was getting to be a tub! And my outlook left a lot to be desired. For one thing, I was a workaholic; I'd known that for a long time. The more devoured by my work I was, the better. And my new job at Wilson was more difficult than I expected. In addition, knowing what Moira would face with Mardoff also made me despondent.

Dragging on a cigarette, I sat slumped on a toilet seat, tears running down my cheeks. After a while I hauled myself up for one more discouraging look in the mirror. My efforts to become a psychologist were clearly exacting a terrible price—I looked far older then I was. My shoulders were slumped in a curiously familiar way. My hairline was receding. Suddenly I saw that I had become my father. I was bent in the round-shouldered stance of the pushcart peddler! Every line of my body screamed, "Defeat!"

For the first time I acknowledged that I must have been more depressed by my father's death than I realized. I had not really mourned for him, but my red-blotched reflection in the mirror, so like his, brought home to me that these tears at last were for him as well as me. Perhaps the bitterness of my conflicts with Mardoff had triggered the deep feelings of rage I harbored toward my father for hurting my mother. That rage kept me from grief at his death, but now that Moira was threatened by Mardoff in the same way my mother was harmed by my father, both my rage and grief were emerging.

Although I had helped Moira a great deal and had enabled her to begin helping herself, I promised myself I would do more to bring what Mardoff was doing to Moira's attention and help her free herself of his evil influence that could impede her progress toward wholeness.

TWENTY-ONE

Warning Signs

In late November I officially ended my work at the clinic. Mardoff had told me that he was going to inform each of my patients by letter that I had completed my internship. Moira's letter would give her the news that she was to transfer to him. I was sitting on my customary anger at Mardoff but was exercising restraint. A hassle with him now could not only lose me my part-time job at the clinic and a final recommendation but, most importantly, jeopardize Moira's transferring to me.

Before leaving for my position at Wilson I didn't tell Moira that Mardoff would be her interim therapist. Though I hoped for the best—that under his treatment she would not regress or otherwise suffer a reversal of the progress she had made—I was well aware that to tell her who she was being transferred to could be emotionally explosive. She had softened her conviction about being "used" by men, but I had no way of knowing what might arouse this resistance again. If it occurred, that might move Moira to end her therapy, as she had once threatened to do. It seemed more comfortable during our final meetings to talk only about her eventual transfer to me. We worked out an agreement to start the transfer in April—five months after my work at the clinic officially ended. I chose five months because it seemed to me that length would absolve me of ethical and legal responsibilities to the clinic. Although she joined me in making these plans, Moira appeared distracted, as though she would rather leave the whole matter to me, and she didn't ask me to whom she was being transferred, nor very much else. I suspected that she knew I was covering up something.

A few days later I met with my old group, the patients who had been with Marcuse and me during our dramatic country marathon. My part-time job would be to work with the new therapist who had been assigned to them. I was startled to meet her at the meeting. Her name was Helen Demar. I had recommended Marcuse for the job, since he had worked with us, but Mardoff had ignored my suggestion and appointed Helen, a pudgy redhead with little experience. I had gathered from him that I was to assume a subordinate, supportive role with this therapist. As the group, Helen, and I got to know each other during an informal interchange, I wondered how Helen and I would work things out. To my surprise, none of the group asked about Moira, and I did not bring her up.

For the next two months my graduate work and my job at Wilson demanded almost all my time and most of my energy. To be paid at last a decent salary for giving therapy was gratifying. However, I soon learned that doing therapy at Wilson was quite different from my clinical experience. At the clinic I had worked with adults who, though neurotic, could function normally and were emotionally independent. The kids at Wilson, however, were in far worse shape: they suffered from serious mental disturbances inflicted on them as babies and young children by abusive backgrounds. Often psychotic or sociopathic, they didn't respond to traditional therapies. I became caught up in a struggle to find effective approaches to their difficult problems. I felt so strongly about this that work at the clinic with my old marathon group and other patients took a backseat. As the weeks went by I left more and more of the responsibility for my old patients to Helen. Although I had been worried about her initially, she proved competent, and I helped her as best I could.

Despite my hectic schedule Moira was often on my mind. During supervisory meetings with Mardoff I quizzed him repeatedly about how she was doing. By turns cantankerous and evasive, he insisted vaguely that she was doing well. I wasn't satisfied with what he told me and found relief in fantasizing that soon I would be able to take her back under my wing again. With that in mind, I stopped asking him about her. Why arouse his suspicions, especially when he wasn't telling me much anyway?

The Ph.D. program at my new university was turning out to be the academic haven of which I had dreamed. The excellent faculty held diverse theoretical positions about psychotherapy that allowed me exposure to a wide range of treatment modalities. I found much to apply to my challenges at Wilson. Again it was brought home to me that psychoanalytic approaches to the Wilson kids were fruitless, so I instituted group therapy and cognitive or behavioral treatments. These, unfortunately, appeared initially to provide little help for my charges, but the experience helped me gain self-confidence and know-how. Meanwhile I continued trying to develop effective treatment methods for them.

Doctoral candidates at my new school were allowed complete freedom in developing their dissertation proposals. Theoretical and experimental proposals were acceptable. Diversity in interpretation was encouraged as well as a recognition that not much genuine validation had occurred of the major assumptions and hypotheses of psychiatry and psychology in general.

The central criterion at the university was pragmatic: Does it work? Treatments were sought that might really help people. Psychoanalytic approaches were valued—but only if it could be shown that they had done some good. By and large, psychoanalysis was confined to obsessive-compulsive disorders and sexual problems.

I found this climate nourishing and gratifying. My early training had aroused in me rebellious convictions against hidebound, rigid approaches. "We've always done things this way; therefore, we must continue to do so." Even if these avenues were demonstrably valueless, I felt that only through flexible grappling with the challenges of existence had human beings gained progress. Encouraged by my new training, I began to think of myself not as a "psychoanalyst" but rather as an eclectic psychotherapist—making my guiding principle the pursuit of whatever genuinely helped patients. My treatment motto became: If at first you don't succeed, try something else!

On arriving at Wilson, I had noted that the kids all suffered short attention spans. They could concentrate on work for about ten minutes at most, then their attention hopped like a fruit fly in other directions. They also suffered language and learning disabilities.

As I got to know them better, I realized that psychoanalytical techniques were hilariously irrelevant for these youngsters. Oedipus complex? Repressed sexuality? Rigid superegos? Forget it! Most of these kids had no idea where their next mouthful of food was coming from. They usually had little connection to their parents, many of whom were either high on drugs or indifferent to their children. Most were raised by brothers, sisters, grandparents, or other relatives. At that point if Dr. Freud had materialized on a Harlem street he would have peered at a world as unlike his Vienna as a lunar landscape. This rough and ready contact with problems for which I was totally unprepared, however, shaped my skills.

My days at Wilson settled into a routine. Arriving at ten in the morning, I supervised the kids who hadn't made it to the local school that day. Part of reintroducing them to the community and, with good fortune, to their homes was getting them to attend the neighborhood school. Most of them hated school. They sensed they were unwelcome both to classmates and to teachers. Many Wilson kids could not read because of their poor schooling and were not able to keep up in a structured learning environment. Not surprisingly, their absence rate was high, and I learned that the school administration couldn't have cared less. So I just conducted therapy as best I could during school hours for the kids who had not attended that day.

Another problem was that those kids who neither showed up at school nor stayed at Wilson roamed the neighborhood, thieving, smoking pot, now and then mugging a senior citizen. The school would phone us to report their truancy, but the school people didn't particularly care about them. We got reports from the kids of brutal treatment by police of those who were caught behaving lawlessly. I had no way to validate these reports—the police never contacted us on those matters. When the truants returned later in the day, some efforts were made to punish them. Usually they were confined to their rooms for the day, but keeping them there became guerrilla warfare.

Many of the children, particularly those who stuck close to Wilson rather than go to school or range the streets, expressed deep fear of the world around us. This was not surprising, since they had probably been reared by abusive, disturbed parents. Many had seen the police beating their parents during drug raids. How could they have avoided concluding that they lived in threatening surroundings?

Since conventional therapies didn't help my young people, I developed the practice of just listening to them talk about their lives and now and then drawing them out with tactful questions. This way of being together worked well with the children who had skipped school and were otherwise unoccupied during the school day. The stories they told me were often terrible and tragic, but at times amusing and flavorfully human. As I tuned into the kids they became more verbal and open. They grew to trust the interest I took in them. I felt frustrated, though, that I could not help them more effectively. Even while I was most engrossed solving their disturbing problems I worried about what was happening to Moira.

Staff meetings at Wilson were held at noon each day. Their official purpose was to review and monitor the childrens' educational and therapeutic progress, map strategies for future work, and train newer staff members in advanced techniques of child therapy.

The approach at Wilson was termed "family system," meaning that the kids' disturbances were judged to have originated in their loveless, manipulative, emotionally chaotic homes. It was thought that if a caring, open, communicative environment could be created at Wilson, this new "family" might help the child grow healthier, stronger, and more able to deal effectively with life.

I soon discovered, however, that the stated purpose of the staff meetings and what they were really about were completely different. In short, they were a steam valve. Working with these disturbed kids was extremely demanding, and it was taken for granted that we needed outlets if we were to maintain our sanity. The staff meeting was a cauldron of feeling during which we redirected at each other our pent-up hostilities and other churning emotions.

A rising current of tension occurred when we gathered for the meetings each morning at eleven. Much of our nervousness had to do with anticipating outbursts and wondering who might be a focus for the group's venting. Babcock never attended these meetings. It seemed accepted that his sole function at Wilson was to dispense tranquilizing medication to the "acting out" children.

During the first staff meeting, perhaps because I was fresh game, I came under fire immediately—from the formidable Dolly. As I might have expected, she gave lectures about how valueless analytic techniques were for the kids. I was getting a little tired of that line of harassment, especially since I'd come to realize how true it was, but I realized I'd have to put up with it for awhile.

"Huh!" Dolly snarled as she played to a grinning audience. "I heard Obler stuffin' that analytical crap into these kids' heads the other day. He even tries it with the real crazies. Think that shit's gonna help? Forget it! Do we need one more whitey shrink in this shithole? I don't think so. The other madman gives 'em pills to shut 'em up. Obler here asks them did they wanna sleep with their mommies! They're making the kids worse with that crap."

The staff roared with laughter. When it died down I asked Dolly, "What other psychiatrist were you talking about, Dolly?"

Dolly rolled her eyes, "I wonder." Everyone, including me, burst into renewed laughter. Dolly couldn't mention Babcock's name, because he was her superior, but all, including me, knew of whom she spoke.

I soon began to think Dolly was one of the most memorable people I'd ever met. She had overcome the effects of a horribly abusive childhood and become a forceful, competent, humane adult. Hired as a secretary, she had so much natural intelligence that she required very little time to figure out what really went on at the agency, which was that the white administrators and the psychiatric staff were predominantly incompetents whose main concern was to protect their jobs. Dolly struck an understanding with them that she would not expose their incompetency. In return she became untitled house director, and she developed into a brilliant administrator.

Since the white administrators and psychiatrists were largely incompetent, the real work with the kids was done by the mostly non-white lower-echelon psychotherapy staff and service workers. In addition to applying their skills and knowledge in a dedicated way, their family and ethnic backgrounds, similar to the young peoples', helped them connect more productively to our delinquents. Under Dolly's regime, she and the effective staff member worked side-by-side with the bureaucrats. Dolly and her team developed at

Wilson one of the finest treatment programs for delinquents in the Northeast. As this came about, however, Dolly permitted the outside world and the board of directors to believe that the agency was run by the administration. One day I asked Dolly why she didn't expose the incompetence of those normally in charge, and she shot back immediately, "Who they gonna believe? Them college-degree white people or a fat, uneducated black lady like me?"

All of us who wanted to really help the kids respected and loved Dolly. We feared her power and honesty—no one wanted to be found wanting in their efforts to help the kids. I was frightened of her at first. However, bit by bit, she came to respect my skills as a psychotherapist. One day she declared to me that I was "the only sincere motherfucker with a higher degree" she had ever met. It was an accolade, and from then on we were comrades.

Dolly was the first strong black woman I had ever known. Although others like her have existed throughout history, in this country and elsewhere, strong black women became highly visible during the black struggles for equality in the United States. The civil rights movement, especially during the late sixties and seventies, reshaped many white people's image of blacks. Afterward 350-pound Dolly and her sisters, aggressive, provocative, and "taking shit from no one," went one step further.

On Moira's first visit to Wilson I pointed out to her Dolly's achievement at becoming an effective person in the face of overwhelming disadvantages. Just before I introduced them I whispered to Moira that under her intimidating facade Dolly was warm and sensitive. We enjoyed a chat during which Dolly seemed to take to Moira immediately. Alone with Moira later, I described to her how Dolly, though uneducated in the formal sense, understood more about people and life than any of us. Moira seemed deeply impressed. It wasn't hard to guess that she was speculating that she, too, could make of her life a version of Dolly's triumph.

Unfortunately, even at that promising moment, I also

began to realize, Moira was encountering storm clouds. The therapy, among other things she was undergoing at the hands of Dr. Mardoff, far from continuing her healing or even maintaining her at the level she and I had attained, was undermining her. Our carefully won gains were being reversed. Sickness was again overtaking her impaired spirit. My fears for her mounted.

As I continued to search for a way to help her, I grew accustomed to the punishing climate of the Wilson staff meetings and came to enjoy it. I even looked forward to it. I relished the verbal and emotional pummeling we gave each other. We were clearly sadomasochistic. One dealt out pain, one received pain—a fine way for human beings to behave —yet these batterings served the important purpose of relieving dammed-up emotions. Both we and our kids benefited; after "getting it all out" we felt better and worked better.

After each meeting I raced to the university for graduate seminars. Two afternoons a week, I was out at the Brooklyn clinic for supervision with Mardoff. Later in the day I met with my old group at the clinic and conducted three private sessions. On alternate days, after supervision with Mardoff, I raced back to Wilson to lead the group of kids who had returned from their wanderings through New York City. My day ended around nine o'clock after squeezing in—if possible—one or two private clients who had started to visit me at Wilson. I saw these patients in a locked room at the back of the house. The children had had dinner and bathed, and counselors were trying to calm them for sleep. Though the rooms were insulated with extra thick plasterboard, my patients and I, trying to focus productively on problems, had to endure hollering and scuffling of all sorts from counselors and kids, which raged until the kids had finally quieted down. It was a hell of a way to start my practice, but I could not pay for an office of my own.

The days were long and arduous. However, my absorption in the ins and outs of the human psyche exhilarated me, and I tumbled into bed each night feeling effective and satisfied. I grew aware that to work to exhaustion was a device used by others of the Wilson staff—it was the only way they could fall asleep after long days in a battle zone.

By February I was looking deeper into my motivations for becoming a psychologist. Why, I wondered, was I trying to help people? I'd assessed earlier in my training that a sizeable concern was to aid myself in overcoming my loneliness by becoming vitally involved with others. However, the brutally honest contact with staff and kids at Wilson made me take another long look at myself. I began to suspect that something else was going on. Had I chosen Wilson, in an unaware way, because what went on there wasn't unlike the calamitous doings in my own and Moira's childhood homes? Moira's relatives had abused each other, and particularly Moira, because they were impoverished and felt personally ineffective—not at all unlike the goings on at Wilson. The staff, while helping the children as much as they could, also hollered at them and disciplined them harshly at times. In this way, on a deep level, they could retain a sense of power in their own often uncertain existences. The kids raped and abused each other, because they had been abandoned and abused. My own childhood held strong similarities to these conditions.

While my reasons for coming to work at Wilson were obviously complicated and obscure, I had no doubt that my stressful relationship to Moira was somehow reflected in my experiences there. I realized that I might have elected to work at Wilson because I felt if I could understand that environment I might better comprehend what had transpired in Moira's sick childhood home.

In January I ran into Moira in the clinic lobby as she was waiting for her session with Mardoff. I hadn't seen her since November. We greeted each other warmly. She looked tired, she had lost weight, and I noted anxiety lines around her mouth and eyes. I was seized by an impulse to hug her; but Gail, the clinic receptionist, was seated nearby, and I knew she was aware that Mardoff would not approve of my doing so. Deciding to be formal, I shook hands with Moira and was dismayed to feel her hand trembling. Unsure of what to say, we just stared at each other.

I didn't want Gail or the other patients to hear what I wanted to tell Moira, so I wrote a note and put it on a table next to where she was sitting. In the note I suggested we resume therapy and asked her to call me at Wilson to talk about it. As she was reading it, Mardoff came out of his office. Moira thrust the note into her bag. As she did so a look of terror flashed into her eyes. I felt enraged. Why should his appearance have caused her such panic? I had a fantasy image of Moira kicking the bastard in the balls while I immobilized him with an armlock. As I gritted my teeth and endured my feelings, Mardoff glared at me disapprovingly. How dare I talk to his patient, his stare seemed to say. I glared back at him as Moira rose obediently and followed him into his office.

Although nothing was mentioned about the incident at my supervisory session with Mardoff later that afternoon, the atmosphere between us was tense. After seeing Moira's panicky expression, I had decided to find a way to transfer her to my care, professional consequences notwithstanding. But I had to confer with her first to make sure she was ready. As I sat there watching Mardoff I asked him how Moira was coming along. He brushed my question off with an evasive answer, then launched into a series of unreasonable criticisms of my work in group therapy. I let them stream in one ear and out the other. They were nonsense; he was obviously getting on my case as a reaction against the deeper issue of Moira. It lay between us like an unexploded bomb.

As the session moved to its close, I chastised myself inwardly for my lack of courage in pressing him harder about Moira. As her former therapist I had a perfect right to ask about the terror-stricken look I had seen in her face. It was not that I had to concern myself any more about reprisal from Mardoff. In times past I had to keep in mind that he could slow or halt the progress of my career. However, at this point, since I was being supervised fully by Babcock, Mardoff posed no threat to me either in my graduate program or with the state board that licensed psychologists. Furthermore, I had decided to sever all connections with the Brooklyn clinic after I had transferred Moira. So I should shortly be home free as far as Mardoff was concerned. Nevertheless, as I sat facing him I realized he still had a powerful effect on me. My impulses to stand up to him conflicted with a desire to flee.

Three weeks later Moira telephoned me. She seemed unsure of following through with her decision to see me; she sounded anxious, distracted. Her indecisiveness worried and angered me. We now had the chance to continue her treatment for which we'd planned and struggled, and she was hesitating. It appeared to me that Mardoff's influence had caused this uncertainty in her. A cold feeling in my stomach suggested that disaster lay ahead. We did, however, set a meeting date for February. As we hung up I thought I heard a loud scream—but whether it was from her, from somewhere in the building, or from inside my troubled head, I'm still not sure.

During the second week of February, on a blustery Tuesday evening, Moira came to Wilson. Appearing distracted, she walked into the lobby of the agency, where I awaited her. I felt a rush of warmth at seeing her, along with rising hope that I could get her started once more toward emotional health.

She wore a plain black dress with a huge wool sweater she hugged about her despite the fact that the room was uncomfortably warm. I wondered if she was trying to disguise the fact that she had lost a considerable amount of weight, since she had once been anorexic. I caught an unhappy vibration from her; she appeared to try to disguise it with a flow of small talk. As we tried to communicate, the background noises of counsellors trying to control unruly kids seemed to make Moira more uncomfortable. Not the most ideal setting for a talk about resuming therapy.

"Let's go back to the room I use for my private patients," I said, "it's quieter." We walked down the hall silently. Following her in, I closed the door and motioned for her to sit down. I took a chair facing her, rather than sitting at my small desk. People at desks broadcast petty authority; I wanted Moira to feel close and comfortable as quickly as possible.

"Well," I said, "it's wonderful to see you. I can hardly believe we've gotten together again at last. How about resuming therapy this minute?"

Brushing aside my friendliness, Moira's face contorted and she shrieked at me: "Why did you leave me in the hands of that scumbag!" She clasped her hands tightly and rocked her upper body back and forth in an agitated way.

I felt agonized and guilty. "What's happened, Moira? Why are you so terrorized and unhappy?"

"Let's face it," she hissed. "Any progress I made has been shot down by that character you gave me to. Now, I'm not stupid. I know you felt you had no choice, you couldn't fight the clinic, but being with him has been horrible." She paused and leaned forward, her voice a whisper. "You know, though, I would have had to transfer to him even if you had fought the policy."

"What do you mean?" I asked, confused.

"I found out there was some kickback insurance scheme going on between the police department and Mardoff. I'm not sure about all the ins and outs of it, but what it amounts to is that officially I was listed as having gone to Mardoff all along, even when I was with you. I have to stay with him. If they find out I've transferred to you it could mean my job, because it might uncover their insurance scam."

She paused, then continued to talk, agitatedly snarling and nearly hysterical. Retracting what she had said moments before, "Still, I'll never forgive you for not somehow preventing my going to Mardoff. I don't care what bullshit justification you gave yourself, you didn't protect me. You could have found a way. It's made me question your judgement as a man and a therapist. Now I'm not sure that you aren't using me to forgive yourself." She gave a deep sigh. "But actually, you're the least of my problems right now."

I broke in. "So, let's start at the top. Or maybe the bottom," I added wryly. "What are your problems right now? We can work out your insurance hassles. If necessary, I'll see you without charging. Whatever damage Mardoff did I can reverse. We'll get you back to where you were and go on from there. I guarantee it. Moreover, I'm sure your job is not on the line. Employers cannot force people to go to any particular therapist or clinic. They've been bullshitting you."

Moira settled back in her chair. She seemed calmer, but wore a somber expression. "It's not so simple anymore," she said wearily. "I'm not the same person I was when you left the clinic. I'm drained emotionally and physically. Now, maybe we could work it out with the police department so I could start to see you. But there's something else—I'm not ready to leave Mardoff yet."

I gasped. "How can you say that after what you just told me?"

She flashed me another in her arsenal of dirty looks, this time contempt. "Sometimes I wonder if you understand me as well as you think you do. Didn't you guess that I'm attracted to him—revolting though he is in many ways? He knows that I need a father figure from our time together before I started sessions with him," she said mysteriously. "He knows he can dominate me the way my mother did, and he's doing it as effectively as she did—maybe more so."

She sighed again. "He got me in his web as quickly as

a hungry spider with helpless prey. He knew the strength I had built up in therapy with you was fragile and that because of my aloneness as a child he could easily make me dependent on him. Never mind the harm it could do to my trying to become my own person! Now he has almost complete power over me." She stared at me intently. "He and his self-serving interpretation of my problems! What it comes down to is that in his view I had manipulated people to control me so that I could get attention from them. I started with my mother, who he says wasn't as bad a person as I made her out to be. According to him I was jealous of her relationship to Janice, so I wheedled attention out of my mother by making unreasonable demands that made her treat me harshly. The idea was to redirect her attention from Janice to myself. Then I got my husband to treat me badly. What the bastard is suggesting is that I am totally responsible for the unloving and brutal treatment I have received." Moira burst into tears, recovered, then continued:

"Mardoff said I secretly craved domination and brutalization. He knows what my weak points are, and he has zeroed in on them mercilessly. He says that I want those close to me, and anyone else I can get, to shit on me, to make me feel like a worthless piece of crap deserving everything they dish out. He says that most women by nature are manipulative and entrapping—they feel that's the only way they can get the security of consistent relationships." Moira sobbed again, this time in an utterly heartbroken way, the tears streamed down her face and into the words she continued to choke out.

"Mardoff says," she went on her voice a hoarse whisper, "that my sickness made me incapable of achieving mature behavior—building caring and responsible relationships. He said that because of my low view of myself as a child I might have blown out of proportion the abuse I experienced. My mother, he thought, might have been more loving than I remember her and, rather than neglecting me, disciplined me for my own good. My father might have taken some frustration out on me, but perhaps I exaggerated what happened."

I felt my jaw clench but said nothing.

She went on. "I was determined to find out if his interpretations included the possibility that my neediness caused me to encourage the rapes. He explained that the rapes could have come about because of my desire to be abused. When I pressed him for a fuller explanation of the rapes and why I had blocked all memory of them, he took my breath away. Angrily he said that he hadn't been going to tell me this for awhile, till I was ready for it, but that the rapes had very likely not happened—that they had been wishfulfillment fantasies, not uncommon among hysterical women. The nuts and bolts of it was that my desire to be raped arose from abysmally low self-esteem and unresolved sexual guilt in wanting to make love with my weak father. He emphasized again that these sick attitudes often occur in hysterics like myself. According to Dr. Wisdom, my rapes were probably pure fantasies. He declared that psychoanalysis has demonstrated that childhood sexual seduction claims made by women are rarely shown to have actually happened. In other words, I had fantasized the molestations."

Moira fell into a sullen silence. Aside from bemoaning to myself the inaccuracy of Mardoff's interpretations, I had a deeper concern: How might I go about resolving her destructive attachment to him?

"You know, Moira," I started, "everything you're telling me is no surprise. Mardoff's hung up on classic analytical interpretations—whether they're on the mark or not. But what does that have to do with your leaving him and our starting therapy again?"

She shook her head. Selecting her words carefully, she answered, "I've never realized how strongly I'm attracted to dominant people. I sense their need to set up that codependency and it appeals to my craving to be a victim. I can't fight it. It's a weird relief to lose my sense of myself as a separate person when a little Hitler like Mardoff gets his hooks into me."

I stared at her ready to disagree. She went on, "Now, don't get me wrong. With part of me I do wish to be with him. After a couple of sessions I had decided to leave. When I was by myself I role-played how I would tell him off and never come back, but I never quite did it. What I did do was keep coming back for more. You guys ought to be grateful you know me. I help you control fragile females, starting with me, and you know how you creeps love to do that!"

I disregarded her remarks about me. They weren't important. What was, was her poor self image. "But your mother controlled you, too—and she was a woman!"

"Right. But she abused me basically because she had no other power in the family, or very little. If she didn't have me to kick around she would have been out of luck. You and Mardoff, as males, wield real power that you abuse. You tell yourselves you're humanistic helpers and healers. Fuck that, and fuck you, too! What's really going on is that through your controlling you're expressing your rage at being dependent on women. Mardoff's a bastard—he holds on to that tortured relationship with his wife and gets his anger out by victimizing me and becoming involved with me."

I gazed into Moira's pained eyes. They were lovely—a tumultuous green sea, now glinting with tears.

My mind raced on several levels. The first had to do with admiration at how perceptively she was reading herself, Mardoff, me, and the situation. She was bright, no doubt about that. With a stir of resentment, I found myself wishing, despite the fact that she was still in bad shape and probably worse now after being with Mardoff, that she could somehow utilize that sharp mentality to mobilize herself—to leave Mardoff and get back into treatment with me. While there was validity to how she saw the negative aspects of Mardoff's and my need to work with female patients, I had knocked myself out to help her and many times risked my career. However, I had to acknowledge that she had sensed my ambition about the case. Indeed, perhaps in the back of my mind was the notion that if the case and my connection to it were recognized in the psychological community, and perhaps in the world at large, my career would benefit. But again, was that so dreadful? Especially since, far from using her in a callous way, I was doing all I could to help her toward full recovery. And if she did recover, why not spread the word?

More immediately, although I had suspected it, I was startled by her intimations that there really was a personal relationship between Mardoff and her. Yet I believed her. I knew Mardoff was too much of a classical analyst to reveal details of his personal life to a patient—unless something else was going on.

"How do you know so much about Mardoff's married life?" I demanded.

Once again I faced Moira's fury. "Wouldn't you like to know all about it," she spat out. "Well I'm not going to tell you. Why should I? If I could, I'd get away from both you characters. But if you and I do start therapy again, you'll just have to trust that what I'm telling you about him is true." She looked into the distance. "Sometimes I feel I'll start treatment with you again, and sometimes I don't. But whatever I decide, the decision is mine and nobody else's. As far as Mardoff goes, the only thing I'm going to say about his and my relationship is that if I do start with you I'm going to continue my relationship with him. And that's all I'm going to tell you!"

I was furious. First she wanted therapy with me again and then she didn't. She may have had grudges against me, but what had happened to the trust we had worked so hard to build up? It was important that I know what kind of connection she and Mardoff had—how else could I work effectively to revive her recovery?

"C'mon, Moira, what sort of relationship do you have with Mardoff?" I burst out. She was about to answer when Hermit burst into the room, Jasslow right behind him. Both boys halted in front of us and stared, Hermit sucking his thumb.

"What are you guys doing here?" I roared at them. "You know you're not supposed to come in here without permission!"

Moira was startled and looked about to jump to her feet and flee. I rose, put my hands gently on her shoulders, and whispered, "Don't go yet." Then I told the boys to leave. Jasslow started obediently toward the door, but Hermit remained rooted, his eyes fixed on Moira and his thumbsucking speeding up. To my amazement, Moira reached out and drew Hermit to her, pulling him gently onto her lap and stroking his hair. They gazed at each other, and both started crying.

"What's wrong?" she whispered to him. He didn't answer, but she rocked him back and forth lovingly. After a while, hesitantly, he whispered to her, audibly enough so that I could overhear:

"Angel and the boys been trying to fuck me in the ass. Jasslow said he'll beat 'em up, but I'm still scared."

Before either of us could react, Chuck entered the room. "Okay, Hermit, wait outside," he directed the boy. Hermit slipped from Moira's lap and darted out. Chuck smiled warmly at us and addressed Moira. "Sorry for this interruption, ma'am. We got so many boys to keep track of, sometimes they get away from us." Chuck's powerful presence, warmed by his honesty and gentleness, affected Moira strongly. She burst into tears again.

After Chuck left to talk to Hermit, I asked Moira how she felt. Drying her eyes, she said, "I'm always moved by neglected, deprived children. Perhaps I see myself in them."

"Do you especially identify with Hermit?" I asked softly.

Moira put her thumb in her mouth and started sucking it. Then she pulled her legs up onto the chair in which she was sitting and doubled over into the fetal position, her head between her knees. It was exactly the position the Wilson kids assumed when frightened.

"Are you all right, Moira?" I said gently.

"I want mah Grandma!" It was the voice of a black child, and not one I had heard her utter before.

Startled, I asked, "What did you say?"

"Please, mister, don't hurt me! I wanna go home to my people! My mamma gonna kick my ass if I ain't home soon." Sobbing and gasping, Moira was speaking in dialect. This voice, different from Marcia's, the British girl, and the sophisticated older man, was new to me. It was childlike and frightened.

My heart sank. I was hearing Moira's desperate need for all the fusion therapy I could bring to bear. When I had left the clinic I hoped she had become more or less integrated, that she had enough therapy to eliminate the need for splitting into other selves. Now I realized that hadn't happened, and that her harmful experience with Mardoff had undoubtedly driven her again toward fragmenting. Reviewing my feelings at the time she and I terminated therapy, I realized I had sensed the presence of other personalities lurking in her, eager to surface. I realized now I had been too eager for success with her. She had improved a lot, but successful fusion in such a disturbed person came slowly.

I recalled other clues suggesting that she needed a lot more help: Memory gaps and inconsistencies, and such distressed physical behaviors as a tendency to curl up either partially or completely in the fetal position—as she had now. Another characteristic symptom was that as another personality would take over, her face would tighten and her eyeballs roll up as if in a hypnotic trance. Her face and hands would shake. When the alternative personality was in place, the tremors would stop, then recur as she became Moira again. Each of these changes took up to five seconds, and when they were over she had no memory of them.

Most of these manifestations had not occurred during

this change, but she had locked herself dramatically in the fetal position.

I decided to approach her directly. I picked her up gently, saying firmly, "Moira, you're not putting me on, are you?" In my arms, she took her thumb out of her mouth, stopped sobbing, and relaxed. As I lowered her carefully toward a standing position, I saw the "change" tremor briefly cross her face. Then she lowered her feet to the carpet, stood erect, and the adult Moira was back.

She gazed at me with a sleepy, composed expression on her face, and I said, "You didn't answer my question."

"What question?"

"I asked if you had been pretending to fragment as a little black girl searching for her mother."

Her eyes widened in surprise. "What are you talking about?" Then narrowed suspiciously. In a weary tone, she said, "I get it. You're pulling one of your manipulations to get me back into therapy with you. It won't work; *I'll* make the decision to rejoin you or not. I'm not going to let you influence me. Now tell the truth—I didn't fragment, did I? You were just making that up to make me want to come back to you."

"First of all, I'm *not* trying to make something up to get you to do what I want. I know you have certain issues with me, and I'm willing to discuss them with you, but you've gotta have a sense by this point that I'm one hundred percent wanting to help you if you'll let me. Now, I'm not sure whether what you did just now was fragmenting in the way you used to. Your conscious self was hidden and you were speaking and acting like a frightened little girl who was sucking her thumb. It happened. I saw it. Does that bring up any memories? Have you ever met anyone like that?"

I could feel anxiety building in Moira, and she changed the subject entirely. Not surprising, I thought, considering she still fragments, that she finds it very tough to acknowledge that fact.

Suddenly Moira began talking again about transferring to me. "It'll take a few months," she said. "If all goes well we can meet in June and begin again. What I want to do is see if I can break Mardoff's hold over me without your help. That would be good for me." She laughed a musical, lyric laugh. "He may need me more than I need him! Meantime, I'd appreciate it if you could work on my insurance coverage. I'm going to need it to pay you. Then, if I can free myself of Mardoff, we can start sessions again in June. How does that sound?"

"That would please me, Moira," I responded. "But I've got to see if I can work a little more on what I just saw. To start with, I did see you, just now, change into another personality. It was upsetting that it was one I never saw before. I may have made a miscall in thinking you had actually integrated all your personalities. I may have been wrong, but don't be discouraged by it—it just means we have more work to do. I do want you back, but not enough to lie about seeing another personality in you. What I feel is most important is that we start again as soon as possible. Your personal relationship with Mardoff is your own business, I can assure you. I don't even want to hear about it," I said curtly. It was not true, but I felt it better to pretend at this point that I felt that way. Eventually I might find ways to get more out of her on that subject.

"Well, I'm glad you feel that way," Moira responded scornfully. "Because you don't have a choice in the matter. We'll probably get together in June; meantime let's try to get the insurance straightened out. If I change my mind about anything, or everything," her face darkened ominously, "I'll let you know."

Quickly she stood up, pulled on her coat, and left. I was stunned. All I knew for sure was that I had to get her away from Mardoff and into sessions with me as soon as possible.

TWENTY-TWO

Seeming Answers

I sighed with relief as Mardoff started our meeting by telling me that Moira had asked his permission to meet with me. My central and powerful determination now was to take a moral stand with Mardoff. I was tired of weaving, ducking, and dodging. I felt I had to get Moira away from him.

Quickly I decided not to tell him about her threat but to keep the conversation firm but light. I acted surprised. "No kidding? I wondered what's been going on—you've hardly mentioned her for months. What do you think about her wanting to see me? Does it have anything to do with whatever you and she have been working on?"

"It doesn't have anything to do with our work, so far as I can see," he replied testily. "And I told her I strongly oppose her meeting with you. But she's made up her mind, said she'd stop therapy with me if I objected. This is all getting out of hand. There's no way I can stop her meeting with you, but I'm going to dictate exactly how you will act and what you will say and won't say." Mardoff was clearly agitated. I had never seen him lose his cool in the face of this sort of issue.

As if confused by his reluctance, I asked innocently, "Why are you so opposed to my seeing Moira?"

He turned red, his face swelled. He was beside himself. "You *idiot!*" he shouted. "You know how inappropriate it is for a therapist to meet with a former patient outside the framework of therapy!" I stared at him. I couldn't believe he had said that to me, considering his own reprehensible behavior. With a herculean effort he got himself under control and apologized for his outburst. He was in charge of himself again but betrayed his agitation by drumming his fingers on the desk. I sensed that for the first time in our relationship I had the upper hand. If I could only dig out of him the full story of what was transpiring between him and Moira, I might be able to win the battle with him at last and get Moira back into treatment with me. I had him cornered; I went for what I hoped would be the kill.

"Wait a minute, Mardoff," I said jovially. "Let's back up for a minute. You seem to be overreacting to a simple request by a patient to meet with her ex-therapist. This happens a lot; patients often want to stay in contact with their former therapists. What's the big deal? Why do you have to exercise total control over whether Moira and I chat? I gotta tell you, you're acting very unprofessionally. You've never shared even a little of what you and she have worked on. And you might have, even as a matter of courtesy; after all, I was very close to her therapeutically for a long time. Now you blow your stack at a harmless request."

Visibly holding himself in check, Mardoff replied, "Maybe it's you who's overreacting now. I admit I got upset at the thought of Moira leaving therapy, and even at the prospect of her meeting you. Her emotional stability is still very precarious, and I'm alert to her resistance. I thought her wanting to meet with you suggested she wanted to regress to a less threatening caretaker."

All my efforts at lightness exploded. "What are you trying to do," I shot back, "set up a competitive triangle among the three of us, to see who can be the closest to Moira, to see who has the most influence over her? Maybe if you told me what she and you have been working on I could understand your course of treatment for her, but your evasiveness has me suspicious of your motives and I deeply care about her welfare."

A look of embarrassment and guilt flashed momentarily in his eyes. I felt smug—it seemed to me I had at last got him on the run. However, to my surprise he turned confidential. He admitted he had been having treatment problems with Moira. I was about to take the bull by the horns and ask him if they had a personal relationship, when the phone rang.

I tried to distract him from answering: "Look," I rushed on, "I could understand if you've run into countertransference problems, like the ones I had when I was working with her. We both know how seductive she can be —you pointed that out to me at the start."

He wavered, looking as though he wasn't going to answer the phone. Then the buzzer sounded off. That meant the incoming call was an emergency. He picked up the receiver and said, "Dr. Mardoff." For several minutes, he just listened to whatever was being said to him. Suddenly he flashed a sardonic smile and seemed to relax. His change in mood was remarkable. My heart beat faster. God, he was shifty! I'd thought I had him where I wanted him, but now I wasn't so sure. I grew anxious.

After he hung up he was his confident, authoritarian self again. Smoothly he said, "Your suggestion that I've become too involved with Moira comes from unresolved projections on your part. As I said, I overreacted to her wish to meet you. I should have realized, as I do now, that she was making a purposeless request in order to resist what I'm trying to accomplish with her. I'll just tell her that meeting with you is out of the question as long as she's in treatment with me." He went on, "I'm no longer worried—there's no chance she'll leave therapy with me." He stared at me. "She's pathetically devoted to me. Like Freud and Breuer's 'Anna O,' she's pathologically dependent on parental figures."

Apparently quite sure of himself again, he continued. "If she insists on seeing you, just suggest she analyze with me her motives to create a triangular conflict among you, me, and her. Then tell her you can't see her. If she insists, make sure she promises to consult with me first. Remind her that while she's in treatment it's not a good idea for her to confer with you as her former therapist."

I was stunned by the turnaround in his attitude, as I had been previously when he made unexpected jumps to new positions in the conflicts between us. "I need time to think about all you've said," I replied. This gave me time to regroup—for one thing I had to find out who had phoned him and what was said. Could it have been Moira? It was crucial to find out. I wanted to finish up with him quickly and talk to Gail. Perhaps I could find out from her who had called.

After agreeing to his wishes, I pointed out to him that I planned to finally leave the clinic by June. "Your leaving will be in the best interests of all concerned," he said, smiling again. I met his eyes. They were hard as steel. *I'm sure you feel that way, you bastard*, I thought. *Gets me out of your hair, and you'd certainly appreciate that.* We stared at each other with supreme dislike.

Just as I was about to take my leave, the phone rang again. This time it was his wife. I could hear them wrangle about his canceling a theater date. Her shouts came over the phone. After the theater issue was thrashed out she started yelling at him about an affair he was having. He began shaking. Her voice was so loud I couldn't help but listen in. I rose to leave, but Mardoff motioned me to stay seated. For a moment or two I did and heard Mardoff say, "Let's hold off talking about our problems until the next marital counseling session." As I headed for the door, I heard her screech, "I'll never divorce you! I'll make your life hell!"

I looked back. Mardoff had hung up and was slumped in his seat, gazing distractedly into the distance.

Walking to Gail's desk, I asked as casually as I could, "How about we go out for coffee after work?"

"Sounds good," she replied. She and I had become

good friends during my internship. Maybe I could find out from her who had phoned; supervisory sessions were rarely interrupted except for emergencies—this must have been something out of the ordinary.

Later that afternoon at a nearby coffee shop, I started the ball rolling by telling Gail that I was leaving the clinic by June. She was all for it. "I'm a great advocator of interns breaking the umbilical cord with their mentors and getting out into the world," she chuckled. I agreed. Then I brought up the subject of Moira, telling of my guessing from her remarks that a personal relationship had sprung up between her and Mardoff. Then I talked of my meeting with Mardoff, how I had tried to pump him about Moira, and how abruptly his behavior had changed after the mysterious phone call. She burst into laughter.

"What's so funny?" I demanded.

"If you're worrying about whether it was Moira phoning, you can relax. It was a black nurse calling from St. Vincent's about an emergency with one of Mardoff's private patients."

"St. Vincent's," I repeated slowly. There was something familiar about the name of the place. For the moment I couldn't recall what it was. I was baffled again. Why would a strictly official call like this change Mardoff's mood so thoroughly? And why would he react in such a strange way to an emergency call?

I pointed these considerations out to Gail, and she replied firmly, "Beats me. All I can tell you is that it was an official call—and I said it was a black nurse because it was clearly a black intonation and accent."

Once more I'd lost all clues. I decided to take Gail fully into my confidence and tell her the whole story, right from the beginning. I told her of my conviction that Moira was a multiple, and I described Moira's alternate personalities, including the sophisticated man who had appeared briefly and the black child who had recently surfaced.

When I finished, Gail sat back and gazed at me in a bewildered way. Did she think I was a mad intern with a feverish imagination? If so, I couldn't blame her—it was a pretty wild story. Nevertheless, I also knew that over the two years of our getting to know each other she had come to trust my judgement and to respect me.

Gail was in charge of the day-to-day operations at the clinic, very much as Dolly was at Wilson. She was a bright, sympathetic person. As we became friends she was for me a strong source of emotional support. She was privy to the inner workings of the clinic, the politics, the latest gossip. Thus she might know about something going on between Mardoff and Moira. I asked her: "Do you think Mardoff is seeing Moira socially—maybe even sleeping with her?"

Gail shook her head. "I don't think he is," Gail answered. "I'm in touch with most of the staff every day, and if something was going on I'd most likely have heard about it. Mardoff has his personal problems, but I think he's too slick to become involved with his private patients, especially one as troubled as Moira. He's had trouble with his marriage for years, and he's had plenty of affairs, but he handles them discreetly. My guess is that he got Moira away from you so that he could work with her and advance his career by publishing a book about his experiences with her. He's a wheeler-dealer; he'd use anyone if he thought he could get some benefit out of it. But he isn't dumb. He watches out for himself every minute."

"Gail, I still think they're having an affair. I've just got to find out what's going on here. Will you help me? It's the only way I can get a handle on how to help Moira."

"I've already told you about the phone call. It was a nurse. What else do you want from me? Are you sure your suspicions about Moira and Mardoff aren't countertransference fantasies?"

"The last thing I need is parlor psychology, Gail," I answered. "All I know is Moira's a guilt-ridden, masochistic religious fanatic with a unique capacity to attract sadistic, domineering people. She's done it all her life. I trust her when she says he needs her. My fear is that they've gotten into a symbiosis that Moira will find extremely difficult to get away from. I feel strongly that something's going on between Moira and Mardoff that's not just a therapist-patient relationship.

"And there's another problem—her insurance coverage. She can't pay for the difference between her current policy and the amount I charge for private sessions. I've offered to see her for free, but she wants to continue to pay through insurance. However, in order to continue qualifying for insurance, through the police department disability status she's on, she has to continue to see a psychiatrist. In her case, Mardoff."

Gail's eyes widened in surprise. "But that's nonsense. It isn't that way at all. It's true that coverage under police department insurance while she's being treated is rather limited, but that limitation ran out six months ago. And any time after that, if she'd gone into private therapy with you or anyone else, the reimbursement would have increased a lot."

I was shocked. Gail knew our insurance coverage inside out, so she was certain to be correct. Apparently Moira had been using the insurance excuse, which she appeared to have fabricated, to justify staying with Mardoff. She could have switched to me any time after I left the clinic in November! Perhaps she misunderstood the terms of her coverage? Or maybe she was demonstrating anger at me for leaving her with Mardoff?

"Gail," I blurted out, "I've just got to see Mardoff's notes on her. Maybe if we look in his files we can find out what's really going on."

"You're out of your head! That wouldn't tell you anything. This lady is manipulating both of you. No question about it. It's the old power game: If you don't love me anymore, I'll switch shrinks. It's becoming a fad among inventive neurotics; they attract attention and don't face up to their real problems by pretending to have multiple personalities."

I wasn't getting anywhere, but I had to keep trying. "Listen, Gail. I'm sure Moira's not manipulative. Something's going on between them. Mardoff is inappropriately involved with her. It might almost amount to brainwashing. All I know is that she can't leave him." As I was talking, I had a sudden insight. St. Vincent's—that was where Moira had fantasized or really been with Mardoff on her three-week absence from therapy. I shivered and went on. "I believe it was Moira who phoned and interrupted my supervisory meeting with Mardoff. Maybe she was frightened of his negative reaction to her request to see me. Maybe she told him she had changed her mind about wanting to see me, and that reassured him, which could have resulted in his suddenly becoming calm. But whatever happened in that conversation if I'm to save her, I need your help now."

Gail took a deep breath, puffed out her cheeks, and blew a long, exasperated, but sympathetic puff. "Oh, what the hell. Why not!" I hugged her with relief and gratitude.

As we left the coffee shop and walked back toward the clinic, Gail recalled two characteristics of Moira's treatment that struck her as unusual in light of how Mardoff customarily worked. "The first," Gail said, "is I've never seen any of the material in Moira's file. That's unusual, because I usually type all Mardoff's notes at the end of each day and place them in the patients' files. Furthermore, Moira has invariably been scheduled as his last patient for her three sessions a week. That's unusual too, because he sees patients at varying times, and I've never known him to schedule someone at precisely the same hour for an extended period."

I nodded. No matter what Gail believed, I felt more strongly than ever that Mardoff and Moira were lovers.

When we got back to the clinic, Gail immediately checked her telephone log. We were startled to discover that during the past five months Mardoff's wife had phoned immediately after each session with Moira. "That's strange," I said, "at least to an extent, because it's puzzling that a wife would call her husband so regularly at the end of the day when presumably he's about to come home."

"Yup," Gail said, obviously beginning to have some suspicions herself. Then we checked the file in which patients' records were normally kept—no sign of Moira's. Gail mused for a moment. "There's a special file in his office in which he also stores some of the patients' records. Let's check that and his desk."

Gail barged into his office. Now that she had the scent of illicit sex, there appeared no stopping her. Deftly using a bottle opener, she pried the drawers open without damaging the locks. Most of the contents were miscellaneous papers, among which we found a letter from his lawyer about a meeting with his wife's lawyer to discuss a divorce. I blushed at our intrusion into his private concerns. But I was trying to save Moira, I told myself, and for that I'd go a long way. There was nothing about Moira in the desk, so we turned to his private file drawers. Gail scrabbled her finger under a tiny shelf behind the files and drew out a key that had been taped there out of sight. Paydirt! We opened the first file drawer, and there was Moira's folder in correct alphabetical order.

We pulled up two chairs and sat down to go through her file together. The first papers I peeled off were the original psychological tests done on Moira, along with Mardoff's psychiatric evaluation. I noticed that she had been given elevated depression scores on her MMPI, the most widely used personality test to measure a patient's psychological dysfunction. A note on the thematic apperception test pointed out that she had fears of losing her identity. My process notes of two years on her case were in the folder, along with Mardoff's penciled notes criticizing some of my diagnostic judgments. Surprisingly, another series of notes in back of the first ones from him praised my treatment skills!

We were about to put the folder back when we came across a bunch of letters, from Moira to Mardoff, marked "private and confidential." We looked at each other, hesitated for a moment, then I picked up one of the letters. I glanced at the postmark. This one was written after Moira had gone into therapy with Mardoff. Opening it, I began to read out loud.

> Dearest John,
> I am indeed a wicked and guilty manipulator, as you suggested the other day. But you are wrong to conclude that the rapes and abuse I went through were only in my imagination. Obler initially felt the same way, but after the evidence was all in, he became convinced of the truth, that I was a child victim.
> I sense you don't believe me because of the suffering you are going through in your marriage. I committed a terrible sin the other day and went through your papers while you were away from your office. I saw the threatening note from your wife and its implication that she was a childhood victim of sexual abuse. It must be hard to be told that your treatment of her is as bad as the abuse she took from her father.
> Perhaps these accusations have poisoned your mind toward women—you now think we're all hysterical and manipulative. Rest assured that I only want to get well and not manipulate you as a parent figure. I need your help. Please try to keep an open mind as to the sort of person I really am.
> Sincerely,
> Your helpless Moira

"Look at this," said Gail. She handed me another letter —this one dated February 16—three days before Moira showed up at Wilson for our first therapy session after being apart.

> Dearest John,
> I have been considering getting in touch with my old therapist Dr. Obler for a friendly chat. I hope you won't read this as another attempt to manipulate the men in my life, to get more attention for myself. I was floored by your suggestion the other day that a major difference between men and women are that men are the truth seekers and

women, in the main, seek security. I don't buy that. My experience of men and women is that both need security. And either can be truth seekers, people who forge ahead in life. Look at Madame Curie, or Florence Nightingale. Perhaps we can discuss this over coffee sometime—

Gail suddenly hissed, "What's that?" We interrupted our reading to listen. "I think I heard a noise," she said worriedly. We heard a key turn in the lock of the clinic's main entrance. Who could it be at this hour? Footsteps approached Mardoff's office. Quickly I moved furniture back as Gail replaced files. Luckily there was a back entrance to the office. As we slipped through it, we heard a key click into the lock.

Gail started. "Let's get the hell out of here," she whispered. "Being discovered could cost me my job." I, too, had a few little worries about being discovered—such as a felony rap and no more career as a psychologist. But I had to find out who had entered the office. I signalled to Gail to be quiet and wait for a moment. "Are you crazy?" she gasped. "We can't stay here. If Mardoff discovers I'm in cahoots with you, I'm finished. My job means more to me than that crazy Moira."

"Steady," I murmured. I felt strangely calm. "This corridor is never used to leave the clinic," I said in a whisper. "If we keep quiet, no one will know we're here and we can do some more snooping later."

We strained our ears. We could hear that more than one person had entered the clinic. They were now in Mardoff's office. Through the wall we could hear a man and woman talking. "It's Mardoff," Gail whispered, "with his wife!" Now I could hear them. "They're having a fight."

We waited, our bodies stiff. Gail wanted to leave, but I managed to get her to stay.

As we stood there, I thought about the letters Moira had written Mardoff. For one thing, why should she have to write him when they met regularly? And unless Mardoff was going off his trolley I could never imagine him referring to her as "guilty" or a "wicked manipulator." As much as I differed with his professional views, I knew him to be too much of a pro to do anything like that. But I was quite taken with her idea that he was projecting his problems with his wife on his female patients.

The voices were very low again. "Can you make out what they're saying?" I asked Gail.

"Shush, listen," she responded.

I put my ear against the wall. Mardoff's wife was speaking. "I'm going to expose you to your colleagues if you divorce me—ruin you professionally by disclosing your psychiatric misconduct to the state psychiatric association, to the press, and to anyone else I can talk to."

Mardoff snarled, "I couldn't care less what you do."

"I'll limit your visiting rights to your kids and hit you with as large alimony demands as I can get."

"Your threats don't concern me," he said. "I've been forced to turn to other women because of your aversion to having sex."

"Yeah, some poor crazy patient who calls you Daddy while you come all over her face and tell her to lick the sticky goo off." She imitated first his and then the woman's voice. After that it got really ugly; she began to describe chapter and verse as to why she didn't enjoy sex with him.

"You're perverted!" she finally screamed and then lowered her voice so much I couldn't hear the rest.

"Did you hear that?" I asked Gail. She nodded. "What were the perversions?"

Gail laughed. "I don't want to talk about it. Either ask him about it or get yourself a hearing aid!"

I put my ear back against the wall. All talking in the office had stopped. Footsteps. Someone walked out of Mardoff's office, and I heard the clinic door slam. I bent down and peeped through the keyhole. I glimpsed Mardoff sitting dejectedly at his desk, dialing a phone number, a letter in his other hand.

I straightened up, motioned, "let's get out of here," to Gail, and we left. We walked for a long time, stopping on the Brooklyn Heights promenade and sitting down on a bench.

For a while we were silent. Then we burst into relieving laughter. We felt like a couple of kids who had gotten away with something.

"Well, I'm not trying to find out for my own gratification. It just strikes me that I was right—he is a womanizer, and the more I know about him the more I might be able to fit it into the picture of his and Moira's connection."

"Are you going to phone her?"

"I'm not sure. I have mixed feelings. For one thing, I really think the black nurse who called could very well have been a split-off personality of Moira's. Another point to think about is how relieved Mardoff was when I told him I would think about all he was saying."

"If you don't see her she won't be able to tell you the perverted details of their romance," Gail teased.

Then, more seriously, she added, "Why don't you talk to her and find out how she feels at this point?"

I rubbed my chin pensively. "Well, I want to be careful. If I push Moira too hard she might run. She seems to have regressed with Mardoff."

We were silent again.

I walked Gail to her home through the cold night air. We lingered on the sidewalk near her home. Suddenly, I felt attracted to her; her dark expressive eyes seemed to suggest she felt the same way about me. I took her hand and said, "I've never had a friendship with a woman that was not just sexual."

And it was true. Women had been a balm for the lifelong anger I felt toward my mother. I understood my anger at my mother, for her failure to nurture and comfort me, but it had never diminished. It had imprinted in me a deep fear of rejection and abandonment. As I looked into Gail's eyes I realized for the first time that sexualizing my connections to women helped protect me against a rearousal of those fears.

Embracing Gail, I kissed her on her cheek. We broke apart for a moment. "And I intend to keep it that way," I murmured into her ear.

And I did keep it that way. Gail helped me.

TWENTY-THREE

Ultimatums

When Moira phoned a week later to announce that we could resume therapy in June, I was overjoyed that she had at last made up her mind, and now that I had her on the phone I could take up my endless quest to dig the truth out of her. I told her the full story of Gail's and my detective work, including overhearing Mardoff's fight with his wife. I emphasized that what we had done was aimed at helping her. Then I asked if she had been the mysterious caller. She refused to answer. She also refused to divulge anything about her relationship with Mardoff, and she berated me for Gail's and my "unprofessional behavior." I sighed. She certainly made it hard to help her.

Afterwards she announced, "I intend to maintain a relationship with Mardoff, even when you and I resume therapy."

Shocked, I asked, "Why?" She said nothing. I pressed her. "Why would you?"

"It's none of your business," she replied. The forcefulness of her voice startled me, especially from a woman who only a week before had a major dissociation episode. I realized that she had probably blocked her memory of that incident and was now presenting me with a kind of Frankenstein's monster: I had helped her become much more integrated and stronger, but she was now using that new strength to select a dangerous path of behavior.

My back was against the wall, as it often was with Moira. Reaching for any question that might open her up a little, I asked as casually as I could, "Moira, why did you tell Mardoff of your desire to visit with me?"

I could hear the receiver rattling sharply. Moira's voice rose as she replied, "It's my responsibility to diminish his jealousy toward my relationship with you. I wanted him to get used to the idea that I would be in touch with you. I figured this would ease the process of my transferring to you. He and I are important to each other. It may take him some time to become comfortable with the fact that I'm not his patient any more."

"Good grief!" I exclaimed. "Are you really planning on having a long-term relationship with that unscrupulous asshole?"

For several minutes Moira said nothing. Then she exploded: "I thought I'd made it clear, Marty. You either accept that Mardoff stays in my life or I'll drop you. Keep your hostility about my private life to yourself and check out your own countertransference problems. Get it through your head that though I'll work with you as deeply as I can and that I appreciate the help you've given me and will probably give to me when we get together again, I'm now running my own life, and I'm not going to answer to anyone about anything!"

I backed off, realizing that opposing her now might get me the exact opposite of what I wanted. "Okay. I won't bring up the subject of Mardoff again—at least not until we start sessions again. But I want you to know that if he is sexually using you to deal with his failed marriage I won't sit by and allow it—abusive unprofessional conduct cannot be tolerated."

She hung up on me. Although I wanted to follow up on my threat immediately, I had to focus for the time being on more immediate concerns.

Eager as I was to begin work with Moira again, I had much to occupy me in the meantime. I was trying to help the young people at Wilson, and I faced completing my dissertation before becoming a licensed psychologist.

To prepare the dissertation was demanding—I had to build into it elements from my studies and my work at the clinic and at Wilson. By June, however, I would be fully qualified. Then I could end my clinic responsibilities and have more time to help Moira complete her recovery.

As I became more acquainted with my young charges, I grew aware that a vicious cycle of prejudice, fear, and discrimination in the society around them pretty much obliterated their chances to lead normal productive lives. Welfare-dependent like their parents before them, they lived in a society indifferent to their ignorance and terror. School systems, helping therapies, programs—none offered promise to these battered children. I, too, had lived a rocky beginning, but the Jewish ghetto child knew that hard work and a little luck could gain him a respectable way of life. I took up the challenge. I would grapple with the institutions that prevented my kids from escaping the prison of a crippled existence. First target: The local school.

The school's attitude toward Wilson was summed up by a comment the principal was known to have made to a city official about the Wilson children: "We just don't want those dirty bastards at our place. Most of our kids are terrified of them. Those pricks on the board think they can force anything on us they want to. Well, I'm gonna make sure my teachers and staff give those kids such a hard time they'll move their spic and black asses out of my place. I'm not going to lower my standards to help those stupid sons of bitches."

That was what I was up against. Angel in particular, I learned, was considered a terror by everyone at P.S. 22. Despite this, I was determined to persuade these enemies to be more accepting of my kids.

My plan was to have a delegation from P.S. 22 attend one of our afternoon group-therapy sessions. I thought that if they saw the children open up and share with each other the brutality of their lives, the visitors would be moved to change their attitudes and want to help them. I asked Chuck to visit the school and extend a warm invitation. Accompanying him on this mission, on his best behavior, was the formidable Angel himself. Chatting with the principal, Chuck informed him that the visitors would be sitting behind a one-way mirror and could view the interactions without being seen. The principal unbent his bigoted viewpoint enough to accept the invitation; we also invited the chief director of Wilson and Babcock. The staff was asked to be on their best behavior during the visit. The day arrived. We put on our best faces and greeted our visitors.

Twenty-three visitors from P.S. 22, with our director, were ushered through the waiting room. Babcock, true to his reputation, was nowhere to be seen. Hermit and Jasslow, decked out in white uniforms, served tea and muffins as the visitors seated themselves in the viewing area. I couldn't imagine where the white uniforms had come from, but I didn't like them. They suggested servant images as if the boys were serving the overlord whites. Later I learned the boys had stolen the uniforms from a nearby thrift shop and, with élan, donned them for the occasion. Our guests were evenly divided between old-time veterans of the public school system—mainly spinsters in their fifties—and young teachers embarking on their careers. I had the feeling that the older teachers would be unfamiliar with group therapy. I got the ball rolling, talking about the format of what we were about to observe. "Please be silent so that you will not be heard in the therapy room."

Angel was leader for the day. He started the meeting with announcements about upcoming sessions. I had stressed to the kids and the staff that making a good impression was crucial, because whether the kids would be released by the courts to return to their homes was dependent on a good report by their teachers.

Angel finished his announcements and took a seat. A silence followed; I sensed tension in the air. I thought it was just nervousness that would evaporate as soon as the boys got talking among themselves in the therapy process. But as I watched, I realized something else was going on. Hermit was sitting with head bowed, ferociously sucking on his thumb. Leaning forward, Jasslow banged his head rhythmically against his knees. The rest of the boys stared distractedly into the distance. Finally Hermit shot Angel an anguished glance and turned to me.

"Mr. Obler, Angel and Joey took me buns last night," he gasped. All the boys shifted uncomfortably in their seats.

"What's such a big deal about them stealing some buns from you, Hermit? You sometimes take things that don't belong to you."

"Me buns! Me *buns!*" squealed Hermit, lifting off the chair so that he could point to his buttocks.

"You mean they raped you, Hermit?" I blurted out, shocked.

"With the Griffin! With the Griffin they done it!" His thumbsucking speeded up frantically.

"Griffin? What do you mean?" I asked, darting a glance around the room. Three of the boys, smirking, jumped to their feet, and each produced a circular can of good old Griffin shoe polish, with which they had lubricated their assault on poor Hermit's rear end.

Gasps and screams from the observers penetrated the

concealing wall. In the horror of the moment, I'd forgotten we were being watched: I ran out into the hall to enter the observing room to try to stop the panic that had erupted. I met a rush of guests in full stampede. Pushed along by this human torrent, I cried out, "Please be calm," but my words were ignored.

The whole pack poured out onto 18th Street. Dolly, sitting at the switchboard, was doubled over with raucous laughter. I rushed out onto the entrance stairway and found two spinster teachers lagging behind, one vomiting and the other looking as though she might at any second. "Wait," I said. "Please. I can explain. This is not as bad as you think. It's natural behavior for them and . . ." I could see I was not making headway with the teachers, one of whom had finished throwing up and was leaning weakly against the other. I raced up the street, trying to get my message across to the retreating delegation. They rewarded me with looks of revulsion. I realized my experiment had failed grandly and that my higher-ups would demand an explanation. Just at that moment, up the street, came Babcock. Having noted the rush of people trooping out of the building, he stopped me to ask, "What's up? Was there a riot?"

My agitation produced unseemly humor. I felt slap-happy. "I guess, Dr. Babcock, those folks don't enjoy buns with their tea!"

He looked at me quizzically, shook his head, and walked away.

He soon found out what had really occurred when word of the fiasco got back to the board of directors. My censurer was one Dr. Mashipian, overall Wilson administrator. He let me know that I would be fired if any further community experiments were tried. He also told me that Robert Lowe Harris, the former Wilson director who had hired me, had interceded on my behalf and helped my cause. He was the family systems expert whose pioneering work had originally attracted me to the Wilson position.

After accepting Dr. Mashipian's reproof, I remonstrated with him. "But look here, doctor. The treatment we're giving the kids now is bullshit. We've got to try new approaches. They're going down the tubes. Sitting and talking to them is useless. I thought this place was famous for a system approach—to work on their problems as part of a systems breakdown among their parents and teachers. I was just trying to get their teachers involved. Now, many of our workers at Wilson are helping the kids a great deal, but we need all the help we can get—from inside and outside the Wilson organization."

He mused a moment. "Look, just talk to Babcock about innovations before you try them. I think highly of your work, and so do others. But your former supervisor in Brooklyn has reported that you get overeager and act too impulsively. We are privately funded; we can't afford scandal."

"Wait a minute," I interrupted. "I just thought such an outing, if it could be done so the board members could meet these kids, would help them understand the reality of the children's lives."

"Forget it!" snapped Mashipian. "Look, don't go off in nutty directions. Keep your nose clean and you've got a future at Wilson. Look at Babcock. He's been here six or seven years and never one problem out of him. A good man; I hardly ever hear from him." *And no one else does, either,* I snarled bitterly to myself. *Is that what it takes to be a success in this field—being a totally noneffective person like Babcock?* Mashipian continued. "Use Babcock as an example. Why don't you do some research at our facility? Use your graduate skills to finish your dissertation. Make home visits." I nodded dutifully, and the interview was over.

Fortunately, things quieted down at Wilson. The administration quickly forgot my well-meant disaster, and Dr. Babcock occupied himself with his radio broadcasts.

Dr. Martin Obler

I began to have some success with the kids on my unit, particularly Hermit and Angel. I used some psychoanalytic techniques having to do with their childhood memories and dreams, and then just felt my way with them. I got them to open up, to tell how they felt about things, and to explore this or that issue or experience in their lives. I could feel their trust in me increasing. They showed increasing self-awareness and self-confidence, possibly the first time in their lives they'd been blessed by such feelings.

I started to uncover similarities in the psychodynamic roots of Hermit's childhood that remarkably resembled Moira's early experiences. His thumbsucking was a defense against the terror of being beaten by his mother, who also beat his six brothers and sisters. From what I gathered, Hermit had stayed regressed to an infantile level while his brothers and sisters developed more normally. One day I understood why: If Hermit could project an infantile need to be protected, he might influence people to protect and defend him. People felt sorry for a tiny, cute kid sucking his thumb. In this way he tried to protect himself from intolerable abusive experiences. Moira had used fragmenting for similar protective reasons. Both thus appeared pathetic and vulnerable to the outside world, but each actually had a lot of basic strength.

Angel's rape of Hermit released in Hermit a lot of material from his childhood—especially his middle childhood—that proved useful in coming to an understanding of Moira's multiple personality defense. I learned from Hermit that because of his small size and inability to defend himself he had been raped frequently. Hermit handled the psychological pain of these assaults by means of his thumb. In effect, he displaced his outrage and hurt onto that finger by sucking it. This gave him a safe outlet. Certainly he couldn't express rage toward his tormentors or he would have suffered the consequences, so his thumb became his outlet, very much as the combative staff meetings at Wilson became an outlet for the feelings generated in us by the demands of life at the agency. Just as Moira detached her pain by channeling it into other selves, Hermit separated from his inner bruises through sucking his thumb.

To my joy, Hermit seemed to understand. "Is dat what I been doing? I's scared of mamma and the boys cause they beat me, so I suck my thumb—it make me feel better; I don't think of the pain so much?"

I hugged him. "You got it, Hermit! Maybe we can help you see that people behave that way toward you, awful as it was, because they had been treated that way when *they* were kids." I was momentarily ecstatic. Using psychotherapeutic approaches, along with good old-fashioned love, patience, and understanding, I had actually helped this troubled little boy to see something he might never have seen his whole life if I hadn't had the chance to work with him. I now saw that despite what Dolly and others had said about the futility of classical analysis for these kids, some of these approaches did have value for them.

Hermit persisted: "I couldn't fight with my fists. I was too small and weak. But my brothers and sisters could. They were tough. I was small and weak. They weren't scared, and I was."

"They were all scared, Hermit. I think you'll come to see that nobody cared for them or gave them love either. The difference between them and you was, they took their shit out on you, but you took it out on your thumb."

Then arrived one of those moments in which a conscientious psychotherapist is compensated for all he or she has been through: As I said those words, Hermit took his thumb out of his mouth for the first time since I had arrived at Wilson.

In that instant I saw why Hermit and Moira hugged each other in my office. It was the same connection Moira had with her schizophrenic brother when both were sick children. She held Hermit tenderly in her arms as though she'd known him for years. This realization made me long to work with Moira again. We were due to meet in April preparatory to resuming therapy in June, and I was determined to let nothing stand in the way of our plans.

Suddenly an idea occurred to me. Why not try to involve Moira with Hermit in some way that might help both of them?

I phoned Moira and made the suggestion. "Well, you've got a nerve to assume I would be meeting with you in April," she responded tartly. "I've told you it all depends on the outcome of my relationship with John. If I do meet with you on April 24th, I might consider visiting Hermit's home. I'd really like to help him. Meantime, don't put any pressure on me to come back to you!"

Annoyed, I said, "Oh, excuse me. Just who is this John? Oh, you mean Mardoff. So you're on a first-name basis— very touching. Has John Boy been brainwashing you into playing this power game with me? Now listen, Moira, I've scheduled our consultation for 10:00 A.M. on the 24th, and I'd like you to join us on our visit to Hermit's home." I banged the receiver down. What a luxury, hanging up on Moira as she had done on me more than once. I knew it was an eminently unprofessional way to express my feelings, but what the hell, I was tired of her wavering and arrogance.

Perhaps hanging up on her might soften her belligerent attitude toward me. If I could interest her in Hermit, it might open the way for her to start therapy with me earlier that June. Here I was, manipulating feverishly again. I seemed to be at it day and night, one way or the other, but I'd become accustomed to the truth that much of therapy is manipulation—indirectly influencing others to behave or think in this way or that, in the interests of edging them toward healthy change. Often, of course, especially with strongly motivated therapy patients, much of the process can be discussed directly. However, where the therapist encounters deeply entrenched defenses against insight and growth, often in the hidden precincts of the unconscious, a frontal approach is unavailing and might even strengthen the patient's hold on neurosis. So I had to find ways of helping Moira and other patients like her despite themselves, and often this could be done only through stratagems of which the patient would be unaware. No manipulation, no progress. The therapist's responsibility, of course, was to do his or her best to ensure that the maneuvering resulted in benefit to the patient. I took a deep breath and struggled to stay objective.

To my surprise, she showed up, on time. When Chuck and Angel opened my office door on the 24th to let her in I was stunned by the woman I saw before me. Was this poor, battered Moira? She radiated beauty and confidence. Her burnished blonde hair fell to her shoulders; her face was full of life and color; a low-cut black dress accentuated her well-shaped breasts.

As I kept my jaw from falling open, she took a seat at my desk.

"All right, Marty," she said in a soft but decisive voice. "I'm here to talk to you as an equal—not doctor and patient. First of all, I don't wish to discuss my relationship with John, which I'm going to phase out by June. At least, I'm phasing out the professional part of our relationship." I was tempted to blurt out, Does that mean you're going to keep seeing the creep as a lover? She seemed to sense what I was going to say, however, and a warning glint in her eye kept me quiet. She had certainly become assertive, that was for sure. Moira continued, "If I still need therapy in June I will resume with you, and I can tell you that the insurance problem with the police department has been solved. I can pay for my own therapy. Now, the reason I've come here today is because I want to do anything I can to help little Hermit. So let's go to his home."

I asked Chuck to get Hermit ready. Moira smiled at me; I could feel a surge of warmth between us. It relieved my angry feelings toward her. There was so much I wanted to know; however, now was plainly not the time to satisfy my curiosity.

Moira melted any still-existing enmity between us by saying, "Listen, I'm sorry I acted so arrogant and controlling."

"No problem," I responded. "I am anxious to work with you again, but I won't pressure you into anything."

"Nope, I'm past being pressured." Moira's smile entranced me.

In walked Chuck and Hermit. Moira rose and gently embraced the tiny boy, who hungrily hugged her back. They clasped hands and walked from the office, Chuck and I following.

We came out of the subway—Hermit, Moira, Chuck, and I—at Fifth Avenue and 116th Street. As we walked along 116th Street we encountered bitter stares. A muttered growl—"What you doin' up here, white man?"—sped our steps. My heart thudded.

We made our way through East Harlem. Littered, filthy streets. Shells of abandoned buildings. Dingy tenements, tiny grocery stores, and bodegas, interspersed here and there with brighter-colored beauty parlors. Battered automobiles were stashed along the curbs where street people, mostly black and Hispanic, tinkered between sips from bag-covered bottles. Hermit was clearly upset about the visit. Moira held his hand tightly and comfortingly, but his eyes shown with terror and he was sucking his thumb again.

I had learned that his memories of home were fragmentary—he knew vaguely that he had lived with his six brothers and sisters and their mother in a three- or four-room apartment. However, he had forgotten what they looked like.

Our arrival at Hermit's building—I had gotten the address from our records—was heralded by a noisy fight in progress within. Shouts, banging of furniture and doors.

Suddenly a teenager raced out of the house and tore past us, ordering us out of his path and almost knocking us down.

"That's my brother," yelped Hermit.

The noise stopped. Chuck rang the bell, and a lovely young copper-skinned girl answered and motioned us to come in. From her resemblance to Hermit, I guessed correctly that it was one of his sisters.

After a short walk through a graffiti-smudged hallway, which reeked of urine and stale liquor, we entered the family's apartment through a second door.

A thin, sickly woman who looked older than she probably was greeted us. She was Hermit's mother. "Hi, Hermit," she shouted welcomingly. Her black eyes looked dazed and she seemed high on some drug. With her was a muscular, ebony-skinned man, apparently her lover, and several younger girls, Hermit's sisters. All had a drugged, distracted manner.

"Hermit," the man said. "How you like Wilson?" Sucking his thumb vigorously, Hermit nodded affirmatively.

"Look, mama!" screamed one of the girls, "Hermit still sucks his thumb like a little baby!"

Enraged, the mother shrieked, "Shut the fuck up, you little bitch. That's your little brother—be nice to him."

Moira seated herself beside the mother on a worn, flowered couch. Chuck took one of two folding chairs and the sisters clustered around a battered recliner; two squashed together in it.

The mother focused a puzzled stare at me. "Watcha bring Hermit home for?"

Chuck explained that every child at Wilson was taken for a preliminary visit with his family before returning to the home permanently.

The mother reacted angrily. "Come *home?* What he wanna do that for? It's good where he is, ain't it? I was thinking that my daughter Jessie"—she pointed to a slim teenager leaning on the recliner—"would be better off there than whorin' on the streets. Which she does, even though she says she ain't." She calmed down and then turned to Chuck. "Can't you find a place at Wilson for Jessie?"

The girl broke in heatedly. "But Mamma! I don't want to go to no shelter place. I got friends at school. Whatcha want to send me away for?" She was visibly frightened at the prospect. I watched her intently. So Hermit's mother was like Moira's mother—a powerful tyrant! I glanced at Moira and saw in her eyes a blankness. I wondered if the domineering manner of this woman was triggering memories of her own mother and whether she was starting to depersonalize.

Hermit's mother then shouted to her kids, "Now y'all get out. I wanna talk to these people private." The kids disappeared as though blown by a gale. Remaining with us, Hermit had taken to pacing back and forth as though expecting some disaster to strike him.

"Take dat thumb out your mouth," bawled the mother. "I sent you away so you could get over that." The boyfriend pulled a pint of scotch out of his jacket pocket and offered it to us. In his agitation, Hermit reached for the bottle and was rewarded with a smack from his mother. He burst into tears, upon which the boyfriend stepped toward Hermit and raised his hand to strike him. Chuck, whom I knew was controlling his rage with difficulty, restrained the man by pinning his arms. Chuck, Moira, and I understood the power relationships going on in that household. Violence and aggression were the watch words, and much of it was channeled toward Hermit, the weakest member.

Influenced by Chuck's quiet but powerful presence, the family calmed down, and I talked to them again about how we wanted to prepare the way for Hermit's return to them.

The mother, however, was not enthusiastic about the possibility. "What I want him back for?" she challenged. "I'm trying to get rid of these other little fucks as it is. I'm sick of not doin' well. I got nothing to give them." She paused for breath, rolled up the sleeve of her blouse, and presented an arm covered with bluish half-healed scabs and fresh red sores from shoulder to finger tip. They were track marks of drug needles. Giving us a moment to register what we were seeing, she added morosely, "Speak to my ma. She always liked Hermit. Maybe she can take him in." She lapsed into silence. I glanced at Hermit; he was fast asleep on the couch.

"Chuck," I said slowly, "do you know anything about the grandmother?"

He shook his head. "I've got the address but nothing else."

"Well, if you're done with us, I gotta go." Hermit's mother stood up and left the room, her boyfriend following. I picked up Hermit and we left. We passed neighbors on the stoop, old people who looked past us. Hermit awoke. I set him on his feet while Chuck asked directions to the grandmother's address from a man sipping beer out of a bottle wrapped in a wrinkled paper bag.

We hailed a cab and drove in silence to a graceful old Harlem brownstone. In a comfortably furnished apartment we met Hermit's gray haired grandmother, a smallish honey-skinned woman who radiated patience and gentleness. She was seated on a small wicker sofa. Hermit ran to her the moment he saw her, and she rocked him lovingly in her arms. As she did so, she related to us a bureaucratic frustration all too common in large cities. "After the court removed Hermit from his mother's house, I couldn't find out where he had been taken. Court workers, social workers, the other officials—none of them could help me find him, though I told them time and again that I wanted Hermit to live with me so I could eventually adopt him.

"It was no use. I was told that at my age I only had the capacity to look after the two retarded foster-care kids I already have. They said Hermit would be too much for me."

She fell silent. Then she stood up and, with a strength that would have done credit to a woman half her age, she carried Hermit to another room. We crowded into the doorway to see what she was up to. Her two older foster boys were playing cards on the floor. Hermit ran to them and leaped on them affectionately, and they hugged and wrestled with him welcomingly.

I glanced back into the living room where we had been talking to the grandmother. Not surprisingly, Moira, under this emotional onslaught, had regressed and was lying curled up and sobbing in fetal position in a worn armchair. Past me swept the aging grandmother, over to Moira, whom she pulled to her feet, embraced, and began to comfort as she would a baby from a crib. My throat constricted, and tears rose in my eyes. Moira responded by hugging the grandmother with the desperation of lifelong hunger. The grandmother seated herself and pulled Moira down with her, cradling her.

At dinner, Hermit related to us horror stories of violence and abuse he had been subjected to in the institution he had lived at before coming to Wilson. Wilson, as Hermit could well attest, was no paradise on earth, but it seemed much better than the upstate facility. The grandmother winked at us as Hermit told his awful stories, as if to say, That isn't really true, I'm sure. He's just making it up! I refrained, for her sake, from pointing out to her that all had no doubt happened exactly as Hermit was describing.

After dinner Moira played happily with the two retarded children. All her contentiousness was gone; she appeared to be an orphan child who had at last found a loving home. For a few minutes Hermit joined Moira and the two boys in play, then he snuggled contentedly against his grandmother on the wicker chair.

The room glowed with contentment and affection.

Good lord, I said to myself, this small old woman has created a haven of security and reassurance just by being who she is—a loving person. Why is such love and reassurance in such short supply? What's wrong?

As I blinked away my tears, I said to her, "Hermit is ready to leave the program at Wilson, and your home seems ideal for him. I'll make sure no problem gets in the way of Hermit's settling in with you. I can arrange foster home placement payments, along with babysitting and other financial aid. If you're willing, he could leave Wilson at any time," I declared. "He needs you."

The woman placed her hands on the two other boys' heads—they had crawled over to her and were leaning against her knees. She started to cry. "I wish I could. I wish I could give them all a home. But the doctors have told me I only have a few months left to live. All I do is worry, Where are they gonna go? You folks have got to help me—we have to find a home for my boys and Hermit. Help me, my time is short."

I sighed heavily. I had no answer. "I'll do what I can. We'll be in touch." I realized it was time to go. We had to drag a sobbing Hermit from the apartment, the only place of love he had ever known. "We can't let you stay, Hermit," I said sadly. "Only the court can grant such permission." I felt anguished at having to tell Hermit this news. Moira seemed to feel the same way. Her face had become fixed in an eerie, distracted stare; she walked stiff-legged. Chuck hailed a cab—we had to get these two traumatized human beings back to Wilson and do what we could for them.

Twenty-Four

Breaking Away

On the cab ride back, my thoughts returned to another calamitous scene: my own grandmother being dragged off to a mental hospital. I was two years old at the time, but the memory of her being carried from our home on a stretcher and placed in an ambulance was still vivid. My father had tears in his eyes—he knew he was seeing his mother for the last time, just as Hermit knew he would probably never see his grandmother again. How strange, I thought now, that my father cried for his mother that day—he had hated her. It occurred to me that a time might arrive when I might see Moira, too, carted off to a sanitorium. I could hear the cries of my mother: "Let de *alter* [old one] go! She was a witch anyway! She got what she deserved . . . old rubbish . . . dirty whore!" Two years later my sister was dragged out of our home by hospital attendants while she clawed at her scalp—"Don't let them take me, Mamma! I'll be good! I swear I will!" Perhaps Hermit was feeling similarly wretched as we dragged him away from the one person he loved, the one person who had cared about him.

We arrived back at Wilson with Hermit and Moira, Hermit sucking his thumb and Moira staring blankly at nothing. Chuck took Hermit off to his office to try to revive his morale, and I took Moira to mine. I led her to a chair, and she sank into it, dead asleep. Though I was dismayed at her reaction to the visit to the grandmother, I thought it might work in our favor. Perhaps it would help persuade her to get back to work with me as soon as possible.

Fighting the fatigue creeping over me, I studied her sleeping face. Beautiful as she was—and her growing self-confidence had enhanced her beauty—the effects of repression and loneliness were still evident in her face. Her lips were now clenched, her forehead furrowed. I knew she was hanging on to Mardoff because of her sick need to attach herself to strong father figures. The delusion she labored under was that if these figures finally gave her the love she had missed as a child, she could then become strong and effective in the world. Only she, however, could achieve that strength; until then, her defenses and fragmentation were the only crutches she possessed for survival.

I was becoming increasingly aware that when therapy is honestly and effectively practiced, it concerns the practitioner as significantly as the patient. Hermit, Mardoff, Moira, and I were victims of the loneliness and depression we shared with our brother and sister human beings. We all faced decay. From the moment of birth we were constantly reminded that we are alone in a universe indifferent to our fears. We fight this existential aloneness by seeking someone with whom to share our separateness, someone who will care and love enough to pay genuine attention to who we are and what is going on with us. Some of us, such as Moira, Hermit, and I myself, spend a lifetime searching for people who will allow us to be our real selves. In therapy, to fill these needs, some of us become the listeners and some become the searchers. In other forums, the listeners become the searchers and the searchers the helpers.

People like Mardoff choose other means to overcome their aloneness. They cannot allow a loving closeness to occur between themselves and another human being, so they foster the illusion of personal power. Wealth, status, and influential position become the guideposts of this path. Mardoff and power seekers like him seek people they can control—in Mardoff's case, in order to ease the horror of his own mortality. They pose a terrible threat to the "love seekers" because they project images of confidence and control. The impoverished seekers are naturally drawn to these facades because they appear to offer love, concern, and strength. My task as a therapist was to persuade Hermit, Moira, and others like them that to search for love in dominant people like Mardoff is bound to fail. They must learn first to nourish themselves and second to recognize and seek people with whom they can genuinely share love and caring.

Only through facing the truth that most of her attachments were expressions of self-hatred would Moira ever live a truly fulfilling life. Each time she experienced a failure with any of these power-seeking father figures, she would be overcome by such panic and despair—mostly on the unconscious level—that she would retreat for sick shelter into one of her fragmented personalities. She had to stop wishing that these figures—including whatever therapist she was with at the moment—would rescue her. If she were ever to attain emotional self-sufficiency and maturity, she would have to learn to face life alone. Then she might find real relationships with adults who cared about her. Fragmenting into partial human beings only allowed her to be a fragment of her whole self.

As I pursued my reverie, Moira stirred and awoke. She opened her eyes slightly and was clearly unsure of where she was. She looked around the room, adjusting herself to returning from whatever inner half-world she had been dwelling in. Suddenly, she opened her green eyes wide. Fully awake, she gazed at me.

"What's going on?" she asked. "And don't ask me where I've been inside myself—I don't remember. Where's Hermit?"

"You're back at Wilson," I said quietly. "Hermit's okay, Chuck is probably putting him to bed. We've all been through a hell of an experience. How do you feel?"

"Strange."

"How do you mean?"

"I'm in deep shit!"

"What does *that* mean?"

"I can't talk about it right now. I feel out of it."

"I know the day has been rough for you, but I think it's best you tell me what kind of trouble you're in."

Moira's face contorted. "I," she said, then stopped, took a deep breath and continued. "Well, it starts with this: I'm having a moment right now that I have once in a while. I can reflect as a whole human being on what I've been going through. I feel like an adult. I know who I am. I sense that I have a center, as I believe most healthy people do. A center they can rely on, anchor themselves to. Whatever happens to them, they have a basic hold on who they are. That's what I mean by center. Now, when I was in therapy with you, I felt my center more and more. The more you and I worked together, the stronger the center became, and the times of amnesia—those blackouts that happened, after which I could remember nothing—happened less and less. Now that I've been with Mardoff again, they're back in full force. The slightest stress and I slip into some unknown place. When I come out of it, I don't remember where I've been or what I've done, but I do know that at least one of those characters who used to come out of me, like Marcia, has come out again. I come back to consciousness and some friend or acquaintance asks me, 'Do you know you were talking like a black woman who was a nurse?'

"A few days ago at the police station I got dressed in some jazzy, sexy clothes we have in our supplies there. A fellow officer asked me later if I had been practicing for undercover duty as a prostitute, and I couldn't imagine what he was talking about. I had blocked it out. I can't take much more of this—being a crazy, frightened person who can't control her identity. I can't live this way."

"Have you told Mardoff about this retrogression? Does it have anything to do with him?"

"From the beginning, Mardoff didn't accept that I was a bunch of split-off people because I was too frightened of the world to cope with it as Moira. He said I was pretending to fragment as a way of seducing him into becoming the powerful father figure I had always craved. He said I knew I couldn't get away with playing the frightened little girl I actually had been, so I used seducing behaviors to get attention from him. And it worked too well. I have become too attached to him. But at this point I don't care what's causing my sickness. I just want to feel like a complete person again."

"Why do you stay with him if he doesn't help you?"

"We've been over all that—let's not go into it again," she said wearily.

"Okay. As long as we can agree to start therapy again in June as we'd been planning."

"I'm ready, but I'm not sure Mardoff will let me go. I'm not in as good shape as I need to be to get away from him. I'm tied to him. A starving person accepts crumbs even when he or she knows it's not genuine nourishment."

I stared at her—finally the truth. "What does that mean, Moira?" I asked gently.

A look of pain came into her eyes. "I can't tell you, I can't. Please understand." She paused and went on hoarsely. "Tonight I saw what I'd been missing when I sat and played with Hermit and his foster brothers. The grandmother was in the background with you and Chuck, and I suddenly felt what it would have been like to grow up loved. You once pointed out that the way to get well as an adult if you've been sick emotionally is to be given love as a grownup that you should have had as a child. But since that didn't happen to me, I've been going through what you call a repetition compulsion. I understand what that is about now: human beings who were emotionally unloved in babyhood and childhood tend to search for people who were like their unloving parents, to try to make those people finally give them the love they crave. That's why I keep trying to get from Mardoff, even though a part of my mind tells me I'll never do it. I can't."

"But you've broken unhealthy bonds with other people, like your husband and Marcia. You fixated on them, too, but got away from the compulsion. What makes him so special? Since you can't work it out with him, make a transfer onto me, and you and I will resolve it healthily."

In her chair, Moira clasped her arms and put her hands around her knees. Holding herself, she began to rock back and forth like an autistic child. Watching her, I felt frightened that she might flee into fragmentation.

To my relief she looked up and at me with a fully sane gaze. "You must be blind, Marty! Can't you see that Mardoff isn't special at all? And he's not domineering, the way he pretends to be. He's actually weak. Both my mother and Mardoff are scared, weak, pathetic people who hate themselves. They have to try to dominate to get some kind of control over other people and themselves. They also need to prevent people from getting too close in a truly loving way. That's what they really need, and that's what would make them genuinely loving and loved. They'd then be healthy at last. But for whatever reason, they can't do this." I was impressed; she was explaining it even better than I could. She continued, "So since they can't tolerate closeness, they have to control powerfully, but they hate the people they control because they hate themselves for not being able to be whole, loving people. They're really the ones begging for help. I feel like I've known this all my life. And I feel guilty, can you believe that? But I do. Because I feel their pain—the pain they feel as they abuse themselves and their dependents. But rather than try to help them it's easier to let them take it out on me as one of their victims."

I'd heard enough. "Wait a minute, Moira! You're making the case that Mardoff is a weak, puny man in the same boat as your mother and father. That's bullshit. He's a manipulative, shrewd, cunning man who knows how to get exactly what he wants."

She shot back. "What makes you think I haven't played the same game with you—making you feel I was the source of the problems in our working together? Perhaps I've guessed that your ego is as fragile as Mardoff's and that my best way to relate to you was to make you feel as powerful as I could. I see into people; I'm very sensitive to what's going on with them. Maybe I sensed that if I give you and Mardoff what you want—making you feel powerful—you will give me the love I never got. But on another level, I know that the people I'm trying to please can't give me love. I'm not really giving them anything either, except to feed into their neurotic needs. It's a useless exchange when you come down to it."

At last I thought I saw a chance to convey an important truth to her. "Okay," I answered, "so you've got your survival defenses in place exactly the way you just described them. But you're defeating yourself! Look, with those defenses you wind up shutting yourself and your life away behind thick walls. You share nothing of yourself—you're alone and isolated. And you pay a terrible price—the difference between a life fully lived, the only life we're sure of, and a life sealed away in the cave of protectiveness you dug in childhood and mistakenly think you have to hide in now. You've got to come out of that cave into the sunshine. Take a stand. Get angry at these people who displace their shit on you. Then you will get what you've always wanted from them. They may not love you, but they sure as hell will see that your needs count as much as theirs."

After staring at me for a long time, Moira pulled out a letter she had written and handed it to me. "It's a letter I've written to Mardoff, and I want your reaction to it before I send it. I wrote it in preparation for our April meeting, right after our last phone conversation in which I set the time and date."

> My Dearest John,
> I have spent a lot of time thinking about our relationship both in and out of therapy during these past few months. It was not a good idea for me to accept your decision to transfer my treatment to you after my previous therapist left the clinic. Too often I allow other people to make decisions for me that I should make for myself. I am con-

vinced now that I should have insisted that I continue with my previous therapist with or without clinical approval. I've come to understand that allowing myself to be transferred to you merely perpetuated my neurotic difficulties. I have a sick need to go along with authority, no matter what the cost to myself. But I think at this point it is in my best interests to take up therapy again with Dr. Obler. I was making steady progress in my work with him; he seems to have a deep understanding of what I need to do to overcome my sicknesses.

Please do not interpret what I'm doing as showing any lack of appreciation of you. At this point, what's most important to me is to continue our private relationship. You have come to mean a great deal to me. I would like to continue working with you until June so we can work out any bad feelings arising from my decision. And I hope that if you have any anger with me, you will not use it to take hostile actions against Marty Obler—I know there are professional rulings surrounding an intern's transfer of patients to private practice that you could invoke to get Obler into trouble. I know I can count on your good wishes for my growth toward recovery as I work with Marty.

I also want to remind you of what I've said before. As a professional you cannot share all your private thoughts, concerns, and life with me even away from our sessions. One of the important values to me of our new relationship will be that we can share more with each other than when we were also a doctor and patient. You have problems, as do we all. But in my new way of connecting to you perhaps I can give you real companionship and emotional support. I certainly hope so. We can discuss this at our next session.

Yours,
Moira

"What do you think?" she asked me when I'd finished reading.

"Great decision," I answered. "But why do you have to insulate the bastard from the truth?" I was about to get on her case for wanting to keep up a relationship with him. Then I stopped myself and decided to let well enough alone.

Get her angry, I thought, *and she might reconsider.* I continued. "But wait a minute. Who am I to say a thing? It's a great letter. Just one suggestion: be careful that he doesn't manipulate you by playing on your guilt. He might change your mind. I'm not sure you're as strong yet as you think you are. Remember how you behaved when that poor old woman told us how sick she is? Just be careful."

"Any other suggestions?"

"First of all, get that letter off today."

Moira laughed, then said, "Now I have a suggestion for you. From now on, don't try to guess what I'm experiencing on your own—check it out with me. Don't assume every time I space out a little that I've dissociated, 'cause sometimes I haven't. And another thing: Do everything you can to find a healthy home for Hermit until I can spend more time with him. I've got a lot to take care of—my family, for example. I don't know whether I'll stay with them or get strong enough to make it on my own, but I'd like to believe that someday I could adopt Hermit. He and I have something very special between us."

"I have to tell you something, Moira. And not as a therapist, but as a friend. Sometimes you seem one of the most fragile people I ever met. Then again you can become, like right now, one of the most insightful, kindest, and strongest people I've ever met. It's confusing."

"I know, I can't figure out why I change either."

Giving me a shy peck on the cheek her face glowing once again, Moira left. I felt marvelous—at last we were going to be working together again. Maybe I could help her to a complete cure. Sadly, that was the last time I was to feel that way with her.

During the next three months Hermit seemed to improve. His confrontations with his mother and the loving visit with his grandmother had reassured him. His thumb-sucking stopped. He had two friendly visits at Wilson with his mother and her boyfriend. His new strength helped him handle his grandmother's death. His mother and her boyfriend did not show up at the funeral. Only I, the two retarded foster boys, and a Catholic priest were present. I wondered sadly what would become of the two children.

Hermit continued to improve. As I worked with him he came to realize that his fate had been like that of many other ghetto kids. His mother, he saw, had been too troubled and ill to keep him with her, but she hadn't purposely gotten rid of him. Each new piece of information from his past that helped him understand himself had a wonderful effect on him. He began to seem happy for the first time since I had met him.

He began to ask whether he and his brothers could live with Moira. I said I would bring it up with her, but Moira's problems might pose obstacles to such an arrangement.

One day Hermit startled me by declaring, "I've decided what I want to do when I get out of Wilson!" He sounded serious—until now he had talked as a child hoping to find someone to live with who loved him.

"What's that, Hermit?"

"I wants to go home to my family. Dey needs me." He was talking with the pride and maturity of a grown man. "I'm gonna ask Jasslow to come with me and live with us. He's got no parents to live with. I'll get a job and get my brudders and sisters off the street. Bad people are going to get 'em hooked on drugs if I don't help 'em. I want to take care of myself, my friends, and my family."

"Hermit, that's a fine idea, but you're just a kid." I was convinced he should not leave Wilson until he had gone through much more therapy. "What kind of job do you think you'll get? Hustling, pushing drugs? You can't even get working papers at your age. Look, I want you to get out of Wilson, too, but we have to find a decent home for you, where you can go to school and live normally."

* * *

In the days that followed Hermit talked continually about helping his family. He actually got some of his brothers and sisters to take part in group therapy sessions at Wilson. They all pitched in to the process enthusiastically, working on communication problems among them and discussing ways to cope with the world around them.

In private therapy with me, Hermit, especially for a thirteen-year-old, applied himself conscientiously to his problems. He accepted the fact that as a withdrawn and vulnerable seven-year-old he could have done little to counteract his victimization by his relatives, the welfare agencies, and the court system. His mother had interpreted his thumbsucking as a serious emotional problem. She had shipped him off as a "youthful person in need of supervision" to the upstate correctional facility he had been assigned to. The abuse he had experienced in his family continued at that institution. He was constantly raped by the older boys, because he was young and handsome. Though bright and well-liked, he was at the bottom of the pecking order because of his lack of physical strength. The therapists, counselors, and teachers he had come in contact with thought he was retarded because of his thumbsucking, occasional retreating behavior (such as his hiding under beds), and his childlike use of language that sometimes bordered on "baby talk."

When he turned thirteen, the upstate institution could no longer keep him, and he was sent to Wilson. At that point it was judged that if placement in his family home or a foster home was not feasible, the court had the power to maintain custody over him. This would mean keeping him in residences for youthful offenders. At twenty-one, he would be tossed into the world, "in his own custody," like an undersized trout into a pool of piranhas. And all this without his having committed any crime. When I was a kid, like most children, my biggest fear was to be sent away if I were "bad." Hermit had done nothing to deserve his fate except to be born to a seriously disturbed mother and an unknown father.

* * *

The time approached for Hermit's fate to be decided. He was now fourteen years old. The best solution would be for him to be placed in a loving foster home; however, they were rare, and, of course, the last place Chuck, Janet, and I wanted to send him was to a youthful offender institution. We hoped we could get the court to release him on his own recognizance. Perhaps we could develop ways to watch out for him.

We were scheduled to appear before Judge Liebowitz at 10:00 A.M. on a Monday morning in family court. This was the same judge who had issued the original petition, when Hermit was seven years old, to send him to the upstate facility for "protection from an undesirable environment." Any change in status was normally a routine procedure, with the court accepting recommendations made by the agency working with the child. Sending a fourteen-year-old into the community without foster parent supervision was unusual, but we were confident the judge would agree, especially if we represented ourselves as willing to do all we could to make sure he fared well. We waited. The judge was late. At five minutes before noon, "All rise . . ." and the judge, tall, well-dressed, distinguished, entered and mounted the bench.

We fidgeted while case after case was adjudicated—family squabbles, child custody, juvenile misbehavior. At 2:30 Chuck, in an effort to get our case moving, asked the court attendant whether we could be next. The attendant whispered to the judge, and we were summoned.

Judge Liebowitz read the report we had submitted. "So you want to send him home to his family. Has he been given job training, schooling, has he been in any serious trouble while with the agency?"

To our surprise, Hermit rose from the chair he had been sitting in at the front of the courtroom, took several determined steps toward the bench, planted his feet and declared, "Your honor, I can talk for myself!"

Startled, the judge stared at Hermit. His left eye began to twitch in an eerily familiar way. I whispered to Chuck, "Is this Babcock's father, or am I hallucinating?"

His honor heard what I said. "Did I hear you mention Babcock's name?" he called to me. "He's with your agency, isn't he? Why isn't he here today?"

"He's only available between five and seven, your honor," I answered. "In any case, it's just a routine procedure, sir. This young man has made remarkable progress, and the staff at Wilson feels he is ready to go back to the community as a responsible person."

I chewed on my lip pensively. Janet, who had had courtroom experience, had told us to say as little as possible. It appeared to me that we had already ruffled Judge Liebowitz. I signaled with my eyes to Hermit and Chuck to cool it and cooperate. But unknown to me, something was going on inside Hermit. I soon found out what it was—an eruption of indignation against the system that had robbed him of freedom, autonomy, and dignity. We were in for it.

Moving his feet a touch farther apart as though to plant them more firmly than they already were, he sounded off: "Your honor, we been here since early morning awaiting your arrival so I can get my papers and go home. I ain't done nothing wrong to be here in the first place, so I'd appreciate—"

"Don't tell me how to run my courtroom, young man," Liebowitz shrieked. "I've seen punks like you for years who need a good whacking. As far as I'm concerned, I don't like the looks of the three of you. I've never had trouble with Wilson before." He rapped his gavel and announced, "I am deferring a decision until a higher Wilson official appears, preferably Dr. Babcock." Hermit appeared stunned. Once again he felt injustice sweeping him along like a chip in a torrent. He walked toward the bench, trying to talk to the judge, who on seeing him approach bellowed to the court guard, "Get that fucking delinquent out of here immediately!"

Back to Wilson we went. As I might have predicted, Babcock was furious on learning what had happened. "I'm getting up to here with you, Obler." I could make out beads of foam around his mouth. "You and your shenanigans. That judge is one of my best friends—a top political figure. Now he wants me to come to court! You know I have no time for that. What's this kid's name, Herman? Hermit? Well, I can't make it to court, but I want you to straighten everything out or you're finished here!"

He took a deep breath and sat back. Calmer, he continued, "You know, Obler, you're not such a bad guy. If you would just do things with a little more prudence. You've been very helpful to me with the sexual research I've been conducting. We could collaborate on the study, then you'd be really useful to the agency. Why do you bother so much about therapy with these unresponsive delinquents? You know how little real good we can do them, no matter how hard we try."

I wanted to ask him why, if he felt that way, he even bothered with his position at Wilson, but I knew the answer: It was a juicy berth he could occupy while pursuing his own interests. I didn't want to antagonize him further. I needed his help to get Hermit released by the court.

"Look, Dr. Babcock," I responded. "I don't know whether you're right or not about treating delinquents. But I do know that Hermit is ready to take care of himself. Even Janet agrees with me."

"Forget this Hermit bullshit, Obler. The kid's better off at Warwick or one of those children's prisons anyway. What's going to happen to him on the streets? He'll just become a mugger or a pusher. Let's talk about my research. What do you say you work more with me? Let's do things a little differently."

"Sounds good to me, sir." I watched him thinking I'll kiss the bastard's ass for a minute or two if it helps. "I'd appreciate the chance to work with you, but I want to get this young man out of here and back home. I discussed it with you a while back and you signed the recommendation report. Perhaps after that we could work on your study together."

"Do what you want, Just leave me out of it. You know I'm on this radio series a couple of nights a week. It takes preparation, and I have no time to waste on junkies!"

I walked out. We were stymied again. Without Babcock appearing in court Hermit would have to wait another year to get released. I was perplexed; what could I do now? However, I needn't have worried—Hermit heard of Babcock's resistance and simply took off. I never saw him again. About six months later Jasslow got a letter from him with a note to me.

> Dear Mr. Oobs,
> That stuff we talked about was good for my head. I am happy. Got a job for $95 a week pushing clothes in the garment center. My girl and I maybe we get married soon. Wasn't much I could do with my family. Mom's out hooking and Lucille is out there too. Look for them on Third Avenue. I'm living with my girl and go to night school for a high school diploma. My teacher is helping me with this letter. I'll come by soon if there's no danger of being picked up by the cops. . . .
> Miss you all a hell of a lot.
>
> Love,
> Hermit

I wrote to Moira and told her of Hermit's escape. Such a letter was as far as she wished me to go toward contacting her at this point; she had made it clear that she needed the three months before we got together to work out her relationship with Mardoff. I prayed it would go as she had said.

The atmosphere in my next supervisory meeting with Mardoff was chilly. Clearly we both looked forward to the end of our turbulent association. Gradually I had transferred my clinic patients to other therapists. When I asked him for his supervisory evaluation and the recommendation letter that was required before I could begin my Ph.D. program, he said he'd take care of the matter, asking that I have forms for recommendations sent to him from prospective employers. During our tense meetings I assumed he was aware of Moira's upcoming transfer. I guessed that he was trying to talk her out of transferring and for this reason had not raised the subject with me. It never occurred to me that Moira might be having a problem dealing with leaving him—first in raising the subject and second in actually walking away. I felt her sounder health these days would give her the strength to make the separation.

I found out differently. By June I hadn't heard from Moira and I was worried. In a few weeks I would complete my clinic responsibilities, and since I wouldn't be attached to the clinic anymore it would be more difficult to help her if she was having problems transferring to me. At the same time, I reminded myself that the situation with Moira, Mardoff, and me was a lot more complicated than I'd been willing to admit. To untangle it would take time—the picture would be clearer only when we'd become more separated from each other and were ready to accept what our three-way tie had really been about.

At the clinic I asked Gail how Moira was doing. She told me Moira had taken a leave of absence from psychotherapy a month before. At the same time, she had also taken an extended leave from her job.

I was stunned. I tried to contact Moira. No luck; apparently she had moved and had left no forwarding address. My first impulse was to rush into Mardoff's office and confront him about her whereabouts and what had happened, but Gail told me Mardoff was as much in a fog about the whole situation as I was. He had no idea what had become of her. I wondered to myself whether Moira had even gotten my second letter telling of Hermit's leave-taking. I asked Gail again whether she or Mardoff had heard from

Moira since April. She said she hadn't, and she was pretty sure Mardoff hadn't. According to Gail though she could tell he was very upset at Moira's termination, he was also very preoccupied with the difficult divorce he and his wife were going through.

The summer came and went. All my efforts to find Moira proved unsuccessful. I checked everywhere I could think of, contacted everyone I was aware she had known. I registered a missing persons report at her police precinct. I got in touch with her husband. His attitude was indifferent and unhelpful. Her mother was outright hostile. I had one clue: Once, in therapy, I had asked Moira if she could envision being free of the control her family had over her. She said that the only way she could see that happening would be if she left everything behind her and wandered like her brother through the streets of New York—a wraith unattached to the world.

I was losing hope of finding her. Then in September I heard from Moira—a scribbled note in my mailbox at Wilson bearing the return address of a city shelter for homeless people.

> Dear Friend:
> I got your letter about Hermit's decision and it prompted me to make a similar move. It looks like resolving the situation with Mardoff will take a lot longer than I had originally expected—thus delaying my starting treatment with you at this time.
>
> Love,
> Moira
>
> P.S. I appreciate everything you have done for me, but please don't try to contact me. I will find you if and when I'm ready.

TWENTY-FIVE

Final Partings

On a windy autumn day I strolled through swirling red, yellow and brown leaves on my way to work. I had concluded that my days at Wilson were numbered. I had received an offer to teach at Brooklyn College. Perhaps academic work might help assuage the loneliness I felt since Moira and Hermit had left. My preoccupation with them had become obsessive. It was interfering with my work on my dissertation. I badly needed a new setting to remotivate my interest in completing a doctorate.

As I approached Wilson, I was startled to see Moira in her police uniform standing by the wrought-iron gates. My heart began to pound. Thank goodness she was safe. She smiled and we embraced. I felt anger and love toward her.

Without a word we walked up the steps into the lobby of Wilson and were greeted by Dolly and Chuck. At first Dolly was alarmed by Moira's uniform, fearing that one of the kids had gotten into trouble, but then she recognized Moira and the two women hugged warmly. I pulled Chuck aside and asked him to take over my next therapy session so I could have a talk with Moira. He agreed.

In my office Moira slipped off her police topcoat. I was shocked to see she had lost even more weight. "How's Hermit?" she asked in an offhand manner that stunned me. She spoke as though we had recently seen each other for lunch!

"Cut the crap," I shouted. "I haven't heard a word from you in months. If you think a minute, you'll remember I told you about him in the letter I wrote to you in June. Did you get my second letter? Where the hell have you been? I think after all we've been through, you owe me an explanation."

Ignoring my rage, Moira asked, "Do you think the kid's okay?"

I cooled off a bit. "I don't know. There's no way I can know. He's out there somewhere, trying to help his brothers and sisters. I think he got a job; he might be supporting them. At least he had the decency to write me, which is more than you did. But don't get me off on Hermit. I want to know what happened to you and me beginning therapy again. Are we still going to do it? Is Mardoff behind your disappearing act? How about a few answers?"

"Answers, answers," she intoned wearily. She put her hands over her eyes. "Listen, if I had any answers I'd tell them to myself. I tried to do what you told me to do—get away from the bastard, get away from the people who mess me up. It's the only way I'll ever grow up and be healthy and strong; so I've tried to make it out in those streets I'm so scared of. But things haven't worked out too well." She paused and caught her breath. "Mardoff had insight. He warned me—hysterical and dependent women have a lot of trouble handling freedom. They want strong men to control them. I guess I learned that I can't make it on my own. I need people like my mother, my husband, and Mardoff running my life. They're all pathological versions of my mother —as all therapists are."

I wasn't about to accept that. "What was that cryptic message you left me suggesting you needed more time to resolve your relationship with Mardoff before you returned to therapy?" I asked.

A long silence this time. Then Moira said softly, "For

people like me there are only two choices in life—selflessness or homelessness."

My heart beat faster, my emotions surging. "That note I got from you had a letterhead of a women's shelter. Is that where you've been living?"

She smiled wanly. "Quite often, during the time I was looking for my brother. I thought I'd find him if I associated with street people. Do you have any idea how many street people are multiple personalities like me? They dissociate just like I do. In a way, they have a strange kind of freedom of a sort you would not understand."

"Free? Free?" I protested, trying to keep my voice even. "You call being out on the streets, hungry and crazy, free? I'd call it being whacked out of their minds, bizarrely schizophrenic, or just plain poor. What kind of freedom is that—half-crazed, all alone in the world, with no one giving a shit about you?"

Moira was pensive. Then she slowly said, "It's a freedom to live without the guilt and pain that goes along with being different. Out there nobody is thought of as a 'crazy.' We're just people trying to get through one day at a time. Our suffering—in terms of comparing ourselves to 'normal' society—has vanished. All that matters is survival. In our world everyone is the same."

I didn't want to talk philosophy. I wanted to know what she'd been doing. I pressed her. "Did you see Mardoff?"

She shook her head. "It was Mardoff I was trying to get away from, you fool, and other power-hungry, dominating control freaks who feed off disturbed sickies like me. But that wasn't all I was trying to get away from. I was also fleeing the weak, puny, self-involved, fragmented, dependent, terrified person you and I knew as Moira. As long as I stayed with my family or in therapy or in Mardoff's grasp I couldn't claim my right to myself."

She continued. "I met a schizophrenic named Maria. She had lived in the tunnels of Grand Central Station since her mid-twenties. She had been a school teacher in the New

York City public school system. From what I learned from her she had been a fine teacher—her mind was excellent. But the staff and children made fun of her because she behaved oddly at times. When she learned she was a schizophrenic, she let herself in for the pain of living in a society intolerant of differences in people. Her illness worsened when she was about twenty-seven and she joined the underclass—crazies like herself living in subway tunnels. She was beaten, spit and pissed on, and raped. But she didn't suffer as she would have if she'd tried to get by in conventional society. Overall, she said that the homeless indigents who became her brothers and sisters treated her better than her family did—those wonderful, healthy New Yorkers she had grown up with." Her forehead was creased in a frown. I sensed she was trying to discern her real feelings.

"And a strange thing happens when you are no longer bound to the stigma of being a misfit and a weirdo: The illness doesn't eat away at you any more. It doesn't matter whether you feel this way, because you've dropped out of 'reality.' The result is the same—you don't suffer. By releasing yourself from the horror of a world you don't fit into, by severing your physical and mental connections to that world, it can no longer hurt you."

She stared at me. Her voice barely audible, Moira went on, "I don't think you can possibly imagine the pain and suffering a mentally ill person goes through each day. When your perceptions and cognitions are always distorted, it is nearly impossible to function competently in a normal world. You marvel at how normal people can do simple tasks that for you present overwhelming difficulties."

Shuddering, she continued, "I don't want to go on talking about this. What's important is that I was not able to make it, and thanks to your help I can't escape into a world of self-delusion anymore. What the world of reality offers me is less than appealing. When I visited home my mother and sister started right in on me, berating me for abandoning my husband and kids. They consulted Mardoff, and all of them forced me to sign a paper saying I was mentally ill when I left and not in control of my actions. Signing that paper means I could be committed to an institution—a life of slavery. I could never escape. Now there's nowhere for me to go, neither forward nor back."

"What do you mean?"

"What it comes down to is that I'm too healthy to go back into madness again, but I'm not strong enough to be independent. So I have to attach myself to people who abuse me, like those remora fish that attach themselves with suckers to the bellies of other fish and live off them as parasites. But the fish I attach myself to are defective and can only damage me." She flashed a sad smile.

"If we don't have at least the illusion of being able to find love, we become one of those people who destroy others. Most people—and I include you and Mardoff—go from relationship to relationship and job to job trying to discover what's going to make them feel better. Mardoff and you feel that the more people you make dependent on you, the more you will feel loved and the more fulfilled and happy you'll feel. Nevermind that in your search you trample people in the guise of helping them find the truth. You don't care where or how you get your needs met or how you go about it. My mother was brutal. She knew I needed her love, and she exploited that need by enslaving me to assure that I could never become independent of her. Because her mother hated her she hated herself. Since she couldn't be loved she turned to control and getting others dependent on her to give her a feeling of personal significance. It was a substitute for the love she could not have directly. That in the process she was destroying my life didn't matter to her in the least. Of course, she was so fogged out by her own troubles she probably never consciously thought she was harming me, and if it had been suggested to her that she was doing so she would have sincerely denied it. But she wouldn't have stopped; I'm sure of that. As she saw it, it was her survival at stake—nothing else mattered." I saw the mute terror in Moira's eyes and was frightened for her. I tried to pat her hand, but she brushed me away.

"So I've been brutalized by everyone—my father, my uncle, my husband, and now Mardoff. They all raped my body or mind, or both, to satisfy their needs for control. That's the way all of you men get love—you may each have different types of impoverishment, but what you have in mind is the same. Get control. I went along with it because I had no choice. I had to grab for any crumbs of attention I could get. My selfness disappeared; people could do what they wanted with me."

She paused, sighed deeply, then continued her doleful observances. "You know, Marty, I've decided there's little difference between victim and victimizer. They're both looking for a sense of feeling needed and wanted. But that difference is important because, as I said, it has to do with choice. The victim feels that he or she has no choice. The victimizer has the illusion of choice: having the capability of selecting a victim makes him successful; he can momentarily circumvent his mortality.

"The only opportunity for the victim is to try to survive alone, free of the need to be victimized. I begged Mardoff for that chance. He wouldn't give it to me."

I burst out: "Why don't you come back to me? I can help you get some real freedom." I felt like begging her on my knees, but I didn't have the nerve. Through all her lamentations I thought I was hearing something positive: she had grown and indirectly may have been asking me to press her to seek more help. If that wasn't the case, why had she showed up at Wilson?

However, she wasn't to be budged. "Therapy with you" she said, her green eyes filling with tears, "is of no further use to me. I have nothing to work out. I'm sure you find that hard to grasp, but weak people like me run out of gas. Awareness is only freeing when the self is strong enough to deal with independence. Let's face it once and for all: because of my early life I had to split into other selves. Our recent work to heal me has failed. Let's leave it at that—let me bow out gracefully." She gave me a look filled with such pain and anguish that my heart shuddered in response.

Moira sat back in her chair and stared at me. I knew what was going on: she wanted me to tell her to leave. She couldn't do it herself. Since then I've seen it happen several times; a patient can't respond to therapy anymore but can't leave. This is simply because they had closeness that for a while rescued them from aloneness. I didn't want her to leave; I wasn't ready to give up on Moira.

"Moira," I said, desperately trying to stall any final break between us, "why don't you take some time to think about your decision?" Despite my perseverance, though, I was running out of hope. Her fate was sealed by Mardoff's implied threat of institutionalizing her. She could no longer flee into fragmentation from the power that she continued to allow Mardoff and her family to exercise over her. I recalled the terrifying dream she had early in her work with me: she would end her wretched existence in a mental institution with only marble walls to protect her. The only path to freedom might lie in her trusting that I could protect her from Mardoff's rage if she broke away from him and her family. But she didn't have that trust. A door was closing between us.

"Marty, it's too late for that. It's too late for anything for me." It was a frail, frightened cry for help that alarmed me more than anything else she had said.

"Don't say that, Moira, please don't say that," I pleaded.

"I'm so tired. I only want some rest, some peace," she said. Rising to leave, she kissed me gently. "Good-bye, Marty," she said with an awful finality.

After seeing Moira, I rushed directly to Mardoff's office. He was between sessions. I waited impatiently for Gail to buzz him. Finally she said, "You may go in."

He was standing at the window and turned to see me. "Can I help you, Obler?"

I had no time for amenities. "I fear Moira is becoming suicidal," I blurted out.

His face became indignant. "And I, Obler," he spat out, "fear you are destined to be the world's greatest fool. I'm telling you for the last time Moira is a manipulative, hysterical woman."

"But the signals are frighteningly clear," I objected.

Suavely but firmly, Mardoff retorted, "Yes they are, Obler, and I'm afraid the real problem here is you just don't know how to read them."

"What do you suggest I do about her threats?"

After a barely perceptible pause, Mardoff replied forcefully, "I suggest you ignore them." Resentment at my intrusion was plain in his voice. I waited. I was about to continue my pleading when Mardoff rose to his feet. "Close the door on your way out."

"But I'm not finished," I protested.

Mardoff broke in, "Yes you are, Mr. Obler. Quite finished." His icy eyes swept my face. "Now get out."

Stopping by Gail's desk, I said anxiously, "Please call me immediately if you hear anything about Moira."

"I will, Marty," Gail said. "I promise."

S hortly after we talked, Gail notified me that Mardoff had transferred Moira to another therapist. I'm sure he was suspicious that she would resume treatment with me. According to Gail, Moira had returned to her family. She would briefly visit each new therapist Mardoff assigned her to, then leave. I knew why he didn't press her to come back to him: He was protecting his ass. In case she really was suicidal, she would be listed as someone else's patient. After she gave in to her family, their hold over her was complete and she could not have resisted. Or perhaps, with some of the strength I had helped her develop, she did resist. I couldn't guess.

It became more difficult to get news of her after that. Mardoff had concluded his connection to me by approving my dissertation and giving me a positive evaluation. After that, he refused further contact with me and instructed Gail and her staff not to discuss Moira's case with me.

By December I had settled into my new post at the university and had finished my internship at Wilson. Moira had disappeared from my life but not my thoughts.

On Christmas Eve I left my office listening to music on the walkman I always carried. As I walked through thick, falling snow across campus, a psychology student from one of my classes fell into step with me. He tapped my shoulder. I took my earplugs out. "Have you heard about the policewoman who shot herself today? She has the same unusual first name as that case you talked about in class—Mariel, no Moira. I guess it's just a coincidence."

I gasped, knowing it had to be her, but did not answer immediately. Finally I managed to say, "No. No, I hadn't heard," then fell silent.

We walked along until he bid me goodnight and took another direction. I continued on through dazed vision. I thought I glimpsed Moira waiting for me outside the iron gates of the hospital entrance. A few steps farther another image accosted me. It was my sister Shirley. Peeking at me as she had done once, from behind the church altar at the mental asylum.

Shaken, I sat down on an iron bench outside the gates. I switched on the radio I was carrying. The story was being broadcast.

The announcer said: "Initially the police had thought the policewoman, Moira McCarthy, was the victim of a robbery attempt. Later investigation showed that she had shot herself in the head with her father's gun."

Moira was dead. As the Christmas bells tolled and the snowflakes fell faster and faster crusting my hair and eyes, I sat sobbing.

Twenty-Six

Reckonings

During those first weeks after Moira's death, I tried to suppress thoughts of her. It was easier to blot out her memory than to deal with it. Indeed, the practice of psychotherapy mandates diminishing memories of patients one has failed with—to obsess on failures inhibits success with later patients. But though I tried hard to forget her, I couldn't.

An associate of Mardoff's asked me to write a case summary of my work with her. In my report to the clinic I wrote this troubled ending:

> The martyrdom defense Moira selected offered her a way to be hostile without either suffering or behaving in a hostile way. It allowed her to gain approval and acceptance without being either destroyed or treated like a mad dog.
>
> Undergoing therapy, Moira gained strength and emotional health that enabled her to become aware of the martyrdom protection and how she used it to survive. Understanding it, she was thus able to relinquish it and seek healthier and better ways to live her life.
>
> Unfortunately, she had no chance to continue the therapy that was healing her. And she did not build into herself a positive foundation for behavior and experience that would take the place of the martyrdom structure. Despite her greater health, this lack of a defensive supporting struc-

ture so demoralized her that she considered death her only solution.

Before the age of five then, the seeds of Moira's destruction had been planted.

One day I was invited to lunch by Marcuse, with whom I had become friends after I ended my internship at the clinic. As we talked about this and that, a sudden image of Marcuse and Moira at the weekend marathon shot through my head.

Marcuse, as sensitive as ever, immediately noticed my change of mood. "What's wrong?" he asked.

"I have to be careful of memories these days, especially those of my time at the clinic. Some of them are terribly painful, especially my strange relationship with one patient."

"Feel like talking about it?" he ventured.

I hesitated. Did I want to talk of my troubling thoughts of Moira? "I don't know," I said pensively. Then I realized I did want to talk about them.

"Remember the policewoman we were with at the marathon?"

"Moira," he said quietly.

I nodded. "You know she killed herself."

"I heard," he said gently. "You must have felt very badly about that."

I sighed heavily. "Guilty."

"Why were you guilty?" he asked. "It wasn't your fault."

"I feel like I abandoned her when Mardoff refused to allow me to see her privately because of the absurd clinic policy about transfer of patients. Before I left the clinic I suggested to her that we could get her transferred after a period of time, handling it in a way not to conflict with the policy. We would do this by having her accept a transfer to another therapist to prevent anyone getting wise to our plan to transfer her to me. Before we could set that in motion, though, Mardoff transferred her to his caseload and, I feel strongly, got involved with her. I suspected it became a sexual and emotional attachment well beyond the limits of therapy. Initially he talked to me about his work with her to a limited degree, but toward the end of her being with him, Mardoff told me nothing.

"After I left the clinic I met with Moira a few times. She told me that Mardoff had indeed become deeply involved with her. As she put it: 'He can't let go of me.' She used that rationalization to stay with him longer than she and I had originally planned. Somewhere along the line, in one talk I had with her, she told me that her family had conspired with Mardoff to threaten to ship her off to a mental hospital if she did not do what Mardoff and her family wanted her to do—which, essentially, was to stay in their clutches. Eventually she did break away from him and her family and dropped completely out of sight, as though she'd vanished from the planet."

I went on to tell Marcuse about my unprofessional conduct in spying on Mardoff. He turned white when I described overhearing Mardoff's fight with his wife in his office. I thought Marcuse was upset because of what I'd done. It turned out he was having other reactions.

"My perception was that Mardoff hated women," I said slowly, "and that somehow his troubling translated to his becoming neurotically involved with Moira to the extent that he couldn't possibly have helped her toward healing. Perhaps he was redirecting his general hostility toward women onto Moira. One moment he would behave positively toward her and in another instant would turn hostile —just as I had heard him do with his wife during my spying on him. If this was true, it might explain why he never accepted my diagnosis of Moira as a multiple. If he could see her as a hysteric who tried to manipulate men for her own ends, he could then justify his behavior in dominating and controlling her as being the only effective approach in dealing with her problems. Thus he could foist upon her his personal problems with women. He kept insisting that I had countertransference problems. Wouldn't you agree with me that his response was a defense mechanism of projection? How many mentors jump right into a therapeutic role with a patient of an intern they supervised, as soon as the intern leaves the clinic? It all seemed very suspicious to me."

"Hold on," Marcuse said. "Stop right there. This is very important. Now, let's go over this whole thing once more. I've got to know the dates when everything happened, as best you can remember."

We went back over details. We reviewed my regret at not standing up to Mardoff more courageously. Marcuse seemed particularly interested in just when Mardoff was vehemently attacking women as a species that could not be trusted. I was chagrined to recollect that I had somewhat agreed with him, influenced by problems I had been having with my wife. I recalled Mardoff's declaration, "You can't trust any of them."

At this point Marcuse was clearly in shock.

"What the hell's going on with you?" I demanded.

His face ashen, he said, "Mardoff's wife committed suicide on the exact day Moira disappeared."

Marcuse paused for a moment to calm himself.

Then he continued. "I'm starting to see the picture now. To start with, every effort was made to keep his wife's suicide quiet. However, Mardoff's disturbances began to be more evident. He was probably involved with other women as well as Moira; he was heard muttering that he had to protect his interns from their seductive manipulative woman patients. He was well out on the edge."

Marcuse looked at me sadly. "Now, I'm not trying to defend his behavior. It was improper, but Moira's leaving and his wife's death were powerful blows. Mardoff hated his wife. He married her out of dependency and a need to control her. I don't want to elaborate on Mardoff's neurotic hangups, but a lot of what he was about had to do with his possessive mother, whom he resented—"

"Wait a minute," I interrupted. "What's this about

Mardoff's neurotic problems? How do you know so much about his relationship with his wife?"

"Because his wife was in analysis with me at the time!"

I was stunned. Marcuse must, then, know a lot more about the whole situation than I had first imagined he did.

He continued. "Mardoff clearly transferred his problems with his mother onto his wife. He became dependent on his wife. She reinforced that dependency by constantly reminding him of all she had done for him—and she had done a lot, including putting him through medical school. Understandably, she demanded gratitude for that."

He took a deep breath and went on. "Resenting his wife in the same way he'd resented his mother, Mardoff sought outlets in infidelities, and he fought bitterly with his wife over them. Under his facade he was a very dependent man who needed women to take care of him. But his ambivalence toward his mother prevented his asking for this care in a grownup healthy way in which he could genuinely give to a mate and genuinely receive.

"Instead, in his desperate quest for love, he insisted on being adored in his female relationships and maintaining tight control over his mistresses."

"One of whom was his patient," I said disgustedly.

Marcuse nodded. "Unfortunately, yes. But," he said, and revealed an important truth: "People like Mardoff are crippled by family conflicts in childhood that made them feel helpless, vulnerable, and unloved. I believe that he was —without consciously realizing it—trying to take back the power he'd surrendered to his overwhelming mother by wielding power over other women. As he found new females, his wife naturally objected. He responded by seeing her as the vindictive, manipulating, controlling mother he hated but needed. The bastard threw his infidelities in his wife's face. She was pretty strong, but his affair with Moira got to her and she began to fall apart."

"I just realized," I broke in, "that you're breaking confidentiality. I'm a fine one to talk—I don't mind bending the rules—but how come you're doing it?"

He gazed at me somberly, caringly. "Because you're suffering too damn much over all this. You're in too much pain, too guilty over Moira's death. Mardoff's wife is gone, Moira is gone, neither can suffer any more. Now, from what you've told me, I can see that Mardoff used you as a pawn in his need to control women. He focused on Moira to carry out his conflicts. When she seemed to be gaining strength to leave him, he had to reimpose control over her—he couldn't let her get away; he needed her too much."

"But I thought he wanted to get rid of his wife."

"That's the double bind. He is driven to get rid of the wife, mother, transferential figure after he has weakened them to the point of powerlessness. At that point, he has gained his unconscious revenge—taken power back from the mommy who oppressed him. She can't, then, gratify his neurosis anymore. At the same time, he can't abide letting go of any woman, like Moira, who needs and adores him. So he has to keep her—but must get rid of her! Until you described your triangle with Mardoff and Moira a few moments ago, I didn't understand what had happened. I've been too close to Mardoff to see it clearly, but I do now."

I took a deep breath. "Are you suggesting he drove his wife and Moira to suicide?"

"Let's just say that the horrible power of the bind—of being needed and rejected at the same time—robbed them of any reason for living."

I let my breath out slowly. In my mind I again glimpsed snowflakes fluttering down on the day of Moira's suicide. Suddenly I could run no more, hide inside myself no longer. I burst into tears. I was racked with the pain of the tragedy of Moira's death. We three had come from past situations where engaging in acts of self-mutilation were imperative for acceptance by our families, for survival itself. Now I could clearly see our roles in this wretched drama: Moira had chosen to play the martyr, suppressing her human needs in an effort to survive her family's assault.

Mardoff played Moira's powerless father, who hid behind a mask of professional power and control. When he lost his grip on his wife and Moira, he had to symbolically destroy them, or face the recognition that he was helpless—an epiphany that would unbearably reinforce his already entrenched self-hate. In this moment, I saw myself as Hamlet's "rogue and peasant slave," because I elected to serve as a kind of brother/co-conspirator who surrendered to his dread of losing family approval by essentially allying myself with Mardoff. Losing "family approval" meant for me endangering my professional status, which, though I had taken risks, I had carefully avoided doing.

Marcuse was gazing at me sympathetically. "What are you thinking about?"

"Do we ever more than skim the surface of what there is to know about each other?" I gasped. "Even we who are trained and supposedly skilled at gazing into the psyche? We know in some corner of ourselves that we are struggling against sensations of impotency and powerlessness. Oh, shit! What does Hamlet say? 'Fie upon it. Fie!' We can't face that we're going to die. We can't face our own insignificance. So we bend the truth to save a little self-respect. What's worst of all is that I feel if I'd gone all out I could have saved Moira!"

Marcuse moved his chair nearer mine, grabbed me with both hands, and gave me two jarring, reviving shakes. "Stop!" He shouted. "It's over. We have to go on living. The past is past, and most of it is incomprehensible."

"Perhaps," I said as we rose and embraced before taking our leave of each other. "But I'm not ready, as yet, to let it go."

TWENTY-SEVEN

Resolution

In the next weeks I was racked by the desire for revenge. All I could think of was Mardoff. Without raising a hand or wielding a weapon he had killed Moira as surely as if he had shot her in cold blood. I had to do something for her and to save all the others who might, in the future, come to him seeking help, only to find themselves in his clutches—but what could I do?

My agonized thoughts jumped from one plan to another. First, I thought of going to the police and then discounted the idea. No one would believe me; even if they did, his crime was so subtle as to defy punishment. Next, I thought of going to the other clinic supervisors, but Mardoff was their boss and, anyway, they would probably think that my theory about his guilt stemmed from professional jealousy. No, the conventional avenues of justice were closed to me.

Still, I could not let the matter rest. And then, lying sleepless one night as I wrestled with my conscience, a plan came to me.

There was a way. I worked on making my plan a reality. As soon as I was ready, I went to Mardoff's office before his clinic hours. This time I did not wait for Gail to buzz him. I barged in.

Mardoff was seated at his desk. He looked up quizzically. "So, Obler, it's you. What do you want this time?" he said, irritation plain in his tone.

"I've come about Moira," I said quietly.

"What about her? You knew she was dead, didn't you," he said matter-of-factly.

His off-hand mention of her death made me livid. "You bastard," I shouted. "You killed her."

He rose to his feet. "You'd better watch yourself, Obler," he spat out. "I'd hate to have to call the police and ask them to forcibly eject you, or worse—suggest you need psychiatric aid."

I stared at him, mesmerized. All the hatred I felt bubbled to the surface. "I wouldn't do that if I were you, Mardoff," I said quietly, forcefully.

"No?" he said disdainfully, "Why not? You haven't come here to threaten me with jail or something, have you?"

I shook my head, "No, you and I both know that as much as I want to, I couldn't carry out that threat. What you've done is beyond the law's reach."

"What, then?" he asked coolly.

"I've come to tell you my plans."

"Very interesting, Obler, but make it fast. I have a patient scheduled very soon."

"This won't take long," I said. "And I think you'll find them worth knowing."

"I'm sure," he smirked.

"I have decided," I looked into his eyes savoring the moment, "that there is only one way to vindicate Moira."

"And just what is that?"

"I'm going to make Moira's case public."

"I don't think so," Mardoff scoffed. "You have no proof."

"No proof that will stand up in a court of law, where you ought to be tried," I said, "but I do have my notes and records. And there are others who know the truth." I stopped short of implicating Marcuse.

"And just what do you intend to do with them?" Mardoff asked coolly.

"Here is a draft of an article I'm writing." I threw it across his desk. "There are no names, of course, but mine. However, that should be enough. If you come forward to accuse me, you will be admitting this article is about you and the public will know everything. It should make a juicy tidbit for the papers." His face had turned white with rage. "I don't think your enormous ego can stand that. And," I went on, "even if you don't come forward, those in the profession will quickly figure out it's you. You'll be damned if you do and if you don't."

"I ought to kill you, Obler."

"You're too much of a coward for that, Mardoff," I replied.

"What do you want from me?" he asked slowly.

"I want you to resign, effective immediately," I said.

"And then you won't publish this garbage?"

"No," I replied walking to the door. "This is just advance notice. I'll publish my report anyway. It's the last thing I can do for Moira."

I left him standing there.

A few days later Marcuse called me at my office at the university. "Mardoff has unexpectedly taken early retirement," he said excitedly. "It was a complete surprise to all of us. Did you have anything to do with it?"

"No," I replied. "It must have been his long-lost conscience." I hung up, walked over to the window and gazed outside.

Spring was making its presence known. Young men and women strolled together arm-in-arm under budding maple trees. How beautiful the scene was. A momentary feeling of sadness came over me. Moira would not see spring again, ever, but, I thought as I gathered my things and walked out into the warm thawing day, at last she has been vindicated. At last she has gotten the justice she deserved.

Afterword

Moira's grave on Long Island was left unattended. Eventually it became strewn with garbage and other debris that I have often cleared away so that the stone marking of her name and birthday will not be buried from sight.

Muttering distractedly about devils having assailed his family—as indeed they had—Moira's brother was found wandering the streets of Bensonhurst. He was institutionalized. Moira's husband remarried and moved to Westchester County. Her mother and sister remained together, immured in their psychotic troublings and surviving mainly on welfare. Her father increased his already heavy drinking and wound up in a halfway house for disabled people run by the police department. His drinking led to intensive memory loss.

Wilson eventually closed for lack of funding. Dolly took a new position directing a program for welfare families. Chuck Hanson works at a state hospital, still helping all those he can. Babcock continued to be a regular on a late-night talk show until the public lost interest. He now works for the government. Robert Lowe Harris, the family systems therapist who had originally inspired me to take the position at Wilson, became a recognized theoretician in family systems therapy and opened an institute of his own. Mashipian became the head administrator at a children's resident facility.

Hermit took charge of his family. He forced his mother into a drug-rehabilitation program, got married, and became a Harlem community leader.

Angel became a pimp and a psychopath. He was known to authorities as a ruthless assaulter of street children and homosexual men in the West Village. Several incarcerations and efforts to treat his problems with drugs left him as menacing as ever.

Of the nine children I worked with as a group at Wilson, seven of them, I regret to say, took to criminal pursuits that earned them drug-related and other felony charges. Jasslow was sent to a mental hospital. Doctors there asked me for a summary of my work with him. He was later diagnosed as a schizophrenic.

Gail finally left her secretarial job to retire on social security and a pension. She spends her time quietly these days.

Mardoff, once a major figure in psychoanalysis circles, retired soon after our final confrontation.

The clinic at which I treated Moira continues to operate as a lower-middle-class outpatient center. Marcuse still works there.

Some of the patients from the therapy group I described on the memorable country marathon completed their analyses with me in private practice, and two have become successful psychotherapists.

Within a span of four years I finished my dissertation, earned a doctorate, taught psychology at Brooklyn College, and established a successful private practice.

My loveless marriage to my first wife ended—she and I were divorced. Later, I met and married the woman with whom I have had a long and happy relationship.

During my second marriage I have become very close to my son and my daughter from my first marriage. With my present wife I have adopted two children, one from South America and the other from the Caribbean. I live a good life. Much of that blessing I owe to the valiant readiness of my patients to cooperate with my efforts to gain healings in them and in myself. These efforts allowed me to become the scientist and healer I am today.

As I say that, I spare myself and my readers any pretense of modesty. I'm proud of what I have accomplished. Hard work and perseverance have gained me my expertise, my feeling of effectiveness. Many I have encountered have contributed to who I am, but foremost is my friend Moira, who taught me how to be an honest human being.